Femmes d'esprit

WOMEN IN DAUMIER'S CARICATURE

Femmes d'esprit

WOMEN IN DAUMIER'S CARICATURE

Kirsten Powell and Elizabeth C. Childs

With contributions by Janis Bergman-Carton,
Lucette Czyba, and Judith Wechsler

The Christian A. Johnson Memorial Gallery · Middlebury College
Middlebury, Vermont

Distributed by University Press of New England · Hanover and London

Exhibition tour:

The Christian A. Johnson Memorial Gallery
Middlebury College
Middlebury, Vermont
June 16–July 15, 1990

The Neuberger Museum
State University of New York at Purchase
Purchase, New York
September 9–December 10, 1990

Copyright ©1990 by The Christian A. Johnson Memorial Gallery,
Middlebury College, Middlebury, Vermont
Library of Congress Cataloging-in-Publication Data

"Femmes d'esprit": women in Daumier's caricature / [edited by]
Kirsten H. Powell and Elizabeth C. Childs; with contributions by
Janis Bergman-Carton, Lucette Czyba, and Judith Wechsler.
     p. cm.
Catalog of an exhibition held at the Christian A. Johnson Memorial
Gallery, Middlebury College, Middlebury, Vt., June 16–July 15,
1990, and at the Neuberger Museum, State University of New York
at Purchase, Purchase, N.Y., Sept. 9–Dec. 10, 1990.
ISBN 0-9625262-0-7
1. Daumier, Honoré, 1808–1879—Exhibitions. 2. Women—
Caricatures and cartoons—Exhibitions. 3. French wit and humor,
Pictorial—Exhibitions. I. Powell, Kirsten H., 1951–   . II. Childs,
Elizabeth C., 1954–   . III. Christian A. Johnson Memorial
Gallery. IV. Neuberger Museum.
NC1499.D3A4   1990
741.5'944—dc20   89-13898
                                                      CIP

Photo Credits:
Erik Borg, Middlebury Vermont: cats. 1, 4, 6, 9, 10, 11, 12, 14,
16, 17, 22, 23, 28, 30, 31, 38, 48, 53, 54; figs. 2.1, 2.3, 6.1, 6.2

Cover: Honoré Daumier, *—Monsieur, pardon si je vous gêne un peu . . . ,*
published in *Le Charivari,* March 8, 1844 (cat. 20). Print Collection, Miriam and Ira D. Wallach Division of Art, Prints and
Photographs. The New York Public Library, Astor, Lenox, and
Tilden Foundations.

Contents

Foreword

SINCE ITS INCEPTION in 1968 The Christian A. Johnson Memorial Gallery has played an integral role in the educational experience at Middlebury. The primary concern of the gallery at many liberal arts colleges is with the traditional academic year, from September through May, when students are on campus and exhibitions and programs are coordinated with the curriculum. At Middlebury, however, the academic year never really ends. No sooner have the undergraduates left than the campus is alive with over 1,200 students and some 200 faculty in residence for intense study of one of eight foreign languages. Because of this large, specialized audience, the Johnson Gallery has taken particular pride in planning our summer program to complement the Language Schools. This year we feel especially privileged to be able to present the exhibition *"Femmes d'esprit": Women in Daumier's Caricature.* Like most worthwhile endeavors, this project has benefited from the input of many people. From the outset, however, the development of this exhibition has been the work of Kirsten Powell, Assistant Professor of Art. She and her co-curator, Elizabeth C. Childs, have brought a contagious enthusiasm to this project, ensuring its success.

From our point of view, this exhibition represents very clearly what the role of a college gallery can and should be. It can be the catalyst for provocative ideas, and it should be the forum for scholars both at Middlebury and elsewhere to share with our community meaningful investigations and analyses of the visual arts. It is in this spirit that the present exhibition was conceived, and we are pleased that it can be shared with you during a summer that celebrates seventy-five years of Middlebury's commitment to the appreciation and study of foreign cultures. The exhibition is, further, a timely tribute to Olin C. Robison as he concludes his presidency of Middlebury College. Over the past fifteen years he has staunchly advocated Middlebury's Language Schools and the enrichment of its fine-arts program.

RICHARD SAUNDERS
Director
The Christian A. Johnson Memorial Gallery

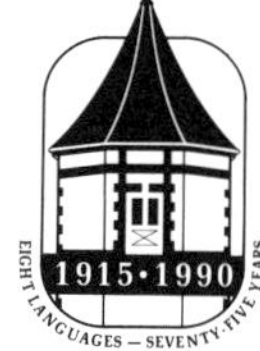

1915 • 1990
EIGHT LANGUAGES — SEVENTY-FIVE YEARS

Acknowledgments

MANY PEOPLE have helped in the preparation of this catalogue and the exhibition it accompanies. We would like to express our gratitude to the administration of Middlebury College and to the Christian A. Johnson Professorship of Art Departmental Enrichment Fund, for funding the project; to Ed Knox, Vice President for Foreign Languages and Director of the Language Schools at Middlebury, for his enthusiasm for the exhibition as part of the cultural activities celebrating the seventy-fifth anniversary of the Middlebury Summer Language Schools; and to Professor Carol Rifelj of the Middlebury College French Department, for her skillful translations of the caricatures' legends. We are also most grateful for the efforts of our contributors—Janis Bergman-Carton, a doctoral candidate at the University of Texas; Lucette Czyba, Professor of French Literature at the Université Lumière Lyon II; and Judith Wechsler, Professor of Art History at Tufts University—for their willingness to participate in this project. As text editor, Fronia W. Simpson carefully supervised the manuscript preparation; as catalogue designer, Catherine Waters accomplished the task of uniting text and image with skill and elegance. Our research was especially aided by Junko Stuveras, Reference Librarian, Butler Library, Columbia University, Paula Berry of The Armand Hammer Collection, Los Angeles, and the staff of Starr Library, Middlebury College. As always, Megan Battey, Middlebury College Slide Curator, lent willing assistance with photographs.

Special appreciation goes to the institutions that lent works to this exhibition and to the individuals who facilitated loan and photography requests. Without the cooperation of Clifford Ackley and Barbara Shapiro of the Museum of Fine Arts, Boston, Susan Stoops and Lisa Leary of the Rose Art Museum of Brandeis University, Colta Ives of The Metropolitan Museum of Art, Roberta Waddell of The New York Public Library, and PNY Fine Prints and Drawings,

New York, this exhibition would not have been possible. We also wish to thank the staff of the Neuberger Museum, State University of New York at Purchase, for their interest in bringing the exhibition to that museum; in particular our thanks go to Dominique Nahas, Director, and Nancy Miller, Associate Director. In addition, we are grateful to Professor Eric G. Carlson of the State University of New York at Purchase for his valuable assistance in this project. Above all, we would like to acknowledge our great debt to the Staff of The Christian A. Johnson Memorial Gallery: Richard Saunders, Director; Christine Taylor, Assistant Curator/Registrar; Ken Pohlman, Preparator; and Mary Ann Brosnan, Secretary. Their tireless efforts, enthusiasm, and humor helped see the exhibition and catalogue to completion. Finally, as true *hommes d'esprit,* John Klein and Luke Powell offered suggestions, encouragement, and support at all stages of the project; to them we extend our deepest thanks.

KIRSTEN POWELL
Middlebury College

ELIZABETH C. CHILDS
State University of New York at Purchase

Lenders to the Exhibition

The Metropolitan Museum of Art, New York

Museum of Fine Arts, Boston, Massachusetts

The New York Public Library,
Miriam and Ira D. Wallach Division of Art, Prints
and Photographs

PNY Fine Prints and Drawings, New York

Rose Art Museum, Brandeis University, Waltham,
Massachusetts,
The Benjamin A. and Julia M. Trustman Collection

Introduction: *Femmes d'esprit* and Daumier's Caricature

ELIZABETH C. CHILDS AND KIRSTEN POWELL

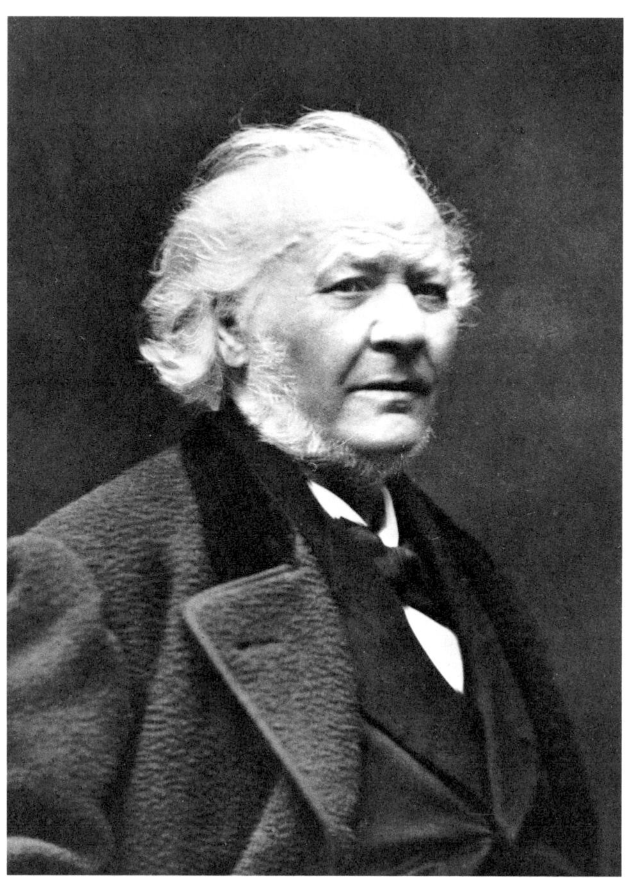

Fig. 1.1 Nadar [Félix Tournachon].
Portrait of Honoré Daumier.
Photograph, ca. 1860. 12 x 8.5 cm.
The Armand Hammer Collection, Los Angeles, California.

IN AN OEUVRE of nearly 5,000 satirical prints, the French caricaturist Honoré Daumier (1808–1879) addressed a wide range of political and social issues with piercing wit and a shrewd economy of formal means.[1] Through his trenchant and often hilarious drawings he debunked contemporary society. Although women feature less frequently than men in Daumier's art, they often play an essential role. In paintings, drawings, and especially in prints, he depicted both real and imaginary women—ranging from happy wives and mothers to zealous bluestocking authors, from feminist socialists to symbolic heroines representing contemporary France and the Republic.[2] The result is a body of caricature that offers insight not only into Daumier's views of the place of women in their society but also into the broader cultural complexities of an era of change in the roles and representations of women. Yet these caricatures are not simple transcriptions of the culture in which they are made. They force us to acknowledge the distinctions between social conventions and their mediation in satire. The stereotypes, ideals, and prejudices of an era all may contribute to the meaning of a caricature; Daumier appropriated such ideas of his times to form his astute commentary.

Daumier lived and worked in a time of social and political change, when the business of publishing satire flourished. An ever-growing middle class provided a willing market for stereotypical images in which the bourgeoisie recognized itself. The invention of lithography by Loys Senefelder in the last decade of the eighteenth century made the rapid printing of cheap images possible.[3] Satirical images were published in daily journals, in bound albums, and on separate sheets as inexpensive works of art, suitable for hanging in one's salon.[4] Subscriptions to these journals were affordable for the middle class; those who did not buy could also see the papers in public reading rooms or simply look at the caricatures hung for viewing in the windows of the publishers' offices.[5]

Daumier created almost all of the lithographs included in this exhibition for publication in one of the most successful satirical journals of nineteenth-century Paris, *Le Charivari*.[6] Founded in 1832 by Charles Philipon, a caricaturist himself, *Le Charivari* was published daily until it folded in 1893. The basic format of the paper remained the same throughout Daumier's career: a four-page newspaper of satirical articles on the social and political life of Paris, with one or more caricatures on page three and advertisements on page four. La Maison Aubert, the firm that published *Le Cha-*

rivari, retained an impressive team of gifted artists to produce satires, including not only Daumier but Grandville [Jean Ignace Isidore Gérard], Gavarni [Sulpice Hippolyte Guillaume Chevalier], Charles Joseph Traviès, and Cham [Amédée de Noé], to name only a few. Typically, the journal's editors would suggest general themes to the artists, such as the "Bas-Bleus" or "Histoire ancienne." The finished satires were then published at intervals as a series, to be enjoyed by the readers over the course of months and sometimes even years. These lithographs were often complemented by related articles which usually appeared in earlier or later issues. The editors hired journalists not only to write articles but also to compose the legends for the lithographs, including those by Daumier.[7] Thus the task of publishing a satire was largely a collaborative effort, and each lithograph was an essential component of a satirical discourse composed of many articles and caricatures. Significantly, that discourse was conceived by an all-male team of journalists and artists for a largely (but certainly not exclusively) male readership.

Daumier was one of the best caricaturists of his time, if not the most prolific or the most famous.[8] His own involvement with *Le Charivari* began at its founding in 1832, and he contributed to the journal throughout his life, with the exception of a hiatus from 1860 to 1863. Thus his career as a satirist spanned the July Monarchy (1830–1848), the Second Republic (1848–1852), the Second Empire (1852–1870), and the first few years of the Third Republic (1870–1940). Daumier was an ardent republican, and his long affiliation with the journal stemmed in part from his belief in the firm moderate republican position maintained by the journal throughout the political tumult of the century.[9] Although it is relatively easy to describe Daumier's overall political convictions as republican, it is more difficult to evaluate his position regarding the movement for women's rights. He espoused the republican ideal of sovereignty by the people, but like many of the great liberal men of his time, his democratic ideals did not necessarily extend to equality for women. Daumier's friend, the historian and writer Jules Michelet, is just one example of a committed republican who staunchly opposed the agenda of female emancipation supported by the utopian socialists.[10]

This exhibition features prints by Daumier in which women appear as main characters or play strong supporting roles. The comprehensive scope of our subject has to date been only partially explored by Daumier scholars.[11] Our present efforts complement the broader revisionist investigation in recent years of the representation of women in nineteenth-century art.[12] Because of this parameter, many of the prints come from series that directly concern activist, progressive women, such as the "Bas-Bleus" and the "Femmes socialistes." The more traditional lives of the wives, mothers, and daughters of the bourgeoisie also provide targets for Daumier's satire. In other lithographs, women assume powerful symbolic roles as allegorical figures. These heroines of Daumier's imagination counterbalance his negative portrayal of bluestocking authors and political activists. Our goal has been to examine Daumier's ambivalent—and from a contemporary viewpoint, often troubling—attitudes toward the women of his society, as expressed in his satirical prints. To focus these issues we have given particular emphasis to the *femme d'esprit* of Daumier's time, the modern woman who is an active participant in her society and who represents the paradoxes of the changing status of women in nineteenth-century French culture.

Although the term *femme d'esprit* is seldom used in France today, in Daumier's time it suggested a wide and even contradictory range of character traits and attitudes; thus it is impossible to isolate one consistent translation in English. Pierre Larousse's *Grand Dictionnaire universel du XIXe siècle,* published between 1866 and 1879, defines *femme d'esprit* (together with *homme d'esprit* and *gens d'esprit*) as someone endowed with keen intelligence and sharp wit.[13] Although the author of the entry on *esprit* gives examples to define the *homme* and *gens d'esprit,* he does not elaborate on the *femme d'esprit,* perhaps because the meaning of the term was far from clear in nineteenth-century usage. Our examination of the term's appearance in a variety of texts reveals its multivalent meaning.[14] In the mid-nineteenth century, the term was often used to describe women of letters and women with progressive political ideals. Yet its application was not limited to feminists—more traditional women could also be described by the term *femmes d'esprit;* depending on the speaker and the audience, such an appellation could be either complimentary or insulting.

Along with intelligence and wit, *femme d'esprit* implies a woman endowed with cleverness, elegance, social agility, and conversational brilliance. Such a woman prides herself on her understanding of character: in 1840 Alfred de Musset observed that "a *femme d'esprit,* for example (a *femme d'esprit* knows so many things!), must not be wrong, I believe, about the real character of people: she must see well from the first glance."[15] A *femme d'esprit* is expected to be highly perceptive: in the serialized novel *Rocambole* by Pierre-Alexis Ponson du Terrail, a male character remarks, "You are thus not a *femme d'esprit,* as I believed, if you would imagine that I only mind your business and not my own."[16]

A *femme d'esprit* can be beautiful and charming. When the writer Delphine Gay de Girardin died, Alfred de Vigny wrote of "this *femme d'esprit,* beautiful and good, all she needed to be completely worthy and more perfectly honored was another mother and a different marriage."[17] A *femme d'esprit* is skilled in the arts of conversation—Louis Duranty wrote in 1860 of a certain "Madame Vieuxnoir! This was a *femme d'esprit,* of beautiful conversation . . . What charm, what genius."[18] Social graces come easily for a *femme d'esprit:* according to Balzac, "good or bad taste depends on a thousand little nuances of this genre [such as the proper way to hold a handkerchief], which a *femme d'esprit* grasps immediately, and which certain women never understand."[19]

This array of characteristics, including intelligence, perceptiveness, cleverness, and verbal skill make up a highly attractive personality from our twentieth-century point of view. And in the nineteenth century, these qualities of *esprit,* when possessed in moderation, were indeed readily valued by men as attributes of an ideal woman, as demonstrated in popular songs and poems of the period.[20] Yet nineteenth-century French society encouraged in greater measure the qualities of obedience, passivity, and intellectual modesty extolled as feminine virtues by Enlightenment authors such as Jean-Jacques Rousseau.[21] In a century of progressive cultural upheaval and subsequent conservative backlash, reactions to *femmes d'esprit* were predictably mixed. Women with too much *esprit* were, some believed, too spirited to be capable of love. This perspective informs a text written by one of Daumier's publishers, Jules Hetzel, who warned men that "it is perhaps not very desirable that the woman one loves have too much *esprit*. . . . It is possibly true to say that a woman who has too much *esprit* almost never has enough heart."[22] A popular song praising women for the broad range of their *esprit* (including the talents of a quick wit and inventiveness) claimed that women also have their mischievous traits, "much like the rose has its thorn."[23] The talents of a *femme d'esprit* could be irritating: Henri-Frédéric Amiel's Madame Lucile "is a *femme d'esprit,* . . . with plenty of spite in her imagination."[24] Although *femmes d'esprit* may be witty conversationalists, in some men's eyes they simply talk too much. Hetzel complained that *"femmes d'esprit* nearly always talk a little too loudly, in too many places, and a little too much for everyone's taste."[25]

According to the negative stereotype of the *femme d'esprit,* an excess of spirit and a poverty of physical charms often go hand in hand. Some male authors described the typical *femme d'esprit* as ugly, as if her lack of conventional beauty has forced her to the seemingly desperate and unnatural measure of relying on her wits rather than her looks. Hetzel, for example, concluded that "when one speaks of *femmes d'esprit,* one inevitably ends up talking about ugly women."[26] Many *femmes d'esprit* supposedly lacked sexual allure. In the Goncourts' *Charles Demailly,* published in 1860, men discuss qualities to seek in a mistress: "'Which mistress suits us? A stupid mistress,' says Franchemont. 'Oh!' says Demailly, 'it is enough if she is not a *femme d'esprit.'*"[27] A *femme d'esprit* is attractive to some men only if she does not brandish her intellectual talents; according to a male character in Balzac's *La Comédie humaine,* she should "never abuse her advantages, for she has to be little and silly in order to catch a man."[28]

The proliferation of these diverse stereotypes of the *femme d'esprit* parallels the emergence of the feminist movement in nineteenth-century France. The shifting meanings of the term provide a linguistic index of conflicting response to the growing demands for the emancipation and equality of women. As part of the idealism that led to the French Revolution of 1789, some women called for a new range of political rights for themselves as well as for greater freedom of expression and more liberal sexual attitudes. Numerous feminist tracts appeared during the Revolution, including Olympe de Gouges's *Déclaration des droits de la femme et de la citoyenne* in 1791. But by 1793 strident attacks against feminism had largely silenced such progressive voices. By 1804 Napoleon's Civil Code not only denied citizenship to women but placed them under the control of their fathers until marriage, when husbands substituted a new authority.[29] A feminist movement rose in reaction to these rigid legal structures, which gained force in the 1830s and 1840s. The egalitarian ideal drew inspiration from the utopian writings of Charles Fourier and the comte de Saint-Simon, both of whom believed that equality for women was necessary for social progress. In particular, the feminists of the July Monarchy focused on issues of suffrage, access to jobs, the right to primary education for girls, and a liberalization of restrictive marriage laws.[30] Although women's claims were supported by the male leaders of the emerging French socialist movements, by the 1840s the republican press, as typified by Daumier's caricatures, had turned against the cause of women's rights. In a burgeoning publishing industry with an expanding audience, women both gained and lost. Women writers found greater opportunity for publication, and their voices were heard. Yet in the flourishing satirical press, an increasing number of insulting caricatures of women writers and activists denigrated their quest for equality, symbolically diffusing their challenge to the status quo.

Daumier was clearly no supporter of feminist politics. The few accounts that survive tell us that Daumier's personal life seems to have centered on a stable and traditional family. An artisan and a member of the lower echelon of the bourgeoisie, he was, it appears, a conventional son and husband of his time, who readily accepted his role as breadwinner. His lithographic work was his most important source of income, first when he was a young man helping to support his parents and subsequently during his married life. Champfleury recalls that most of Daumier's artist friends had to balance their artistic ambitions with the need to earn a living from their art in order to support their families.[31]

In 1846 Daumier married Marie-Alexandrine Dassy, a twenty-four-year-old seamstress from a working-class family, who, like most young women of her class, had lived at home until the time of her marriage.[32] Financial security was always a concern for the couple, and Daumier's wife may have continued to do some sewing for additional income. While not a mother, she was primarily a housewife and she is listed on Daumier's death certificate as having no occupation.[33] Arsène Alexandre, Daumier's biographer, knew Madame Daumier and described her as a "good housekeeper and a *femme d'esprit.*"[34] Far from being a *bas-bleu,* Daumier's wife did not strive to be included in her husband's artistic circle.[35] She was, nonetheless, a literate woman (unlike Daumier's own mother) who followed the politics of her time by reading newspapers.[36] She was also a petite bourgeoise who enjoyed modest extravagances during the couple's more prosperous days: in 1849 Daumier stayed in Paris to work while he sent his wife to the seashore for a month.[37] For much of their married life, they lived on the Quai d'Anjou on the Ile St.-Louis—an area inhabited by a mixture of classes, ranging from old prosperous families to the bohemian circle of Baudelaire and a new influx of workers from the ninth arrondissement to the north.

Here, at the very heart of the city, Daumier was well positioned to be a critic and chronicler of modern Paris in all of its diversity.

As the prints in this exhibition amply demonstrate, women fulfill essential roles in Daumier's satires of modern life. As Judith Wechsler observes in her study on gender and gesture, physiognomic and gestural conventions inform Daumier's satirical depictions of women of all classes, ages, and occupations. Elizabeth Childs's study of his prints of domestic life indicates that while the artist was sympathetic to the gender roles both men and women play in the traditional family, he could also be a brutal and irreverent critic of the vanity, snobbery, and materialism he perceived among the bourgeoisie. He also extended harsh judgment, as Janis Bergman-Carton demonstrates in her essay, to the intellectual and politicized women of his day, whom he characterized as unattractive, selfish, promiscuous, and irresponsible shrews. As Lucette Czyba shows through her comparison to the women in Flaubert's novels, such stereotypes were common in literature and antifeminist journalism as well. Although glancing at Daumier's "Bas-Bleus" and "Femmes socialistes" prints might lead one to accuse the artist of uncompromising misogyny, the larger picture is far more complicated. Daumier joined his colleagues in the satirical press in taking potshots at the rising feminist movement and in extolling only conventional roles. But, as Kirsten Powell demonstrates in her essay on the "Histoire ancienne" series, Daumier is more sympathetic to the women of history and mythology, to whom he often assigns symbolic functions through clever inversions of traditional gender expectations. When Daumier distances women from present reality by giving them allegorical identities, he employs them as idealistic symbols and as surrogates for the artist himself, in that they, too, comment on the significant issues of modern life.

Daumier's double standard is telling—he accorded only to fictional women the critical voice and political power sought by liberal women of his time. His contradictory art expresses a wide range of his society's ambivalent attitudes toward the position of women. Yet his satires are not hollow caricatures based on unexamined idealism or rigid prejudice; these images resonate with the artist's shrewd observation of human nature. Although Daumier reduces his subjects to easily graspable caricatures, he also universalizes them by endowing them with disarming familiarity and plausibility. If Daumier's *femmes d'esprit* belong firmly in the nineteenth century, they often convincingly embody some of the desires, ambitions, and commitments that shape the lives of many women today. But these images also demand that we reflect on the authority asserted by stereotypes and consider how in both Daumier's time and our own representation often reinforces the ideology of one audience only at the expense of another.

NOTES

1   Loys Delteil published 3,959 lithographs in the eleven volumes of his catalogue raisonné, *Le Peintre-Graveur illustré: Daumier* (Paris: Chez l'auteur, 1925–1930). Eugène Bouvy catalogued an additional 991 wood engravings in *Daumier: L'Oeuvre gravé du maître. Reproduction de toutes les planches; notices sur chaque ouvrage et sur chaque planche, introduction historique et index alphabétique*, 2 vols. (Paris: Maurice Le Garrec, 1933). The present exhibition includes only lithographs, which are referred to throughout this catalogue by their number in the Delteil catalogue (abbreviated as D.).

2   The catalogue raisonné of the paintings, drawings, and watercolors by Daumier was published by K. E. Maison, *Honoré Daumier: Catalogue Raisonné of the Paintings, Watercolours, and Drawings*, 2 vols. (London and Greenwich, Conn.: New York Graphic Society, 1967–1968). The most efficient method for locating Daumier's works in all media on any particular subject is to consult the comprehensive index by Louis Provost, *Honoré Daumier: A Thematic Guide to the Oeuvre*, ed. Elizabeth C. Childs (New York and London: Garland Publishing, 1989).

3   On the early history of lithography in France, see *De Senefelder à Daumier: Les Débuts de l'art lithographique*, exh. cat. (Paris: Maison de l'histoire bavaroise), 1988.

4   On the history of the satirical press, see Jules Brisson and Félix Ribèyre, *Grands Journaux de France* (Paris: Jouast Père, 1862); Philippe Roberts-Jones, *La Presse satirique illustrée entre 1860 et 1890* (Paris: Institut français de la presse, 1956); and John Grand-Carteret, *Les Moeurs et la caricature en France* (Paris: La Librairie illustrée, 1888).

5   On public reading rooms and the proliferation of private libraries where, for a subscription fee, one also could have access to satirical journals, see Theodore Zeldin, "Newspapers and Corruption," in *France 1848–1945: Intellect, Taste, and Anxiety* (Oxford: Clarendon Press, 1977), chap. 11.

6   On the history of the administration of *Le Charivari* during Daumier's career and for a discussion of the subscription patterns of the journal, see Elizabeth C. Childs, "Honoré Daumier and the Exotic Vision: Studies in French Caricature and Culture, 1830–1870," Ph.D. diss., Columbia University, 1989, chap. 1 and appendix. See also Ursula E. Koch and Pierre-Paul Sagave, *Le Charivari: Die Geschichte einer Pariser Tageszeitung im Kampf um die Republik, 1832 bis 1882* (Cologne: C. W. Leske, 1984). On the development of the market for satirical prints in Paris during the early July Monarchy, as well as a detailed account of Daumier's relationship to Philipon, see James Cuno, "Charles Philipon and La Maison Aubert: The Business, Politics,

and Public of Caricature in Paris, 1820–1840," Ph.D. diss., Harvard University, 1985.

7   For a discussion of the authorship of Daumier's legends and the editorial process of *Le Charivari,* see Childs, "In Collaboration: The Publishing of Satire," in "Honoré Daumier and the Exotic Vision," pp. 43–51.

8   David Kunzle stresses that Cham created more satires than Daumier, and that during their lifetimes Cham was the better known of the two satirists; "Cham, the Popular Caricaturist — Cham and Daumier: Two Careers, Two Reputations, Two Audiences," *Gazette des Beaux-Arts,* ser. 6, vol. 96 (December 1980): 213-24.

9   The studies of Daumier's republican politics are far too numerous to mention here. One excellent brief discussion is T. J. Clark, *The Absolute Bourgeois* (Greenwich, Conn.: New York Graphic Society, 1973), chap. 4. For the most complete bibliography of the Daumier literature (to 1980), see Provost, *Honoré Daumier: A Thematic Guide,* pp. 237-64.

10 On Michelet's politics and antifeminist position, see Claire Moses, *French Feminism in the Nineteenth Century* (Albany, N.Y.: S.U.N.Y. Press, 1984), pp. 158-61.

11 Among the studies to have addressed the issue of women in Daumier's caricature are Philippe Roberts-Jones, "Les Femmes dans l'oeuvre lithographique de Daumier," *Médecine de France* 23 (1951): 29–32, and Ann Morrissey, *Daumier on Women: The Lithographs,* exh. cat. (Los Angeles: University Art Galleries, University of Southern California, 1982), pp. 7–21. For studies of caricatures of progressive women, see Cäcilia Rentmeister, "Daumier und das hässliche Geschlecht," in *Honoré Daumier und die ungelösten Probleme der bürgerlichen Gesellschaft,* exh. cat. (Berlin: Neue Gesellschaft für bildende Kunst for the Schloss Charlottenburg, 1974), pp. 57–78, and Françoise Parturier and Jacqueline Armingeat, *Daumier: Intellectuelles ("Les Bas-Bleus" et "Femmes socialistes")* (Paris: Editions Vilo-Paris, 1974).

12 See, for example, the summary of recent scholarship on Degas's representations of women in Kathleen Adler, "Angles of Vision," *Art in America* 78 (January 1990): 181 note 1. An important compendium of feminist essays, several of which address the representation of women in nineteenth-century art, is Linda Nochlin, *Women, Art, and Power and Other Essays* (New York: Harper and Row, 1988).

13 Pierre Larousse, *Grand Dictionnaire universel du XIXᵉ siècle* (Geneva and Paris, 1866–1879; Slatkine Reprint, 1982), s.v. "esprit"; "Homme, femme d'esprit, gens d'esprit. Personnes dont l'esprit brille par sa finesse, son tour ingénieux et piquant." We would like to thank Janis Bergman-Carton for first bringing the phrase *femme d'esprit* to our attention and for the many insights we gained from reading a longer, earlier version of her essay published in this catalogue.

14 The following examples have been culled from the Treasury of the French Language (ARTFL) Database at the University of Chicago, a textual data base of 1,700 French texts, from the seventeenth to the twentieth century. For use of the data base, see "Current Research Using ARTFL," *The ARTFL Project Newsletter* 5 (Winter 1989–1990): 1-5. We would like to extend our thanks to Junko Stuveras of the Butler Library at Columbia University for her assistance in running a search for the phrase

femme d'esprit. A recent statistical analysis of gender terms from the ARTFL data base is also relevant to our study. From his analysis of the word *femme* in texts over four centuries, Mark Olsen shows that during the first half of the nineteenth century women play an increasingly important role in the cultural *mentalité.* According to Olsen, while the appearance of the word *homme* in printed matter roughly doubled in use from the seventeenth to the nineteenth centuries, the relative frequency of *femme* quadrupled by the second half of the nineteenth century, although use of both words declined in the first half of the twentieth century (p. 9). Moreover, Olsen's research indicates the extent to which "woman" was paired with the concept of possession during Daumier's day: the second most frequent word to precede *femme* during the nineteenth century was *sa,* while *ma* is the third most frequent collocate between 1800 and 1850; only in our century does the neutral, nonpossessive *la* appear as one of the top *ten* collocates (p. 10). As Olsen observes, "The frequent collocation of *femme* with possessives suggests that the definition of woman depends, in no small part, on being 'possessed' by someone, typically a male" (p. 11). Olsen also notes that by the mid-nineteenth century, age distinctions made up the most frequent categorization, outnumbering moral, physical, and social attributes; youth, in particular, is a category of description that increasingly appears, jumping in rank from forty-eighth in the eighteenth century to sixth in the nineteenth century (p. 12). See Mark Olsen, "*Histoire des mentalités* and the Treasury of the French Language: A Quantitative Approach," unpublished paper delivered at the Western Society for French History Annual Meeting, New Orleans, October 20, 1989.

15 "Une femme d'esprit, par exemple (une femme d'esprit sait tant de choses!), ne doit pas se tromper, à ce que je crois, sur le vrai caractère des gens: elle doit bien voir au premier coup d'oeil"; Alfred de Musset, "Un Caprice," in *Comédies et proverbes,* ed. F. Gastinel, vol. 3 (Paris: Les Belles-Lettres, 1957), p. 223.

16 "Vous n'êtes donc pas une femme d'esprit, comme je le croyais, que vous vous imaginiez que je fais simplement vos affaires et non les miennes"; Pierre-Alexis Ponson du Terrail, *Rocambole,* ed. C. A. Ciccione, vol. 3 (Monaco: Editions du Rocher, 1963–1965), p. 169.

17 "Delphine Gay de Girardin, une mort très prompte vient d'enlever en huit jours cette femme d'esprit, belle et bonne à qui il n'a manqué pour être complètement digne et plus parfaitement honorée, qu'une autre mère et un mariage différent"; Alfred-Victor, comte de Vigny, *Mémoires inédites,* ed. J. Sangnier (Paris, 1863; reprint, Paris: Gallimard, 1959), p. 176.

18 "Madame Vieuxnoir! C'était là une femme d'esprit, de belle conversation . . . que de charmes, que de génie!"; Louis Duranty, *Le Malheur d'Henriette Gérard* (Paris, 1860; reprint, Paris: Gallimard, 1942), p. 192.

19 "Le bon ou le mauvais goût tiennent à mille petites nuances de ce genre, qu'une femme d'esprit saisit promptement, et que certaines femmes ne comprendront jamais"; Honoré de Balzac, *Les Illusions perdues,* ed. A. Adam (Paris, 1843; reprint, Paris: Garnier, 1961), p. 182.

20 See the poems "Esprit des femmes" and "La Femme bel esprit" by Louis Janet, ed., *L'Esprit des femmes* (Paris: Louis Janet,

1820), pp. 1–3, 28–29. For example: "It is not always beauty which makes us cherish a woman: *esprit* and kindness have more power over our souls" (Ce n'est pas toujours la beauté / Qui nous fait chérir une femme: l'esprit et l'amabilité / Ont plus de pouvoir sur notre âme), p. 3.

21 For example, the ideal woman in Rousseau's *Julie ou la Nouvelle Héloïse* (1761) is characterized as one who knows her place: she happily assumes her role as a nursing mother, and she effaces her own intellectual abilities. The connection between Rousseau's ideas and the representations of motherhood is explored in Carol Duncan, "Happy Mothers and Other New Ideas in Eighteenth-Century French Art," in Norma Broude and M. Garrard, eds., *Feminism and Art History: Questioning the Litany* (New York: Harper and Row, 1982), chap. 11.

22 "Il n'est peut-être pas très à désirer que la femme qu'on aime ait beaucoup d'esprit . . . et il est peut-être vrai de dire qu'une femme qui a beaucoup d'esprit n'a presque jamais assez de coeur"; Pierre Stahl [Jules Hetzel], *L'Esprit des femmes et les femmes d'esprit* (Paris: Michel Lévy, 1853; reprint, Paris: Hetzel, 1882), p. 6.

23 "Vous avez l'esprit du moment . . . Vous possédez l'esprit léger . . . Vous avez l'esprit inventif . . . La Femme a son esprit malin / Comme la rose a son épine"; in the song entitled "Esprit des femmes" in Janet, ed., *L'Esprit des femmes,* p. 3.

24 "Madame Lucile . . . est une femme d'esprit, qui a du naturel et de l'entrain, avec assez de malice dans l'imagination"; Henri-Frédéric Amiel, *Journal de l'année 1866,* ed. L. Bopp (Paris, 1866; reprint, Paris: Gallimard, 1959), p. 386.

25 "Les femmes d'esprit parlent presque toujours un peu trop haut, un peu trop partout, un peu trop pour tout le monde"; Stahl [Hetzel], *L'Esprit des femmes,* pp. 7–8.

26 "Quand on parle des femmes d'esprit, on en arrive forcément à parler des laides"; in Stahl [Hetzel], *L'Esprit des femmes,* p. 64.

27 "'Quelle est la maîtresse qui nous convient?' 'Une maîtresse bête,' dit Franchemont. 'Oh!'—dit Demailly—'il suffit qu'elle ne soit pas une femme d'esprit'"; Edmond and Jules Goncourt, *Charles Demailly* (Paris, 1860; reprint, Paris: Charpentier, 1876), p. 202.

28 "Une femme d'esprit n'abuse jamais de ses avantages, il faut être petite et sotte pour s'emparer d'un homme"; Honoré de Balzac, "La Maison Nucingen," in *La Comédie humaine* (Paris, 1838; reprint, Paris: Gallimard, 1936), p. 624.

29 For a discussion of the status of women and the law during the nineteenth century, see Jean-François Tetu, "Remarques sur le statut juridique de la femme au XIX siècle," in *La Femme au XIX siècle: Littérature et idéologie* (Lyon: Presses Universitaires de Lyon, 1979), pp. 5-17.

30 For a detailed account of these developments, see Moses, *French Feminism,* and Barbara Taylor, *Eve and the New Jerusalem: Socialism and Feminism in the Nineteenth Century* (New York: Pantheon Books, 1983). An excellent study of the development of feminism in the last half of the nineteenth century is Patrick Kay Bidelman, *Pariahs, Stand Up! The Founding of the Liberal Feminist Movement in France, 1858–1889,* Contributions in Women's Studies, no. 31 (Westport, Conn.: Greenwood Press, 1982).

31 These friends, many of whom also lived on the Ile St.-Louis, included the painters Jean Meissonier, François Bonvin, Charles Daubigny, and the sculptors Jean Feuchère, Michel Pascal, Antoine-Auguste Préault, and Adolphe-Victor Geoffroy-Dechaume. Champfleury [Jules Fleury], as quoted in *Daumier raconté par lui-même et par ses amis,* ed. Pierre Courthion (Vésenaz-Geneva: Pierre Cailler, 1945), p. 80.

32 Courthion, *Daumier raconté par lui-même,* p. 252.

33 Roger Passeron, *Daumier* (New York: Rizzoli, 1981), p. 295.

34 Arsène Alexandre, *Honoré Daumier: L'Homme et l'oeuvre* (Paris: H. Laurens, 1888), as quoted in Catherine Camboulives, *Daumier: Scènes de la vie conjugale,* exh. cat. (St. Denis: Musée d'art et d'histoire, 1988), p. 21.

35 The painter Théodore Rousseau's account of his visits with Daumier at Barbizon in 1865 reveals that Madame Daumier did not feel comfortable joining the evening meetings of the male artists and that she "modestly declined" Rousseau's offer to loan her a set of men's clothes so that she would feel more at ease among them; see Passeron, *Daumier,* p. 279.

36 Evidence that Madame Daumier followed contemporary politics is found in "Lettres à Didine ou les bains de mer de Madame Daumier," in Jean Cherpin, *L'Homme Daumier: Un Visage qui sort de l'ombre* (Provence: Arts et livres de Provence, 1973), p. 58.

37 This trip was both a vacation and an escape from the cholera outbreak in Paris; see Cherpin, "Lettres à Didine."

La Bourgeoise:
Public and Private Life in Daumier's Caricature

ELIZABETH C. CHILDS

THE NINETEENTH-CENTURY HISTORIAN of caricature John Grand-Carteret made an erroneous but telling generalization about the work of Daumier when he said that it lacked in "two capital elements—*la jeunesse and la femme*" (youth and woman).[1] It was unfair, he continued, to expect these elements in Daumier's work, "as if an artist could be at the same time deep, comic, graceful, and pretty. . . . Assuredly, humanity, as this great painter saw it, could not be beautiful." Henry James similarly observed that "when a man leaves out so much of life as Daumier—youth and beauty and the charm of woman and the loveliness of childhood . . . when he exhibits a deficiency on this scale . . . it is interesting . . . to put one['s] finger on the reason why we are not scandalized. I think this reason is that, on the whole, [Daumier] is so peculiarly serious."[2]

First, it must be noted how wrong both of these distinguished writers were in their assessments of Daumier's oeuvre. Youth and women abound in Daumier's lithographic work. As Judith Wechsler shows in her essay in this catalogue, over one-fourth of Daumier's lithographs include women—hardly a negligible proportion. Children appear in hundreds of images as well.[3] What Grand-Carteret and James did not find in Daumier's work were many "lovely" children or "beautiful, charming" women. The hundreds of mothers who appear in Daumier's satires are certainly young women —but the majority of them do not fit these authors' conventional definitions of grace, charm, or prettiness. The art of caricature does not idealize beauty; it seizes on widely accepted stereotypes of physical appearance and exploits them for expressive ends. The result can be pretty but is more often common, and even ugly. James attributed the want of feminine beauty in Daumier's art to the serious nature of the artist. It is only the sober force of Daumier's comedy, James argues, that prevents it from scandalizing us by its lack of female beauty. In the realm of such serious art, he seems to imply, women are out of place.

James is right to claim that Daumier is peculiarly serious in his comedy—the artist sought to mix universal observations about human nature with the humor of anecdote and circumstance. But both James and Grand-Carteret, blinkered by their own preconceptions, overlooked the hundreds of caricatures of ordinary and unidealized young women in the simple business of everyday living—as mothers, wives, shopkeepers, maids, and even as writers and political activists. Scenes of their rituals of courtship, marriage, fashion, and social intercourse make up one of Daumier's most significant subjects throughout his career.

The mundane and even ridiculous moments of life inspire many of Daumier's satires. Many exemplify what Baudelaire termed the significative comic (*le comique significatif*). This kind of humor relies on those events that make men and women laugh in ordinary situations. Such comedy elicits only a smile or chuckle of recognition rather than a guffaw of surprise or the hilarity inspired by burlesque.[4] This theory of the comic includes, but is not limited to, the laughter of little children:

It is the joy of receiving, the joy of breathing, the joy of confiding, the joy of contemplation, of living, of growing up. . . . Also, generally, its manifestation is rather the smile, something analogous to the wagging of a dog's tail or the purring of cats.[5]

Baudelaire's significative comic depends on anecdotes, on fleeting impressions of trivialities—in short, on the response to the transient moment which is at the heart of his more general concept of *modernité*. For Baudelaire, caricature was an appropriate medium for the expression of this humor because "trivial images, sketches of the crowd and the street, and caricatures are often the most faithful mirror of life."[6] These are precisely the moments that Daumier represents in his satire of the bourgeoise, the ordinary woman of the urban middle class.

The subject of bourgeois culture was a safe and popular one for the satire of Daumier and the editors of *Le Charivari*. During most of the July Monarchy (after 1835) and the Second Republic, when political caricature was subject to the prior approval of the censor, the choice of inoffensive social themes permitted the journal to sidestep the dangers of suppression. *Le Charivari* was particularly successful throughout its long history in preserving its sharp satirical edge and its moderate republican position in spite of the presence of censorship.[7] Part of that success depended on a judicious emphasis on social satire.

Daumier amused his bourgeois readers with what James called "the large cracked mirror" of his caricature.[8] The bourgeoisie of the nineteenth century is a broad concept that defies simple definition.[9] Although its members were all ostensibly of the middle class, they ranged from aristocrats with dwindling resources to the prosperous and educated artisan. Professions of its members included the highly respected domains of business and politics as well as the more unconventional careers of some writers and entertainers. Daumier was sufficiently successful, educated, and financially secure to be described as a member of the lower bourgeoisie.[10]

Yet he intentionally promoted his identity as an artisan and, in his art, demonstrated great sympathy for the values, dreams, and frustrations of the working class. The inspiration for his witty but often scathing satire of bourgeois culture may have derived from his ambiguous social position on its fringes: he kept just enough distance from it all to retain his sense of humor.

Daumier's view of the bourgeoise embraces a wide range of her adult experience. Most of his prints revolve around her primary identities as wife and homemaker. Marriage among the Parisian bourgeois was usually a matter of convenience, duty, or ambition. Although sympathy and romantic love played important roles, marriage was primarily an arrangement between families, in which men took the initiative and women accepted paternal decisions.[11] Marriage was a means of acquiring greater wealth and social position not only for the couple involved but for their entire families. A guide to domestic life, popular throughout Daumier's life, advised that "marriage is in general a means of increasing one's credit and one's fortune and of ensuring one's success in the world."[12] The negotiation of dowries, or the property brought by a woman to her marriage, was of particular importance. In the eyes of the law, a dowry bought a woman a protector and a manager for the administration of the property she was considered incompetent to handle.[13] For the young man, a generous dowry could often mean a crucial advantage in business. But wives had to be chosen with great care; marriage was binding for life, for during Daumier's lifetime divorce was illegal. Although divorce had been allowed on certain grounds both after the Revolution of 1789 and again in Napoléon's time, it had been abolished altogether in 1816. Although feminists of various political persuasions struggled to win back this basic right, divorce was only reinstated in 1884.[14] Daumier's virulent caricatures from 1848 of "Les Divorceuses" (Advocates of divorce) as homely, childless, and licentious ideologues (cat. 31, 32, and 34) suggest his firm support of the conventional commitments of marriage.[15]

Daumier was clearly amused by the rituals of courtship. He often focused on the mischief and deception practiced by young lovers. In one print (cat. 1) he parodies a young couple who carry on a covert flirtation throughout a music lesson, in spite of the chaperoning presence of the young woman's mother in the background. The tutor teaches his pupil two social skills essential to her future: how to play the piano (a supposedly feminine grace important for entertaining hus-

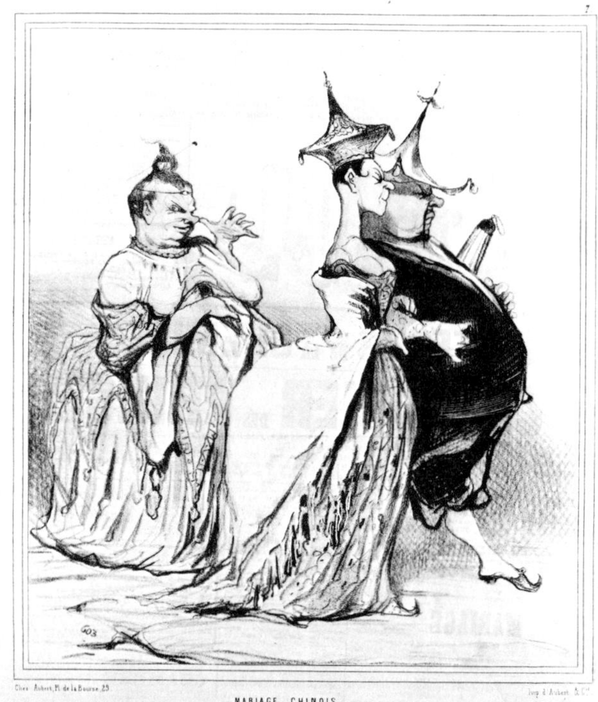

Fig. 2.1 Honoré Daumier.
Mariage chinois. L'adresse du pêcheur à tendre ses filets, l'habileté du chasseur à saisir le gibier, les ruses du maquignon pour cacher les vices rédhibitoires de son cheval, rien n'est comparable à l'adresse, à l'habileté, à la ruse que déploie une mère pour marier sa fille. . . . Les pauvres chinois ont beau se méfier des appâts, du miel et de la glu, il en tombe toujours quelqu'un dans le traquenard maternel.

The strategy with which the fisherman attracts his fish, the cleverness of the hunter in seizing his game, the ruses of the horse dealer in hiding the defects of his horse, none are comparable to the cleverness and the ruses used by a mother to marry her daughter. . . . Poor Chinese men are smart to be suspicious of baits, honey, and glue. Someone always falls into the mother's snare.

"Voyage en Chine" (Travel in China), no. 7; published in *Le Charivari,* April 28, 1844 (D. 1195).
Private collection.

band and guests alike) and how to receive the attentions of an admirer without arousing suspicion.

Daumier's view of the manipulative games of courtship and the economic politics of marriage could be quite cynical. In his series "Voyage en Chine" he uses the satirical device of a fictional exotic setting to comment on the social conventions of bourgeois French culture.[16] In *Mariage chinois* (fig. 2.1) an obese mother-in-law thumbs her nose at the obése groom, who leads away his prize—a rather ugly, squinting bride. She has hoodwinked the man by assisting her daughter to catch a respectable mate, whose financial station is suggested by his Chinese parasol imitative of the bourgeois umbrella. The theme of the domineering mother-in-law, who ruled as tyrant over her daughter's interests, runs throughout popular literature: the serialized book *Les Français peints par eux-mêmes,* for example, devotes a chapter to "La Belle-Mère" (The mother-in-law), the unfortunate "invention of civilization."[17] By projecting one of the most common male complaints—the tyrannical mother-in-law—into an exotic setting, Daumier distances the problem and permits his male audience to laugh with sympathy and relief at a familiar scene.

Elsewhere in the "Voyage en Chine" series an anxious husband watches his new wife browse through antiques in *Mariez-vous donc . . . en Chine* (cat. 2). The legend cautions that any Chinese woman—no matter what her dowry—will lead her husband to financial ruin through her spending. A stinging irony of the satire resides in the fictitious Chinese setting, for it was well known in France that real Chinese women were obedient and powerless wives who seldom appeared in public.[18] The shopping spree was a pleasure of the Parisian bourgeoise, and a spendthrift wife could destroy any advantage a husband had gained through a large dowry. In such prints Daumier mocks the materialism and the manipulative behavior of a class that conceived marriage as "the greatest financial operation of their lives."[19]

The laws regulating marriage in the mid-nineteenth century were directly based on Napoléon's Civil Code of 1804, which granted women few of what today are considered basic civil rights. Women were prohibited from conducting business contracts, testifying in court, or bringing lawsuits without their husbands' permission. The Napoleonic Civil Code also dictated certain marital duties:

Husband and wife owe each other fidelity, support and assistance.

A husband owes protection to his wife; a wife obedience to her husband.

A wife is bound to live with her husband and to follow him wherever he deems proper to reside. The husband is bound to receive her, and to supply her with whatever is necessary for the wants of life, according to his means and condition.[20]

The Napoleonic code formed the basis of the secular marriage ceremony, held at a couple's local town hall. Daumier's print *A la mairie* (cat. 3) parodies a couple at the moment of their vows. A short groom, eyes cast down, acquiesces to the ceremony, while the bride, taller and more assertive, eyes the mayor with irritation as he reads the edict proclaiming her submission to her husband. Her hands grasp the table indignantly, and her expression conveys her distaste for the terms of her new contract. Daumier's joke here depends on an inversion of conventional gender roles. This satirical structure is one that also appears in the "Histoire ancienne" series, which Kirsten Powell discusses in her essay in this catalogue. Here, the groom is passive while the bride is aggressive. Moreover, the groom's tractable posture emphasizes by contrast the bride's resistance, just as the smaller stature of the groom exaggerates her unusual height.

The ideal wife of mid-century Paris embodied the virtue of obedience required by the law. She was also quiet, reserved, and skilled in the domestic arts. An "exactly proper" wife is described by one male writer of the time as "judicious, practical, active, acting as hostess in her parlor with grace and relieving her husband of all domestic worries. With this, she is also sweet, courageous, pretty; as simple and natural as one could desire, modest and reserved, making sure never to bother anyone, and to make her home agreeable for everyone."[21] She was also an attentive and devoted mother. As Janis Bergman-Carton and Lucette Czyba demonstrate in their essays in this catalogue, Daumier ridiculed the ambitions of the *bas-bleus* women writers by characterizing them as poor housekeepers, unfaithful wives, and irresponsible mothers. When women with literary ambitions turn to their books and manuscripts, domestic havoc reigns: babies drown (cat. 23), and neglected husbands struggle with laundry and sewing (cat. 21 and 22).

Daumier's view of marriage stresses pragmatic responsibilities but is nonetheless often sentimental. Grand passions and great events do not figure in his landscapes of married life. He focuses instead on the ordinary moments and small significant actions that make up the patterns of everyday existence. In Daumier's domestic world both men and women take pleasure in the simplicity and harmony of their shared lives. His contented wives do not display great intellect and wit; the *esprit* of the *bas-bleus* vanishes before the hearth and home of conjugal love. The opinion that love necessarily represses one's esprit is extolled by Jules Hetzel, one of Daumier's publishers, who writes,

In Daumier's series "Moeurs conjugales" the romance of courtship gives way to routine and familiarity.[23] For example, Daumier brilliantly captures the mutual ennui of two Parisians who, after six months of marriage, have come to know each other too well (cat. 4). In a striking composition of diagonally reclining figures, the yawning faces of the wife and husband mirror one another: like their lives, their figures are fused together. Their well-appointed parlor suggests that they have succeeded in filling their lives with possessions if not with interesting conversation.

Daumier even invades the privacy of the marital bedroom; here couples read in bed (D. 634), gaze at stars outside their window (D. 648), play with their children (D. 627), or fall into bed exhausted after a night of dancing (D. 679). Some of these prints of the early 1840s were surely inspired by Daumier's own relationship with his future wife, Marie-Alexandrine Dassy, as both the artist's own features and Marie-Alexandrine's nickname, "Didine," appear in images in the "Moeurs conjugales" series (D. 667 and 679). Daumier alludes to passionate love only occasionally and then indirectly in his prints: for instance, one new husband stands by his bed, rubbing his hands with glee the day after his wedding, declaring his newfound happiness as his passive wife sleeps (D. 517). Daumier's depictions of people in bed ring true; heads back, lips parted, his couples slumber and snore through the night, at peace with their lives and their love (fig. 2.2). They are often joined by infants or dozing cats at the foot of the bed—all enjoying a simple pleasure of life. Such prints embody Baudelaire's sense of the significative comic. Like the purr of a cat, our response to such natural and uncomplicated images is reflexive—we smile as we recognize the private moments of our lives.

Although simple in their subjects, these representations of domestic life are not facile. The bedroom functions in these prints as a symbolic space, as important a setting as the parlor in other images. Daumier's bedrooms signify domestic and marital order. The curtains that enclose the beds for warmth in the winter serve in several caricatures as framing elements, like stage curtains drawn back to reveal a miniature drama. Moreover, the cloak of night's darkness in these bed-

room scenes offers Daumier the opportunity to dramatize the contrast between intense blacks and brilliant light areas that set off the faces of his subjects.

The setting of the bedroom is not limited to Daumier's depictions of modern life; it appears in the "Histoire ancienne" series as well, as a symbol of restored marital order. The subject of *Ulysse et Pénélope* (cat. 39) is the couple's potentially erotic reunion ending their long separation following the Trojan War. In Daumier's unsensual rendering of this middle-aged couple in bed, Ulysses sleeps contentedly while Penelope gazes affectionately on her spouse's face. Their marriage is clearly restored. Such marital order is transgressed in other satires of modern life when the bed is abandoned. For example, a restless *bas-bleu* author leaves her bed and her husband in the middle of the night to pace the floor as she thinks about her novel in progress (D. 1225). Daumier's message is clear: proper wives should be content with their assigned place in marriage. In these various bedroom scenes Daumier represents the intimacy of the private sphere with disarming candor. His subject of familial accord is consistent with the proliferation of informal domestic scenes in art during the July Monarchy. In numerous prints blissful, nurturing mothers and loving patriarchs tend their contented families. This romantic idea informs representations not only of bourgeois families but also of the family of the Citizen King, Louis-Philippe.[24]

Although Daumier portrayed the satisfactions offered by marriage, he also believed that it is far from a perfect state. In a world of marriages based on convenience, duty, and social ambition, with no possibility of divorce, it is not surprising that extramarital affairs were common among the bourgeoisie.[25] Daumier's vision, however, excludes the common reality of both institutionalized and informal practices of prostitution, which figure so prominently in the work of Edgar Degas and Henri Toulouse-Lautrec in the following decades. Occasionally Daumier alludes to a man's fond recollections of past affairs, memories often inspired by the sight of a familiar woman on the street (D. 581 and 2395). In one bold composition, a fashionably dressed bourgeois gazes wistfully into a shop window displaying four corsets (cat. 5). A network of diagonal lines draws our attention to his own middle-aged, bulging paunch. In contrast to his relaxed torso stand the stiff corsets, which trace the contours of four distinct female figures. These remind him of his slender first love; of a wench named Cocotte and "big Mimi," both with curvaceous figures; and of his wife, endowed with the

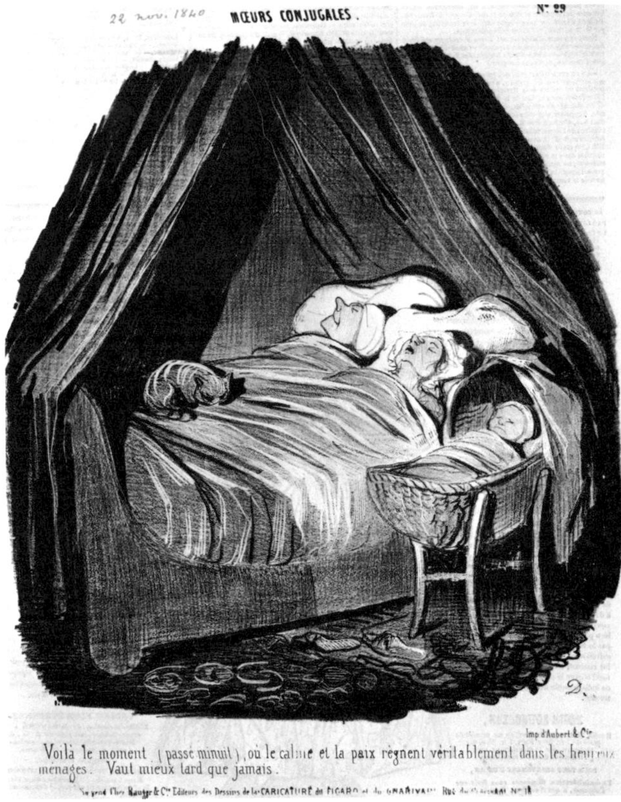

Fig. 2.2 Honoré Daumier.
Voilà le moment (passé minuit), où le calme et la paix régnent véritablement dans les heureux ménages. Vaut mieux tard que jamais.

Finally the moment (after midnight), when calm and peace truly reign in happy homes. Better late than never.

"Moeurs conjugales" (Married life), no. 29; published in *Le Charivari,* November 22, 1840 (D. 652).
The Armand Hammer Collection, Los Angeles, California.

thickest waist and hips of the lot. The corsets become ciphers of past liaisons, reducing the women in his life to sets of measurements. This gentleman's materialist habits, evident in his sartorial splendor, here extend to the consumption of women, whom he regards as one more genre of products to be displayed, acquired, and enjoyed by the bourgeois.

In Daumier's satires, however, the blame for actual infidelity falls heavily on the shoulders of the wives. Daumier's prints about adultery star not the betrayed wife but the cuckolded husband who discovers his spouse in a wide range of compromising situations: strolling with another man (D. 645 and 1667); enjoying an illicit rendez-vous in a carriage (D. 658); or accepting a good-night kiss from her lover under her husband's bedroom window (D. 663). The betrayed husband usually figures as a helpless victim; even when he confronts his wife, she gains the upper hand. In one instance a wife shields her lover from her husband's violent threats (cat. 6). As the woman cautions her husband with "Would you kill your children's father?" the husband recoils in realization of the scope of his wife's infidelity. Far from hysterical or contrite, the wife commands this scene as she thrusts herself between the two men, advancing as her husband retreats. Meanwhile her lover cowers beneath the table; the tablecloth that hides him merges with the skirts of his lover's dress to suggest his violation of a most private sphere. Daumier's strong-willed and unfaithful bourgeoise here insists on her right to be the mistress of her house in more than one sense of the word.

Apprehension about sexual infidelity merges with fear of miscegenation in a print depicting the encounter between the Parisian bourgeoisie and exotic Algerian soldiers known as Turcos (cat. 7). These soldiers from North Africa, who served as riflemen in the French army, played critical roles in the international military campaigns of Napoléon III during the Second Empire. Following their triumphant entrance into Paris in August 1859, a regiment of Turcos camped in the Bois de Vincennes, where they were visited by crowds of admiring Parisians, stimulated by racist curiosity to see how the supposedly barbaric heroes lived. Numerous caricatures by both Daumier and Cham in the series "Au Camp de St. Maur" parody the attraction these foreign men held for the women of Paris.[26] In one print a bourgeoise, strolling through the Turco camp on the arm of her husband, gazes admiringly at the soldiers. Her husband warns her away, reminding her that because she is pregnant, she must be careful not to catch one of their glances, lest she give birth to "a little Negro." The husband's anxiety derives from his wife's sexual attraction to the soldier, but he masks his fears of adultery and miscegenation through an appeal to his wife's superstitious beliefs about pregnancy. French folklore held that the imagination of a pregnant woman could influence and even deform the fetus. The pregnant body, the old wives' tale goes, is a sensitive conductor of the sensations of the outside world or the impressions of the mother's mind, and the appearance of an unborn child may be permanently altered by the mother's experience, or even by her dreams and fantasies.[27] Therefore, according to the superstition, this bourgeoise must control her imagination for the sake of her unborn child. In actuality, social convention demands that she control her flirtatious urges in public for the sake of propriety and respectability.

The public life of the bourgeoisie is a central element of Daumier's satire throughout his career. This is particularly true of his prints published during the Second Empire, when he uses the bourgeois to comment on important changes in the nature of public experience. The Paris of the July Monarchy was essentially still *vieux Paris,* medieval neighborhoods made up of winding streets and small houses. Yet an urban explosion had followed industrialization, and the rapidly growing working class, made up largely of provincials who had moved to the city, crowded into inadequate quarters. The population had risen from 547,800 in 1801 to over 1,000,000 by 1848.[28] By mid-century the city was in a physical crisis: housing, sewage, transportation, water systems, and even cemeteries had all been stretched far beyond their capacities. With the advent of the Second Empire, Napoléon III began an ambitious program of urban renewal under the direction of his prefect of the department of the Seine, Baron Georges-Eugène Haussmann.[29] Under Haussmann the city was completely transformed not only by new fresh water, sewer, and gas-lighting systems but also by the construction of an imposing network of public parks and grand boulevards. These boulevards served several purposes, such as the improvement of general access to important public services such as markets, train stations, and business districts. Moreover, the newly widened streets and generous sidewalks facilitated the movement of large crowds (including, significantly, the dispatch of imperial troops during times of civil revolt). Thus, the streets of Second-Empire Paris, lined with shops, restaurants, and outdoor cafés, became a new stage for modern life, and much of the social activity that had occurred in the privacy of homes moved into the public sphere. Vast new apartment complexes, funded by ambitious speculators, also appeared along these boulevards, providing new housing for the affluent but often displacing families of more modest means.

The rise of a new city meant the inevitable destruction of the old. Prints depicting the modernization of Paris typically emphasize the extent of the architectural ruins and the labor of the wrecking crews (fig. 2.3); Daumier focuses less on the physical process of demolition and more on its social consequences. His bourgeois often find themselves caught between their desire for the new elegance and progressive future promised by Napoléon III and their nostalgia for the past. In a print from 1853, the first year of Haussmann's renovations, a couple pauses to watch the demolition of the apartment building in which they had made their first home (cat. 8). The husband bemoans the loss of their nuptial chamber, commenting that "those masons have no

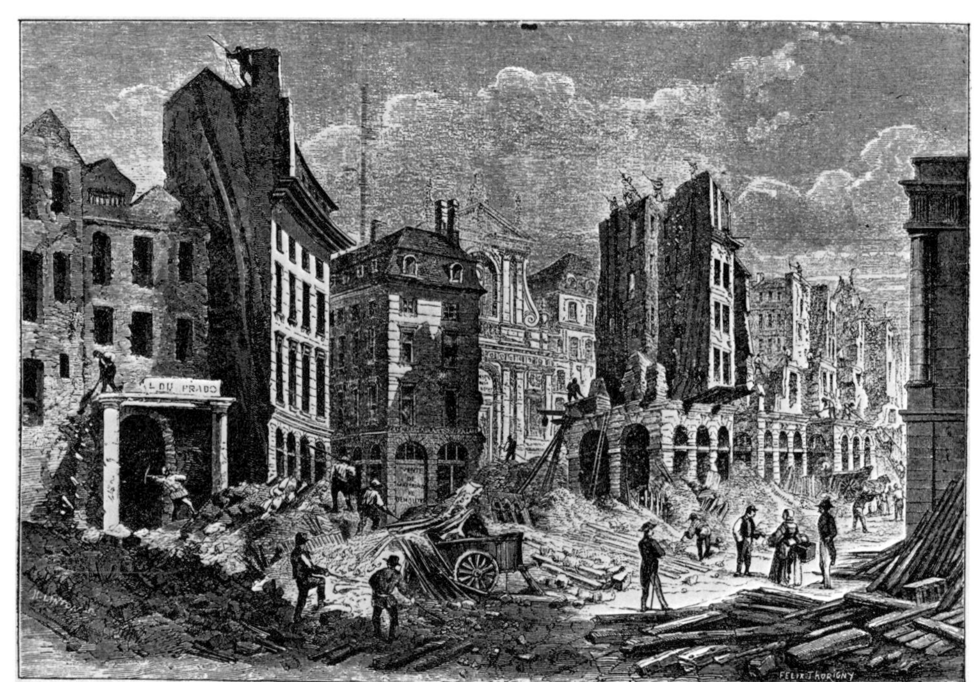

Fig. 2.3 Félix Thorigny. *Percement du Boulevard Sébastopol—Aspect des démolitions de la rue de la Barillerie.*

Construction of the Boulevard Sébastopol. View of the demolition of the rue de la Barillerie, 1859.

Illustration in Charles Simond, *Paris de 1800 à 1900 d'après les estampes et les mémoires du temps,* vol. 2, 1830–1870 (Paris: Librairie Plon, 1900), p. 534. Private collection.

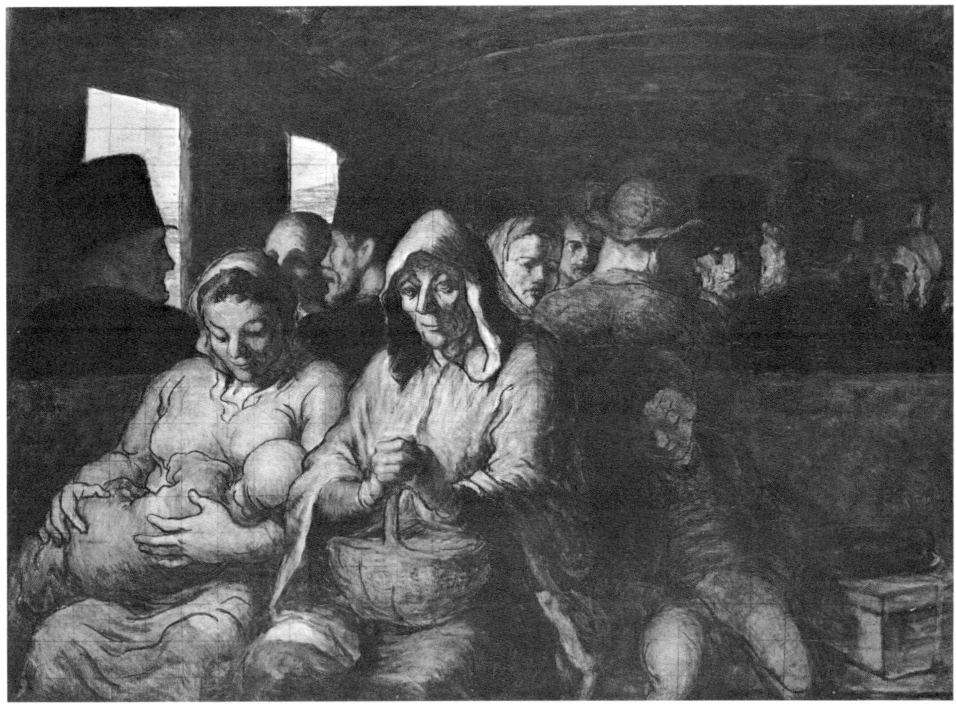

Fig. 2.4 Honoré Daumier. *The Third-Class Carriage.* Ca. 1863–1865. Oil on canvas, 25¾ x 35½ in. (65.4 x 90.2 cm). The Metropolitan Museum of Art, Bequest of Mrs. H. O. Havemeyer, 1929. The H. O. Havemeyer Collection (29.100.129).

respect for anything, they don't honor memories!" Critics of Haussmann's plans often bemoaned just such a price exacted by the modernization: "City without past, full of minds without memories, of hearts without tears, of souls without love!"[30] Daumier's bourgeois couple gazes upward over a broken wall toward the mason perched on the higher floors where the less expensive apartments were usually located. The now prosperous couple, confronted with the wreckage of their previous (and perhaps more modest) home, also witnesses the destruction of their private realm of dream and memory. As with many of the prints in Daumier's "Moeurs conjugales" series of the previous decade (see fig. 2.2), the bedroom symbolizes the private domain that here is crassly violated and transformed into a public spectacle. Here, the couple's memories are assaulted by a society that emphasizes uniformity and newness at the expense of individual experience.

Daumier's critiques of the renovation of Paris may have even broader implications. Most of his satires of the reconstruction program appeared in *Le Charivari* during the early years of the Second Empire. Following a period of considerable liberty for the press during the Second Republic, Napoléon III reinstituted a harsh policy of press censorship that forbade any criticism of himself or his regime.[31] Yet as Francis Klingender argues, Daumier's focus on the theme of demolition criticizes Napoléon III indirectly by lambasting his destruction of the older, more democratic city and by questioning the value of the elegant plaster facades that primarily served the needs of the middle class.[32] The destruction of old Paris resulted in not only a loss of charm and romance but also the city of the workers and the revolutionaries of 1789, 1830, and 1848. One American observer of the Paris of 1867 longed to "revive the memories of . . . the talk of a cosy old café, the traditions of the first revolution—the spirit whereof yet gleams from the savage eyes of many a surly *ouvrier,* on his long walk from his work to the suburbs."[33] Like this observer, Daumier was skeptical of the advances as he watched Napoléon III oust both the Second Republic and a valued way of life. Daumier's satire stresses that even the bourgeois couple, the supposed beneficiaries of all this rebuilding, also suffers a poignant and important loss in the wake of modernization.

Public life of the bourgeoisie is a central element of Daumier's satire. In his scenes of the street, the omnibus, and the train, Daumier parodies the convention that a proper bourgeoise remains aloof when in public. On buses during the Second Empire, proper men and women sat in silence:

The same account relates that men who do manage to
engage women in conversation on a bus may look forward to a probable conquest when the bus ride is over.
In this world the bourgeoise retains her reputation and
her position by maintaining her silence. Daumier's
timid and indignant women recoil reflexively when in
the proximity of male strangers (cat. 15 and 16). As
Judith Wechsler demonstrates in her essay, the gestures
and bearing of Daumier's bourgeoise reflect the social
conventions that require her to remain utterly reserved
when alone in public.

In his painted images of crowds on buses and
trains, Daumier moves beyond the satire of middle-
class propriety to the idealization of the working class.
In monumental compositions such as *The Third-Class
Carriage* (fig. 2.4), he often heroicizes women and children, in this case excluding men altogether. In the
foreground the massive figure of an imposing old
woman dominates the family group of a young mother
and two children. Daumier's bold outlines in this
unfinished painting share the graphic vigor of the caricatural line of his lithographs. As in his satire, these
representative figures summarize the experience of an
entire class. Through the image of women Daumier
asserts the solidity of the family within the broader
structure of society. Three generations of workers, organized in pyramidal harmony, testify to a continuity of
social patterns unshaken by the fast-paced modernization of Second-Empire France. This affirmative vision
of the family informs many of Daumier's paintings of
the poor women of Paris. In his compelling portrayals
of laundresses, for example (see fig. 6.3), strong women
simultaneously tend their work and their children. As
these fatigued laborers mount the stairs leading from
their workplace on the Seine, their children follow not
only in their steps but also in the established patterns
of their mothers' lives.

In contrast to these sober and monumental compositions of lower-class women, Daumier's treatment of
the bourgeoise is primarily satirical. His prints often
feature the middle-class *parisienne* in public with her

husband, as companion to his interests and follies. One
of caricature's most pompous couples is Monsieur and
Madame Prud'homme, who appear with regularity in
Daumier's caricatures of the Second Empire (cat. 9).
Prud'homme, the archetypal bourgeois, is pretentious,
materialistic, and small-minded.[35] His fat belly, jowl-
framed face, balding head, and bombastic gestures
suggest a man at middle age, too lazy and too sure of
himself to question his conventional values. His wife
usually appears in the supporting role of partner to his
shortcomings. As a similarly rotund and fashionably
dressed figure, her great concerns include looking pre-
sentable and carrying herself with the pomp and dignity required by her station in life — not only on the
boulevards of the new Paris (D. 2589) but even when in
the Egyptian desert (D. 3748) or in her swimming costume at the beach (D. 2593).

Although Daumier's bourgeoise often serves in public only as a decorative backdrop to her husband's actions, in one hilarious group of prints debunking modern fashion, the shoe slips onto the other foot. The
pretensions of the fashion-conscious had amused Daumier throughout his career,[36] and the exaggerated
forms of crinolines provoked even greater extremes for
his satire. The crinoline was a stiff petticoat con-

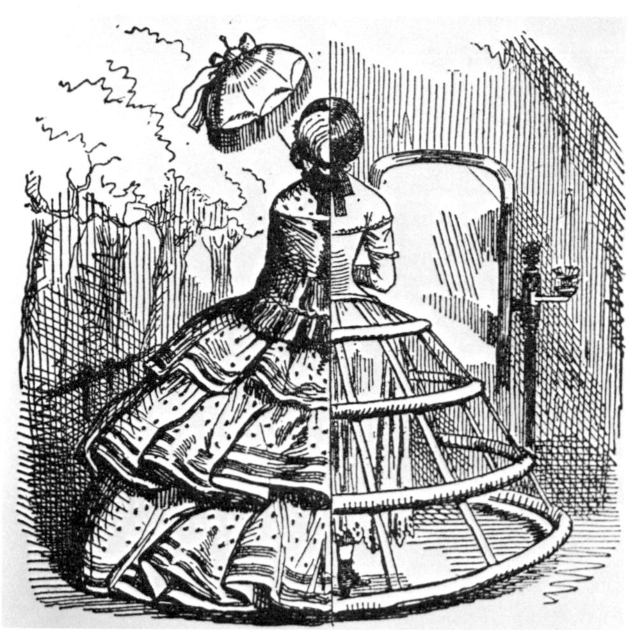

Fig. 2.5 Anonymous.
Dress and the Lady.
Woodcut in *Punch, or the London Charivari,* August 23, 1856, p. 73.
Columbia University Librairies, Butler Library, New York.

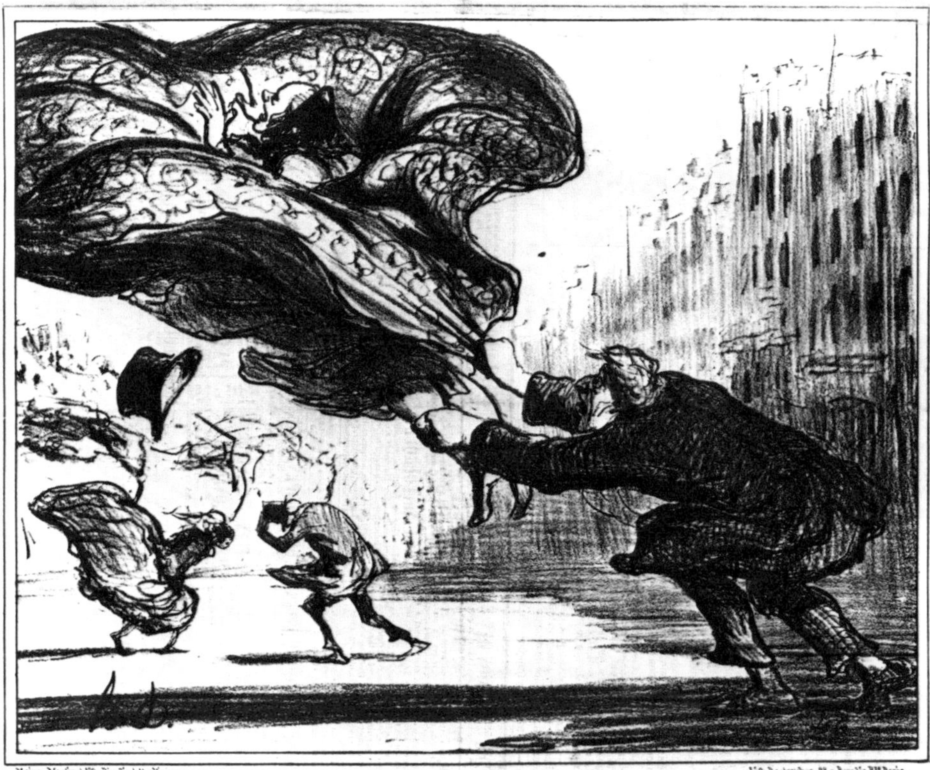

Fig. 2.6 Honoré Daumier. *Danger de porter des jupons-ballons à l'époque des coups de vent de l'équinoxe.*

The danger of wearing hoopskirts at the windy period of the equinox.

"Actualités" (Current events), no. 383; published in *Le Charivari,* April 3, 1857 (D. 2917).
The Armand Hammer Collection, Los Angeles, California.

structed of concentric hoops, made first from cane, iron, and rubber, and finally, with greatest success, from steel wires (fig. 2.5). Invented around 1855, the crinoline derived its name from the horsehair (*crin*) that had been used since the July Monarchy to stiffen petticoats. Such a rigid structure was needed to support the voluminous skirts made of the crisp but lightweight muslins and silks popular at the time.[37] Extremely slim waists were the ideal of feminine beauty, and women struggled to reduce their waist measurements to less than twenty inches through some rather torturous devices.[38] Crinoline petticoats, in conjunction with tightly laced corsets, created the highly desirable illusion of even slimmer waists. Moreover, the rigid skirts swayed with the moving body, permitting the attentive male observer treasured glimpses of such forbidden features as the ankle or even the calf. This subtle form of flirtation was the special domain of the supposedly unavailable married woman. Young single women were generally expected to dress and behave more soberly, in a manner befitting their innocence and

advertising their suitability as wives rather than mistresses. In bourgeois culture the pursuit of high fashion was an approved pastime more for the experienced matron than the naïve unmarried girl: chic and charm were both skills to be cultivated after marriage, under the appreciative eye and with the financial support of a husband.[39]

Daumier exposes how fashion can dominate women's lives. His bourgeoise does not wear her crinoline; rather, her crinoline wears her. In prints published in the series "Actualités" and "La Crinolomanie," massive skirts sweep recklessly through the boulevards of Paris.[40] Daumier's women fight for the precious space of the sidewalk, knocking into each other like ruffled bumper cars (D. 2625, 2627, and 2758); the great expanses of the skirts even invite confused chickens to nest in the moving cages of steel hoops (D. 2916). In one print, an acrobatic bourgeois manages to escort his wife only by stretching elastically across vast expanses of skirt (cat. 10). The woman's haughty expression and stiff posture suggest her pride not only in her own taste but in that of her husband, who has the good fortune to escort her.

Daumier also exaggerates the tendency of the moving skirts to reveal tantalizing portions of leg. In one print, the wind whips the billowing crinoline of a bourgeoise over her head and threatens to carry her off like a balloon, in spite of her resourceful husband, who desperately grabs the ankles of his air-borne wife (fig. 2.6). In another print Daumier's ladies jump from a hot-air balloon only to float safely to the ground in their inflated skirts which serve as parachutes (D. 2759). Crinoline skirts also knock aside whoever happens to be in their way. In *Plus que ça d'ballon . . . excusez!* (cat. 11), a tall and skinny bourgeois, pinned to the wall by the passing bourgeoise, is overpowered by her elephantine skirts. His baffled expression suggests that he, like the cuckolded husband in earlier prints, is the helpless victim at the hands of willful women. Daumier may have displaced the serious debate about the position of women in his society into this burlesque comedy about bourgeois *moeurs;* the image of the bourgeoise who imposes her silly crinoline on men in the street may suggest Daumier's view that women who demand an increased presence in the public sphere are as ridiculous and unwelcome as this fashion.

The parody of the crinoline was widespread in Europe in the 1850s and early 1860s. In the British magazine *Punch, or the London Charivari,* for example, the anonymous satires of the cumbersome, dangerous, yet often revealing petticoats also turn on the same punch lines as those used by Daumier.[41] The success of Daumier's caricatures of the bourgeoise results not only from his jokes, often the same as those seen in the satirical journals of his era, but also in his draftsmanship. Although Daumier's prints are anecdotal and humorous, they are nonetheless strong formal compositions. Daumier is attracted to the motif of the crinoline not only by an opportunity to lampoon high fashion but also by the simple contours of the huge, rounded skirts with which he fills the foreground of his compositions.

During the Second Empire the public sphere became as important as the private sphere for Daumier's commentary on the bourgeoise. A large proportion of his prints feature grand women on grand boulevards. They promenade through streets and parks on the arms of proud husbands; they circumnavigate the treacherous obstacles of Haussmann's reconstruction projects; they compete for seats on the crowded omnibuses. They inhabit their city with exaggerated airs of authority and confidence. Daumier also uses the street as a stage

for making poignant contrasts between wealthy and poor women. An emaciated worker comments on how well fed a bourgeoise looks in her crinoline (D. 2969); an exhausted street sweeper reflects that the long, wide skirts of the bourgeoise cleans half the street for her (D. 2970); and the haggard expression of a half-frozen sweeper—who offers to knock the snow off the crinoline skirt of a passing bourgeoise—suggests she feels more repressed anger than goodwill toward the wealthier woman (D. 3089).

The bourgeoise essentially disappears from Daumier's caricature in the late 1860s, along with his other subjects taken from the daily life of the middle class. With the loosening of press restrictions during the so-called Liberal Empire after 1867, Daumier's satire turned almost exclusively to direct political commentary. In these later years his allegorical and symbolic figures eclipse the quotidian women of the previous decades. Even though the bourgeoise often apparently plays a supporting role to her husband in the melodramas of Daumier's satire, she is actually a central character. Often driven by her vanity or her desire for status and wealth, she plays a ready partner to the social and materialist ambitions of her spouse. For an audience made up largely of republican middle-class men, Daumier's satires published in *Le Charivari* elicited both the vicious laughter of disdain and the humor of the recognition of one's own follies. Many of his images of the bourgeoise permitted his male readers to laugh at their own class by making their women— their wives, mothers, and mistresses—the brunt of the jokes. Daumier's images also reinforced a conventional model of familial obligation in traditional marriage, a model he appears to have followed in his personal life. Even as he satirized the vanity and pretensions of the bourgeoise, Daumier championed her conventional roles as wife and mother. At a time when women were challenging these accepted norms, Daumier's art reaffirmed the resistance of his audience to such change.

NOTES

Broadly speaking, a bourgeoise is a woman whose beliefs, attitudes, and practices are conventionally middle class; a bourgeois is her male counterpart; and the bourgeoisie is the social class to which they belong.

1   John Grand-Carteret, *Les Moeurs et la caricature en France* (Paris: La Librairie illustrée, 1888), as quoted in Henry James, *Daumier: Caricaturist* (Emmaus, Penn.: Rodale Press, 1954), pp. 25–26.

2 James, *Daumier: Caricaturist,* p. 28.

3 The wide range of Daumier's lithographs featuring women and children is evident from even a brief consultation of Louis Provost, *Honoré Daumier: A Thematic Guide to the Oeuvre,* ed. Elizabeth C. Childs (New York and London: Garland Publishing, 1989).

4 This latter genre of humor is described by Baudelaire as *absolute* humor. Baudelaire develops his definitions of these types of the comic in "De l'essence du rire et généralement du comique dans les arts plastiques" (1857); reprinted in Charles Baudelaire, *Curiosités esthétiques: L'Art romantique* (Paris: Garnier Frères, 1962), pp. 241–63. For a discussion of the significative and absolute comic in Baudelaire's theory of caricature, see Ainslie Armstrong McLees, *"Argot plastique:* Baudelaire and Caricature," Ph.D. diss., University of Virginia, 1980, pp. 49–53.

5 "C'est la joie de recevoir, la joie de respirer, la joie de s'ouvrir, la joie de contempler, de vivre, de grandir . . . Aussi, généralement, est-ce plutôt le sourire, quelque chose d'analogue au balancement de queue des chiens ou au ronron des chats"; Baudelaire, *Curiosités esthétiques: L'Art romantique,* p. 253.

6 "[L]es images triviales, les croquis de la foule et de la rue, les caricatures, sont souvent le miroir le plus fidèle de la vie"; Baudelaire, "Quelques Caricaturistes français" (1857), in *Curiosités esthétiques: L'Art romantique,* p. 265.

7 On the history of censorship of the satirical press in general and of *Le Charivari* in particular, see Elizabeth C. Childs, "Honoré Daumier and the Exotic Vision: Studies in French Caricature and Culture, 1830–1870," Ph.D. diss., Columbia University, 1989, chap. 1.

8 James, *Daumier: Caricaturist,* p. 30.

9 A useful discussion of the confusing and often contradictory uses of the term "bourgeois" is found in Peter Gay, *The Bourgeois Experience: Victoria to Freud: Education of the Senses,* vol. 1 (New York: Oxford University Press, 1984), pp. 17–44.

10 On Daumier's background and that of his wife, see Childs and Powell, introduction to this catalogue.

11 On marriage among the bourgeoisie, see Theodore Zeldin, "Marriage and Morals," in *France 1848–1945: Ambition and Love,* vol. 1 (Oxford: Oxford University Press, 1979), pp. 285–314. See also James F. McMillan, "Marriage and Motherhood in the Bourgeoisie," in *Housewife or Harlot: The Place of Women in French Society, 1870–1940* (New York: St. Martin's Press, 1981), pp. 29–36; Anne Martin-Figier, "La Maîtresse de maison," in Jean-Paul Aron, ed., *Misérable et glorieuse: La femme du XIXᵉ siècle* (Paris: Editions complexe, 1984), pp. 117–34; and Erna Hellerstein, Leslie Hume, and Karen Offen, eds., *Victorian Women: A Documentary Account of Women's Lives in Nineteenth-Century England, France, and the United States* (Stanford: Stanford University Press, 1981), pp. 118–33.

12 Joseph Droz, *Essai sur l'art d'être heureux,* 7th ed. (Paris, 1853), as quoted in Zeldin, *Ambition and Love,* p. 288.

13 Zeldin, *Ambition and Love,* pp. 357–68.

14 On the history of the legalization of divorce in France, see Antony Copley, *Sexual Moralities in France, 1780–1980: New Ideas on the Family, Divorce, and Homosexuality. An Essay on Moral Change* (London and New York: Routledge, 1989), chap. 5; and

Roderick Phillips, *Putting Asunder: A History of Divorce in Western Society* (Cambridge: Cambridge University Press, 1988), pp. 422–28. On the issue of divorce as part of the feminist demands at mid-century, see Claire Moses, *French Feminism in the Nineteenth Century* (Albany, N.Y.: S.U.N.Y. Press, 1984), pp. 141–42.

15 Several prints from the series "Les Divorceuses" (D. 1769–1774) are discussed by Judith Wechsler in her essay in this catalogue. For an in-depth examination of the theme of divorce in the satire of *Le Charivari,* see Lucette Czyba, "Féminisme et caricature. La Question du divorce dans *Le Charivari,*" in the forthcoming proceedings of the colloquium "La Satire imagée et la caricature entre la République et la Censure de 1830 à 1900," held in Frankfurt, 1988.

16 On this series, see Childs, "Honoré Daumier and the Exotic Vision," pp. 239–72.

17 Anna Marie, "La Belle-Mère," in *Les Français peints par eux-mêmes,* vol. 2 (Paris, 1842; reprint, Paris: Furne, 1853), pp. 285–88.

18 The stereotype of the servile Chinese wife was one who stays at home and who should be "only a pure shadow and a simple echo" (qu'une pure ombre et un simple écho). See the serialized, fictional travel account of Old Nick [P. E. Forgues], *La Chine ouverte: Aventures d'un Fan-Kouei dans le pays de Tsin* (Paris: H. Fournier, 1844), p. 330.

19 Paul Bureau, *L'Indiscipline des moeurs* (Paris, 1927), as quoted in Zeldin, *Ambition and Love,* p. 291.

20 Hellerstein, Hume, and Offen, eds., *Victorian Women,* p. 162.

21 "La femme de Marc Monnier est exactement ce qu'il lui fallait, judicieuse, pratique, active, faisant avec grâce les honneurs de son salon et débarrassant son mari de toute préoccupation domestique. Avec cela douce, courageuse, joie; simple et naturelle autant qu'on peut le désirer, modeste et réservée, attentive à ne jamais faire de peine à personne et à rendre sa maison agréable pour tout le monde"; Henri-Frédéric Amiel, *Journal de l'année 1866* (Paris: L. Bopp, 1866; reprint, Paris: Gallimard, 1959), p. 1962.

22 "On peut avoir de l'esprit avant de s'aimer, il est indispensable d'en avoir après s'être aimé; mais en avoir beaucoup pendant qu'on s'aime, c'est inutile, c'est peut-être périlleux, et c'est très probablement le signe qu'on ne s'aime guère. L'amour n'est si bon que parce qu'au fond il est un peu bête, il nous simplifie"; P. J. Stahl [Jules Hetzel], *L'Esprit des femmes et les femmes d'esprit* (Paris: Michel Lévy, 1853; reprint, Paris: Hetzel, 1882), p. 11.

23 The series "Moeurs conjugales" (Married life) includes D. 624–683. The most comprehensive study of the prints in the series, as well as other scenes of married life, is Catherine Camboulives, *Daumier: Scènes de la vie conjugale,* exh. cat. (Saint-Denis: Musée d'art et d'histoire, 1988).

24 On the image of the family in prints of the July Monarchy, see Michel Melot, "'La Mauvaise Mère': Etude d'un thème romantique dans l'estampe et la littérature," *Gazette des Beaux-Arts* 79 (March 1972): 167–76.

25 On the widespread presence of adultery (a crime punishable by imprisonment or a fine) and prostitution in nineteenth-century French culture, see Zeldin, *Ambition and Love,* pp. 303–12.

26 For a discussion of the Turco series "Au Camp de St. Maur,"

see Elizabeth C. Childs, "Die Turkos in Paris: Ein Sonntagsvergnügen der Weltstädter," in *Die Rückkehr der Barbaren: Europäer und Wilde in der Karikatur Honoré Daumiers,* exh. cat. (Hamburg: Hans Christians for Kunsthalle der Stadt Bielefeld, 1985), pp. 315–29, and Childs, "Honoré Daumier and the Exotic Vision," pp. 34–42, 145–63.

27 Paul Gabriel Boucé, "Imagination, Pregnant Women, and Monsters in Eighteenth-Century England and France," in G. S. Rousseau and Roy Porter, eds., in *Sexual Underworlds of the Enlightenment* (Chapel Hill: University of North Carolina Press, 1988), pp. 86–100. I am grateful to Michael Marrinan for first drawing my attention to this article.

28 David H. Pinkney, *Napoléon III and the Rebuilding of Paris* (Princeton: Princeton University Press, 1958), p. 151.

29 For a study of Haussmann's plans and achievements, see Pinkney, *Napoléon III and the Rebuilding of Paris,* and Howard Saalman, *Haussmann: Paris Transformed,* Planning and Cities series (New York: George Braziller, 1971).

30 Louis Veuillot, *Les Odeurs de Paris* (Paris, 1867), as quoted in Robert Herbert, *Impressionism: Art, Leisure, and Parisian Society* (New Haven and London: Yale University Press, 1988), p. 1.

31 See "Décret organique sur la presse," printed in *Le Moniteur universel,* February 18, 1852, which strictly limited the freedom of the press. An excellent general history of the French press that considers the role of censorship is Irene Collins, *The Government and the Newspaper Press in France, 1814–1871* (Oxford: Oxford University Press, 1959).

32 Francis K. Klingender, "Daumier and the Reconstruction of Paris," *Architectural Review* 90 (August 1941): 57. Klingender observes that during the Second Republic Daumier had already satirized Louis-Napoléon as a plasterer who, along with his mason Thiers, aspired to rebuild the structures of the republican government (D. 2081).

33 Henry Tuckerman, *Papers about Paris* (New York, 1867), as quoted in Herbert, *Impressionism,* p. 1.

34 "On s'assoit à côté les uns des autres sans rien dire—les femmes abaissent leur voile, les hommes ramènent leur chapeau sur leurs yeux. . . . Qu'on vous pousse involontairement du côté de votre voisine, elle retire son genou d'un geste superbement indigné, et vous écrase de son dédain. Qu'un voyageur candide et novice essaye d'entamer la conversation, on lui répond par monosyllabes, puis on finit par ne plus lui répondre du tout"; *Les Petits Paris: Paris en omnibus* (Paris: Librairie d'Alphonse Taride, 1854), p. 54.

35 On the history of Prud'homme in caricature, see Judith Wechsler, *A Human Comedy: Physiognomy and Caricature in Nineteenth-Century Paris* (Chicago: University of Chicago Press, 1982), chap. 4.

36 For example, several prints in the "Voyage en Chine" series of 1844—such as D. 1194—mock the fashions of the bourgeoise.

37 On the history of crinolines, see Norah Waugh, *Corsets and Crinolines* (London: B.T. Batsford, 1987); Elizabeth Ewing, *Fashion in Underwear* (London: B.T. Batsford, 1971); and Almut Junker and Eva Stille, "Die Bürgerin als Dame der Gesellschaft: Krinoline und Turnüre, 1840–1890," in *Zur Geschichte der Unterwäsche, 1700–1960,* exh. cat. (Frankfurt:

Historisches Museum, 1988), pp. 117–23. I would like to thank Carol Rathore of the staff of the Costume Institute Library of The Metropolitan Museum of Art for her kind assistance in my research.

38 Ewing, *Fashion in Underwear,* pp. 50–53.

39 On the different attitudes toward fashion among married and unmarried women of the bourgeoisie, see Valerie Steele, *Paris Fashion: A Cultural History* (New York: Oxford University Press, 1988), generally, and esp. pp. 156–60.

40 Daumier's prints featuring crinolines include D. 2968–2973. For a complete listing of his forty-five lithographs with this subject, see Provost, *Honoré Daumier: A Thematic Guide,* p. 109.

41 For example, the idea of a lady whose skirt causes havoc in the street is the basis of both Daumier's print (cat. 11) and the article "Melancholy Accident," in *Punch* (August 16, 1856). Jokes about crinolines are ubiquitous in *Punch* during the years 1856–1858. Satires based on the exposure of women's limbs due to the effect of wind or unexpected movement of the crinolines appear on December 20, 1856; July 24, 1858; and August 21, 1858. Other humorous satires feature ladies floating through the air (September 6, 1856); a man wearing a crinoline-style overcoat to avoid the grasp of thugs (December 27, 1856); a lover hiding behind a young woman's skirts (October 4, 1856); and schoolboys who use the back of their mothers' full skirts as shelves for their schoolbooks (August 22, 1857). For a discussion of crinolines in the pages of *Punch,* see Christina Walkley, *The Way to Wear 'em. One Hundred Fifty Years of "Punch" on Fashion* (London: Peter Owen, 1985), pp. 12–16, 72–74.

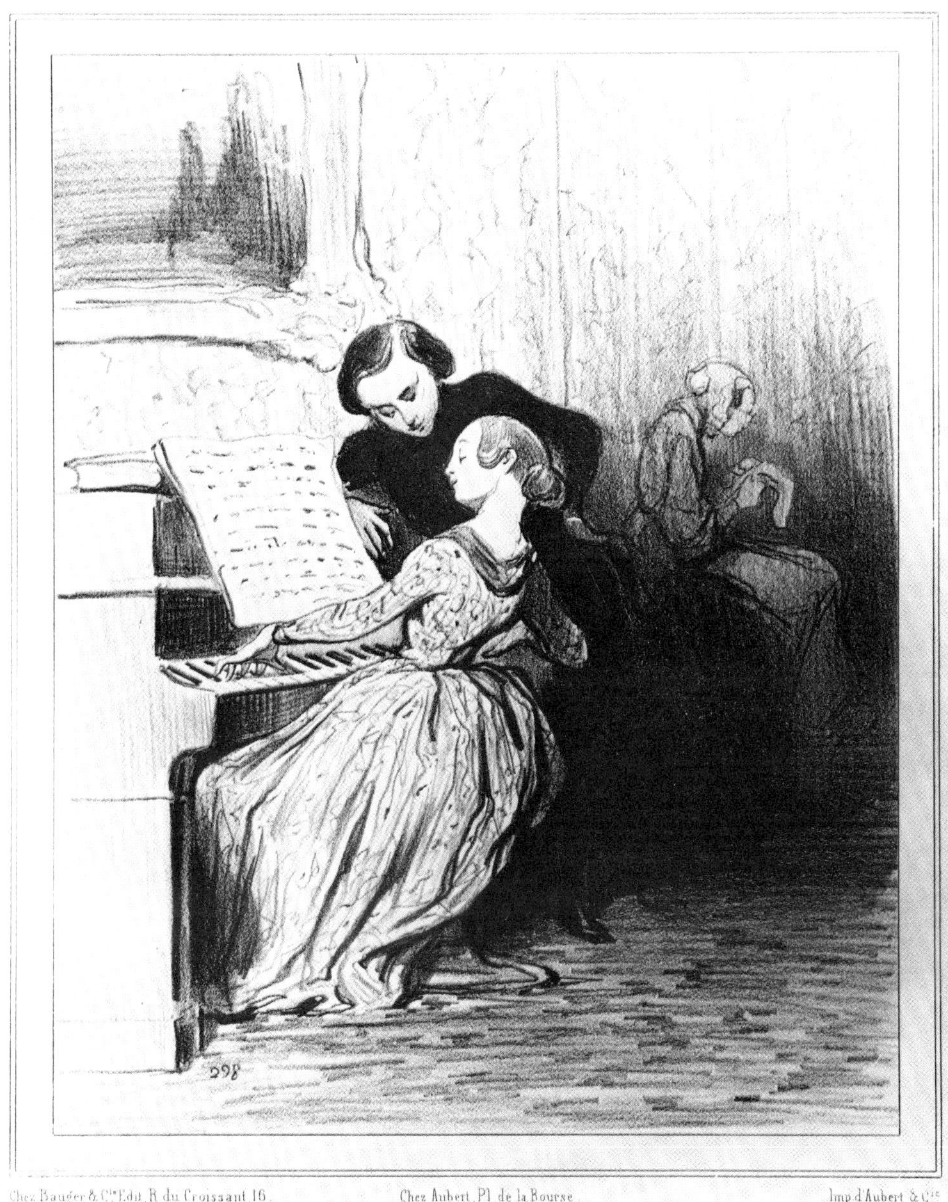

Cat. 1

Si vous saviez combien vous êtes jolie! faites semblant de jouer —
Taisez-vous do. — Vous ne m'aimez pas si—Et je serai toujours! la
mi.

If you only knew how pretty you are! pretend you're
playing—DOn't talk.—You don't like me SO—I hope
you'll always like MI.

"Les Musiciens de Paris" (The musicians of Paris), no. 6;
published in *Le Charivari,* March 6, 1843 (D. 924).

LENDER: The Metropolitan Museum of Art, Bequest of
Alexandrine Sinsheimer, 1959 (59.534.61).

Cat. 2

MARIEZ-VOUS DONC . . . EN CHINE

Une chinoise qui n'apporte rien à son mari met le ménage dans la gêne car sa toilette coûte beaucoup.
Une chinoise qui apporte quelque chose met le ménage dans l'embarras car sa toilette coûte davantage.
Une chinoise qui apporte beaucoup met le ménage dans la misère: ses caprices mangent tout!

WHY DON'T YOU GET MARRIED . . . IN CHINA

A Chinese woman who brings nothing to her husband puts the household in financial difficulties because of the cost of her toilette.

A Chinese woman who comes with something puts the household into debt because her toilette costs more.
A Chinese woman who brings a good deal puts the household into poverty: her caprices devour everything!

"Voyage en Chine" (Travel in China), no. 8; published in *Le Charivari,* April 22, 1844 (D. 1196).

LENDER: Museum of Fine Arts, Boston, Bequest of William P. Babcock.

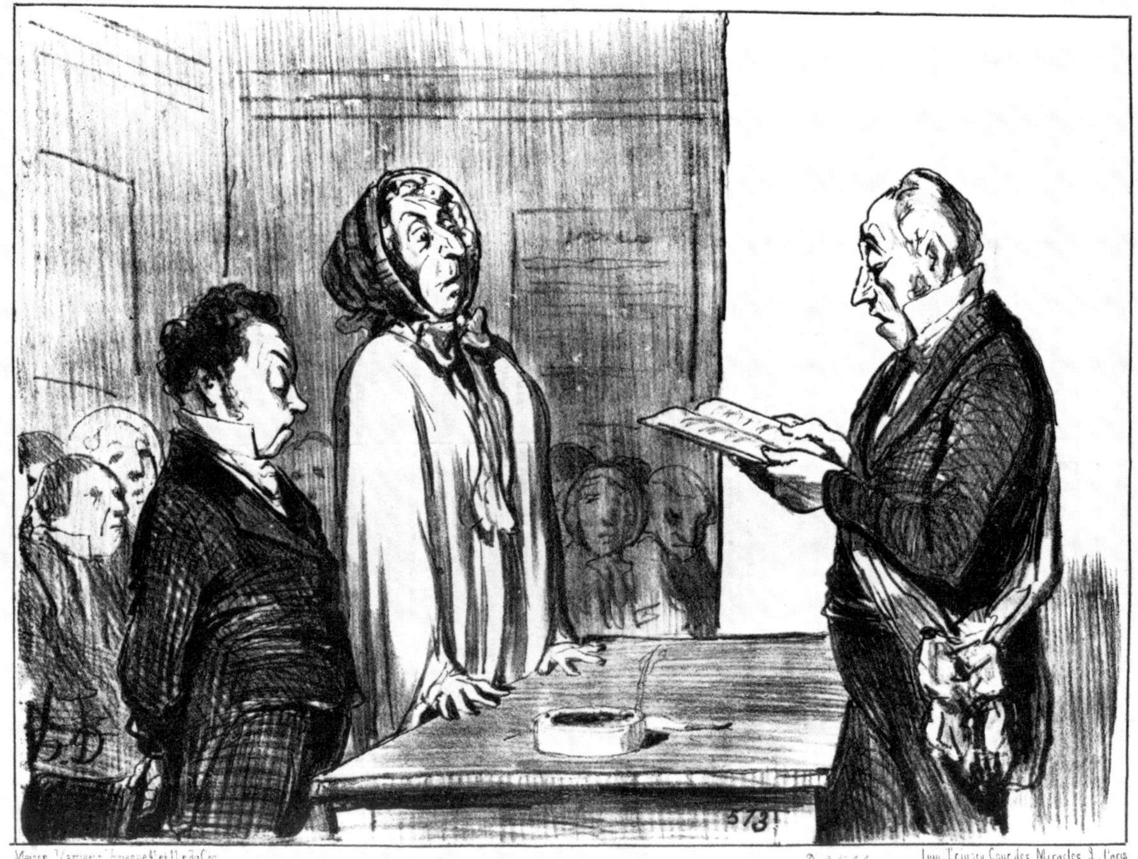

Cat. 3

À LA MAIRIE

La femme doit obéissance et soumission à son mari (Code civil, — titre du mariage).

AT CITY HALL

The wife owes duty and submission to her husband (Civil code, — article on marriage).

"Croquis parisiens" (Parisian sketches), published in *Le Charivari,* February 2, 1854 (D. 2566).

LENDER: The Rose Art Museum, Brandeis University, Waltham, Massachusetts, The Benjamin A. and Julia M. Trustman Collection.

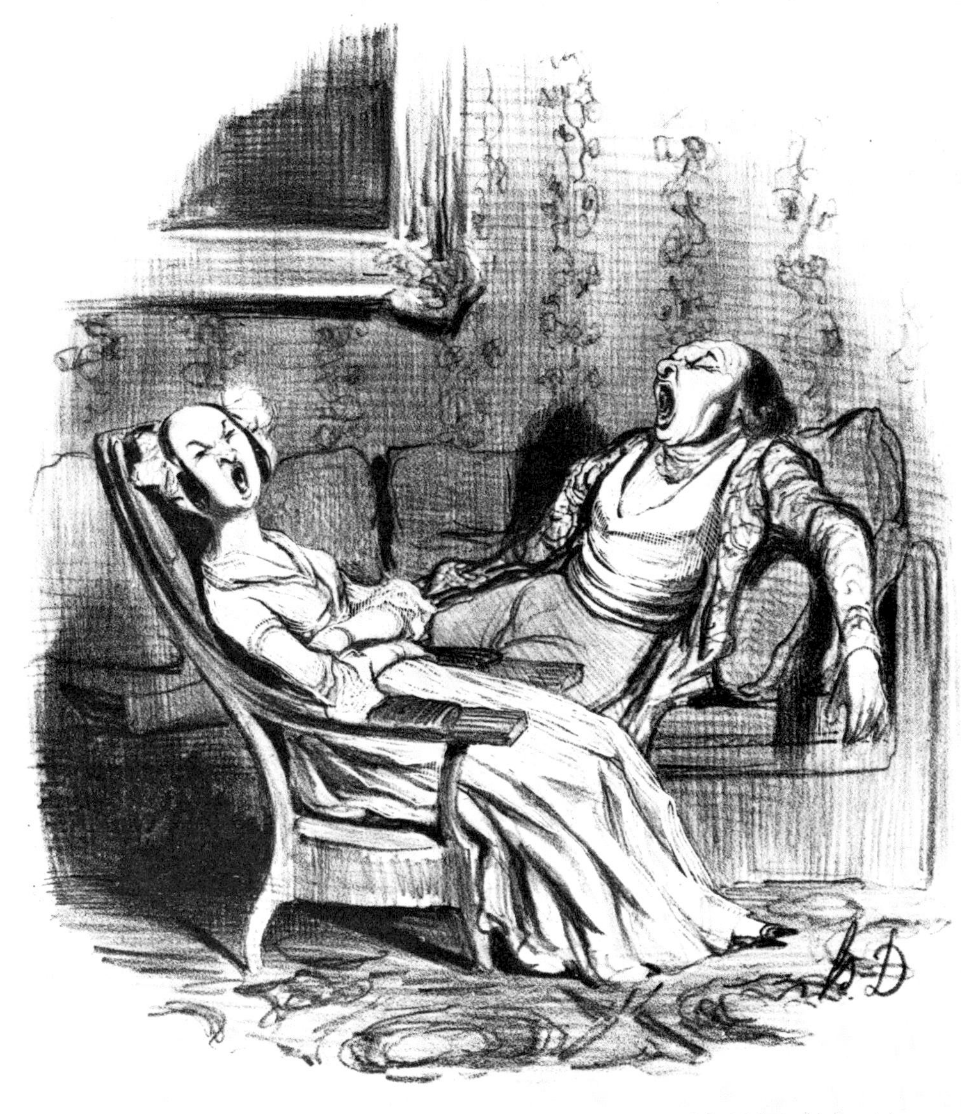

Cat. 4

Six Mois de mariage. La Sympathie est le lien des âmes.

Six months of marriage. Sympathy is the bond between souls.

"Moeurs conjugales" (Married life), no. 7; published in *Le Charivari,* July 28, 1839 (D. 630).

LENDER: The Rose Art Museum, Brandeis University, Waltham, Massachusetts, The Benjamin A. and Julia M. Trustman Collection.

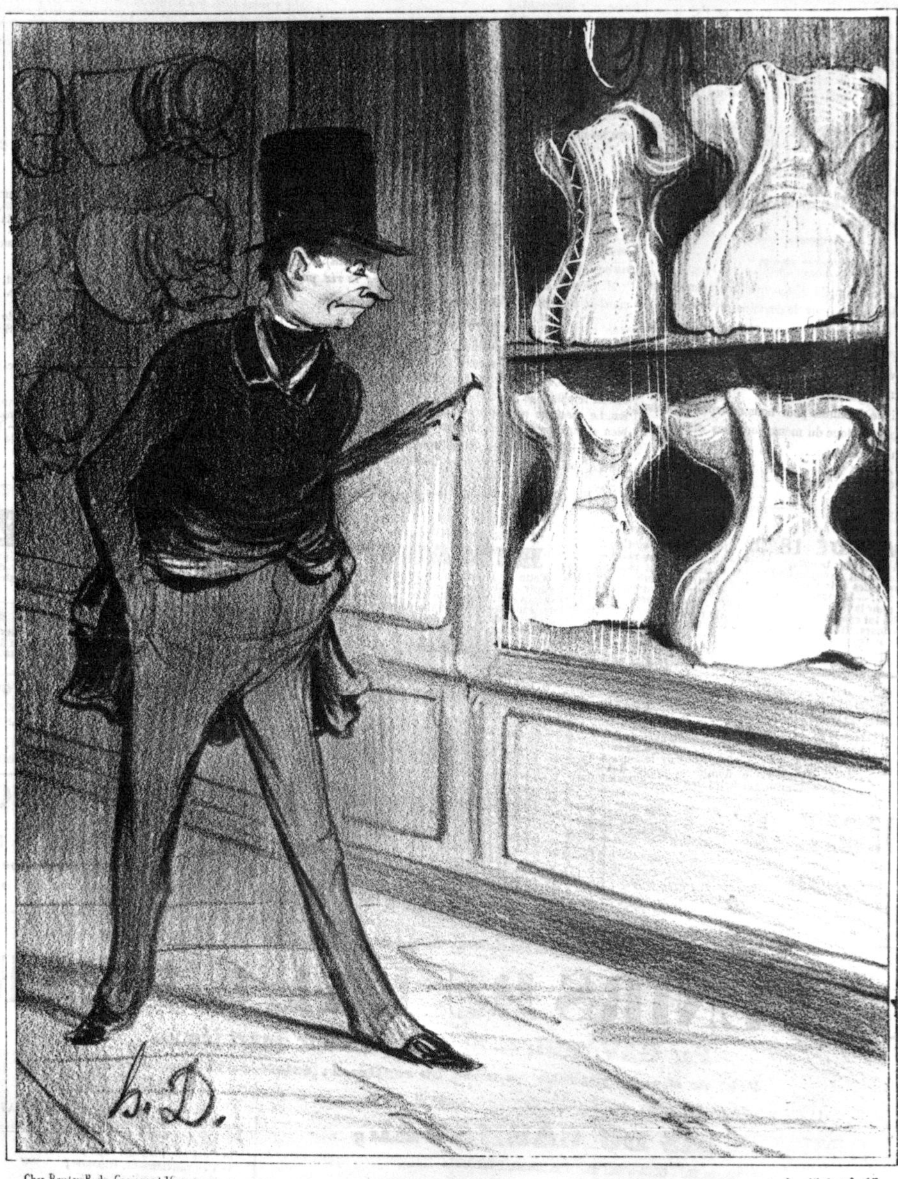

Cat. 5

C'est unique! j'ai pris quatre tailles, juste comme celles-là dans ma vie; Fifine ma première! Cocotte, cette gueuse de Cocotte! la grande Mimi, et mon épouse là haut dans le coin.

It's unique! I've had my arm around four waists, just like those, in my life; Fifine, my first! Cocotte, that wench, Cocotte! big Mimi, and my wife up there in the corner.

"Emotions parisiennes" (Parisian emotions), no. 17; published in *Le Charivari,* February 7, 1840 (D. 711).

LENDER: Print Collection, Miriam and Ira D. Wallach Division of Art, Prints and Photographs. The New York Public Library, Astor, Lenox, and Tilden Foundations.

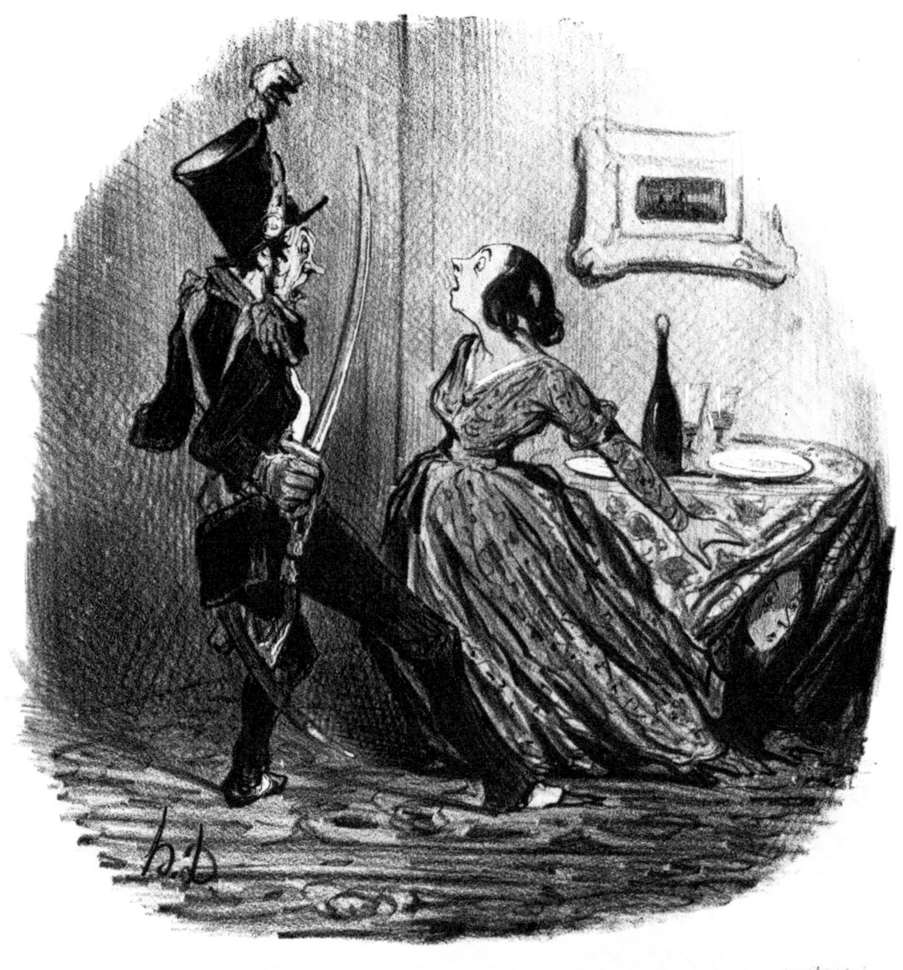

Cat. 6

Malheureux! Tu veux donc tuer le père de tes enfants?

Wretched man! Would you kill your children's father?

"Moeurs conjugales" (Married life), no. 31; published in
La Caricature, February 21, 1841 (D. 654).

LENDER: PNY Fine Prints and Drawings, New York.

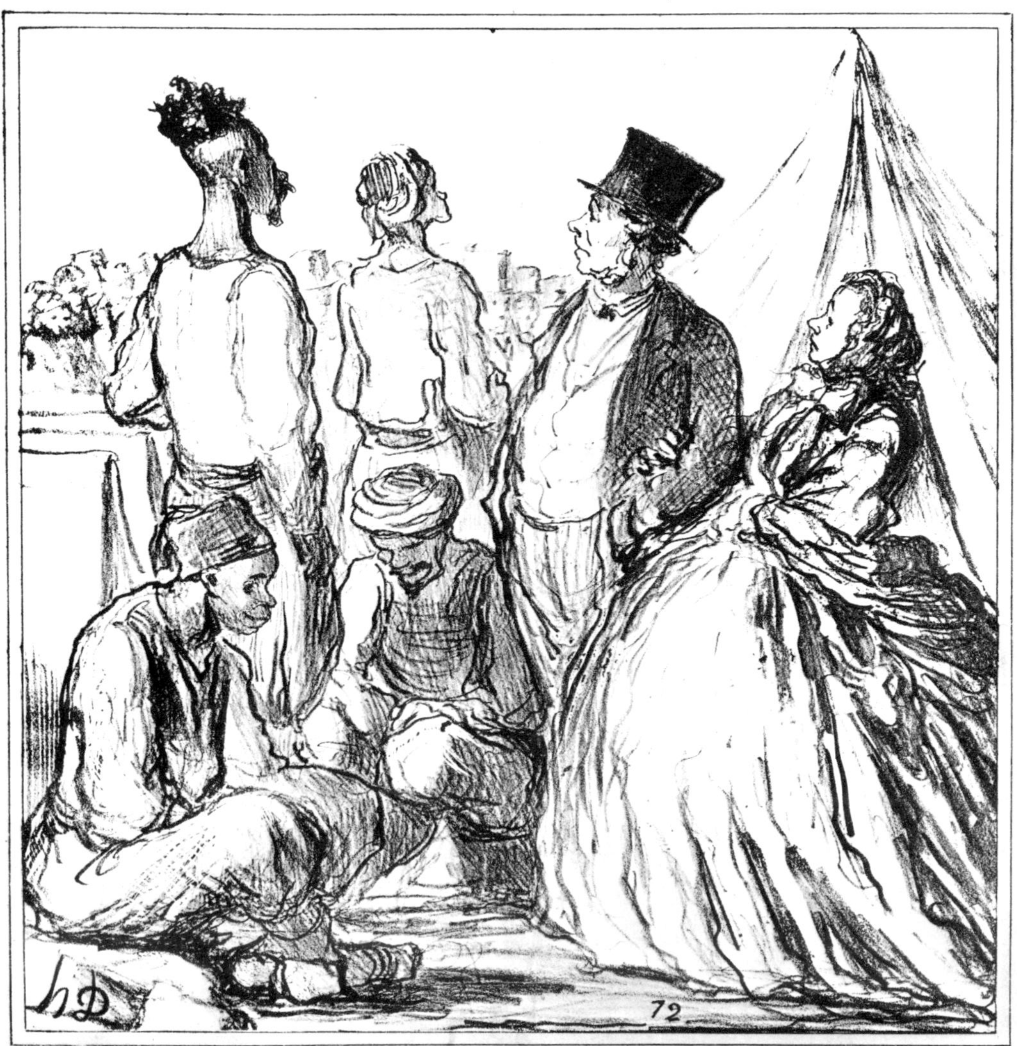

Cat. 7

—*La Dame.* —*Oh! mon ami . . . , quel beau turco! . . . quel beau turco!! . . . laisse-moi le contempler encore un peu! . . .* —*Le Mari.* —*Non . . ., allons-nous en . . . tu oublies, bichette, que tu es dans une situation intéressante . . . je crains que tu n'attrapes un regard . . . et que tu n'accouches d'un petit nègre! . . .*

—The wife. —Oh, my dear . . . what a handsome turco! [Algerian soldier] What a handsome Turco! Let me look at him a little longer! . . . —The husband. — No, let's go . . . you are forgetting, my dearest, that you are in a delicate condition . . . I'm afraid you will catch a glance and give birth to a little Negro!

"Au Camp de St. Maur" (At the St. Maur Camp), no. 2; published in *Le Charivari,* August 15, 1859 (D. 3193).

LENDER: The Metropolitan Museum of Art, The Elisha Whittelsey Collection, The Elisha Whittelsey Fund, 1962 (62.650.348).

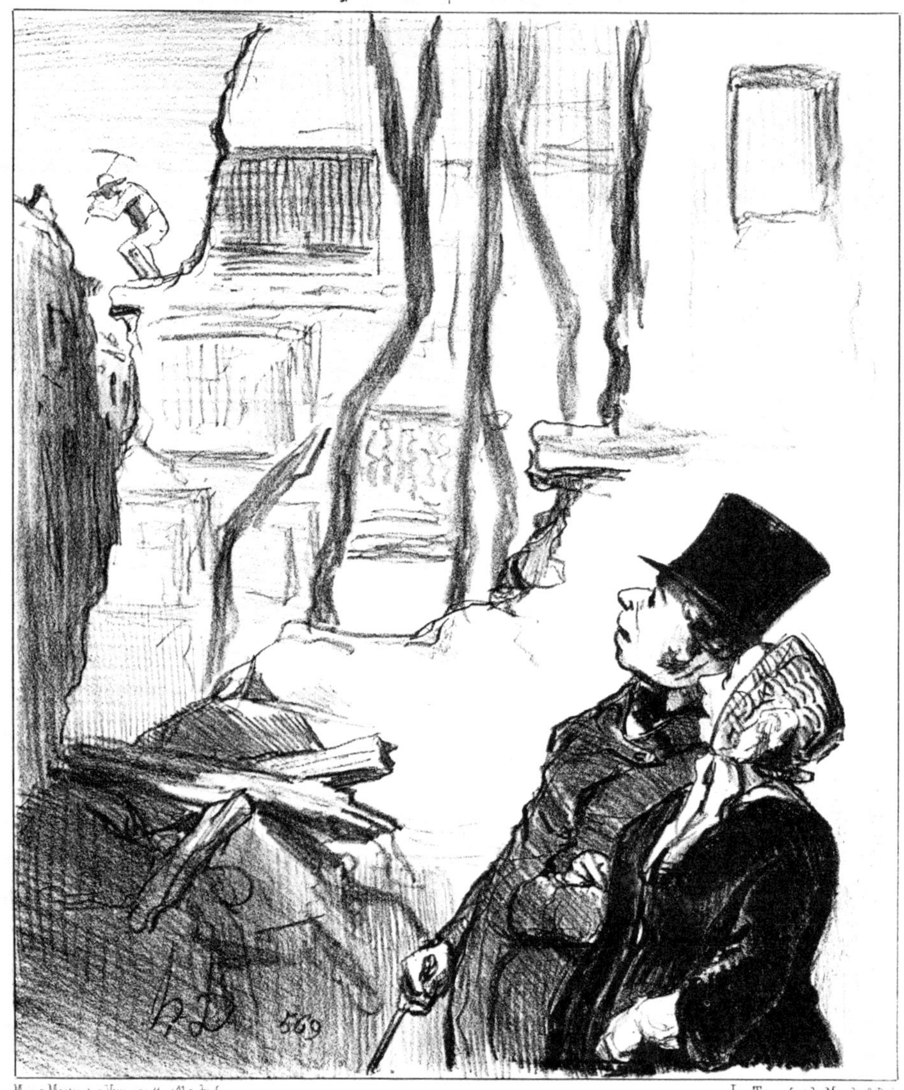

—Voilà pourtant notre chambre nuptiale, Adélaïde . . . . ces limousins ne respectent rien, ils n'ont pas le culte des souvenirs! . . .

Cat. 8

*Voilà pourtant notre chambre nuptiale, Adélaide . . . ces limousins
ne respectent rien, ils n'ont pas le culte des souvenirs! . . .*

That was our nuptial chamber, Adelaide . . . those masons
have no respect for anything, they don't honor memories! . . .

"Croquis parisiens" (Parisian sketches), no. 3; published in
Le Charivari, December 13, 1853 (D. 2429).

LENDER: The Metropolitan Museum of Art, Bequest of
Edwin De T. Bechtel, 1957 (57.650.116).

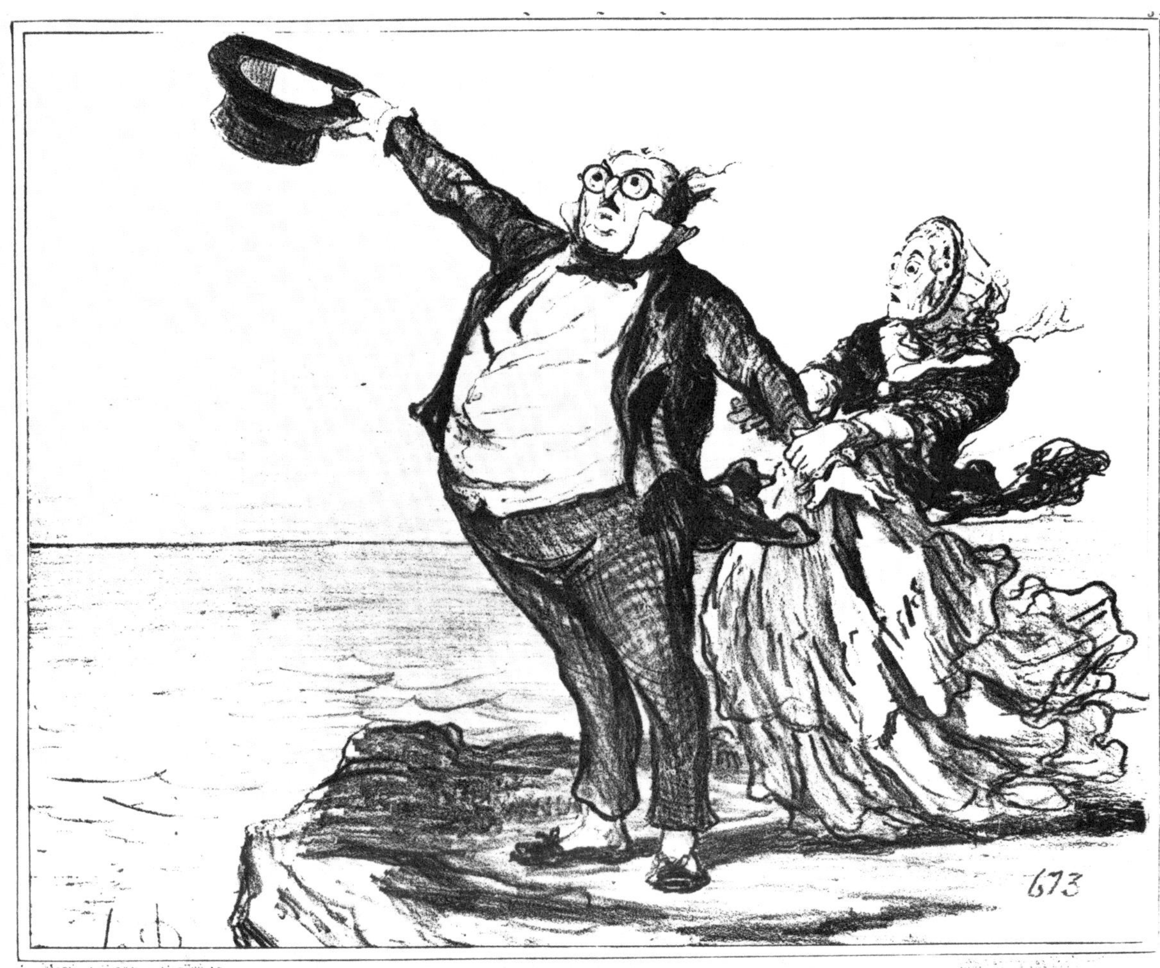

— Laissez moi, Madame Prudhomme, laissez moi saluer de loin, quoique je ne les connaisse pas, ces voyageurs qui quittent l'Europe pour aller à travers les plaines liquides, planter leurs tentes dans les prairies Américaines ...

— Puisque ce sont des allemands, ils ne te comprendront pas ....et puis d'ailleurs, j'ai peur que tu tombes à l'eau, il y a peut être des requins !

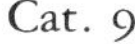

Cat. 9

—Laissez-moi, Madame Prudhomme, laissez-moi saluer de loin, quoique je ne les connaisse pas, ces voyageurs qui quittent l'Europe pour aller à travers les plaines liquides, planter leurs tentes dans les prairies Américaines . . . —Puisque ce sont des allemands, ils ne te comprendront pas . . . et puis d'ailleurs, j'ai peur que tu tombes à l'eau, il y a peut-être des requins . . .

—Allow me, Madame Prudhomme, allow me to salute from afar, although I am not acquainted with them, those travelers who are leaving Europe to traverse the liquid plains and plant their tents in the American prairies . . .

—Since they're Germans, they won't understand you . . . and then, besides, I'm afraid you'll fall into the water, maybe there are sharks . . .

"Croquis aquatiques" (Aquatic sketches), no. 3; published in *Le Charivari,* September 14, 1854 (D. 2594).

LENDER: The Rose Art Museum, Brandeis University, Waltham, Massachusetts, The Benjamin A. and Julia M. Trustman Collection.

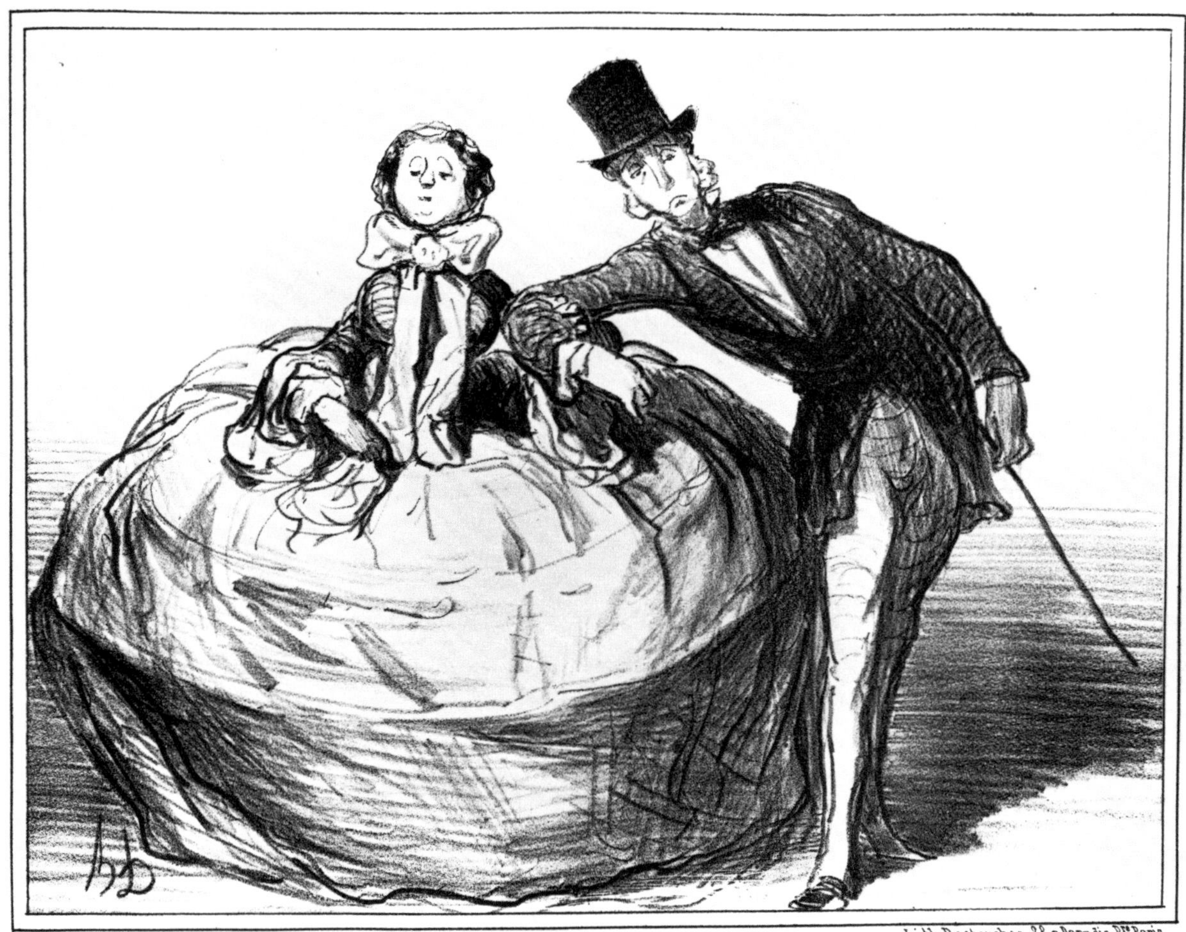

_ Saprelotte ! si les femmes continuent à porter des jupons en acier, on fera bien d'inventer, pour leur donner le bras, des hommes en caoutchouc .

(Réflexion d'un mari qui a toujours eu un mauvais caractère et qui commence à prendre en outre un mauvais pli.)

Cat. 10

Saprelotte! si les femmes continuent à porter des jupons en acier, on fera bien d'inventer, pour leur donner le bras, des hommes en caoutchouc.

Great heavens! if women go on wearing steel petticoats, they'd better invent rubber men to give them their arm.

"Actualités" (Current events), no. 437; published in *Le Charivari,* August 19 and September 9, 1857 (D. 2973).

LENDER: The Rose Art Museum, Brandeis University, Waltham, Massachusetts, The Benjamin A. and Julia M. Trustman Collection.

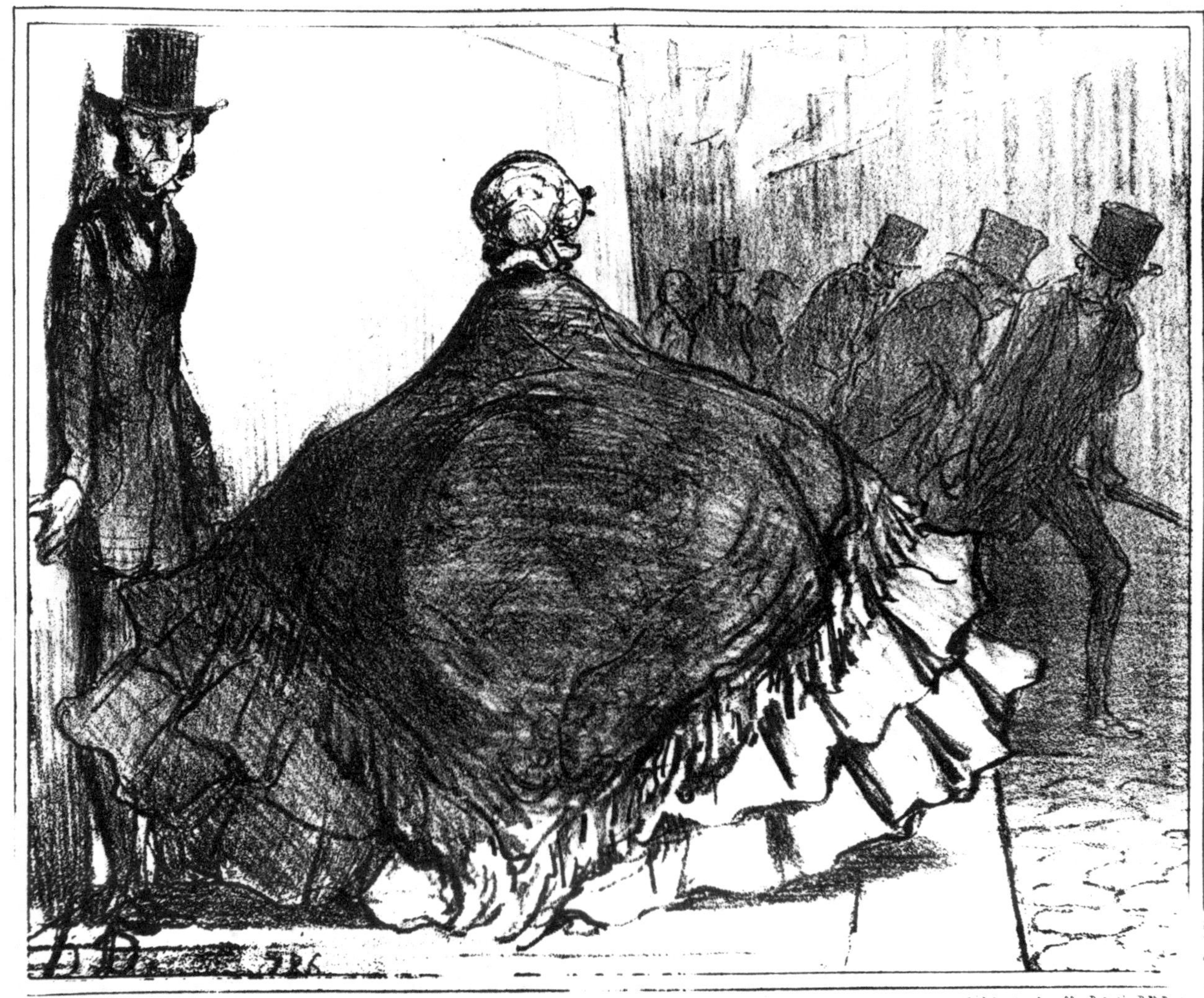

Cat. 11

Plus que ça d'ballon . . . excusez! . . .

Their behinds can't get any bigger than that . . .
Excuse me! . . .

"Actualités" (Current events), no. 199; published in
Le Charivari, June 13, 1855 (D. 2626).

LENDER: The Rose Art Museum, Brandeis University,
Waltham, Massachusetts, The Benjamin A. and
Julia M. Trustman Collection.

Daumier: Gender and Gesture

JUDITH WECHSLER

Bearing, gesture, and facial expression reveal attitudes, actions, and reactions of both types and individuals. The signs of the body, its language, signal thoughts and feelings directly, at least to a contemporary audience. The gestures that Honoré Daumier depicts in his lithographs and the contexts in which he places them communicate social and political stances. Captions are a gloss.

More than any other caricaturist of his time, Daumier was a master of expressive anatomy. Through a study of the body language he deploys and the differences between the ways he presents men and women, we can deduce a set of attitudes held by both the characters portrayed and the caricaturist himself.

A Classification of Daumier's Women

Daumier produced 3,959 lithographs,[1] of which 1,208 include women. Of these, 793, or about two-thirds, depict women in the traditional roles of wives and mothers, in domestic settings and other daily circumstances, including leisure activities, which are categorized in this essay as "the quotidian." About 11 percent of the images, or 134, are allegorical figures, usually political, representing countries, institutions, or principles. Series depicting women activists, such as "Les Bas-Bleus" (The bluestockings or women of ideas), "Les Femmes socialistes" (Socialist women), and "Les Divorceuses" (Advocates of divorce) comprise 5 percent, or 66 of the total. There are 34 working women (concierges, waitresses, shop attendants, servants, an artist's model), 40 performers, and 4 other professionals, of which 2 are writers and 2 are painters. Some 136 women appear in such miscellaneous series as "Les Baigneuses" (Bathers), "Croquis aquatiques" (Aquatic sketches), "Physionomies tragiques" (Tragic physiognomies), and "Voyage en Chine" (Travel in China).[2]

Daumier's women are not beautiful, elegant, charming, or sexy. In a sense, Daumier works against the grain, as these qualities predominate in the descriptions of the *parisienne* in both the literature and illustrations of the time. Daumier's relatively rare comments on fashion, as in the prints about crinolines, are characteristically humorous (cat. 11). He does not represent the demimonde and women of pleasure. These types were favored by his contemporaries Constantin Guys and by Gavarni in his series "Les Fourberies de femmes en matière de sentiment" (The duplicity of women in matters of sentiment) published in two parts: the first, consisting of 12 prints in 1837; the sec-

ond, with 52 lithographs, published in 1840–1841. Gavarni's series "Les Lorettes" of 1841–1843 concerns the mercenary aspects of romance.[3] In his *Physiologie de la parisienne* Taxile Delord observes that women pass their lives "commanding, obeying, desiring, pursuing," and he comments on their greed and narcissism.[4] Daumier shows few of these aspects. For the most part his representations of women are benign, if the women keep in their place. His bourgeoise, petite bourgeoise, and working-class women are on the whole good folk, loyal wives, proud mothers. Couples are frequently seen together at home, though not without occasional boredom, frustration, and anger, as in *Six Mois de mariage* (cat. 4). Women are shown gossiping, as in D. 503, 560, 564, 592, 682, 1719, and 2263. Among the many scenes of outings, particularly in the series "Pastorales" and "Croquis d'été," some show discomfort and frustration, as in the case of a family caught in a rainstorm (D. 631, *Tu te plains toujours, tu n'es jamais content;* You are always complaining, you're never content).

Couples are often shown taking delight in their children: D. 513, *Est-il joli! . . . Ce chérubin! . . .* (Isn't he pretty, the angel), and D. 522, *L'Education au Biberon ou les douceurs de la paternité* (The education of Biberon or the sweetness of paternity). Delteil 570, *Douze Ans et demi et trois premiers prix* (Twelve and a half years and three first prizes), shows a couple laden with books walking with pride behind their wreath-carrying son; a variation of the motif recurs in D. 632.

Daumier is exceptional in his sympathetic and romantic depictions of older couples. Examples are D. 519, *Toujours jolie* (Always pretty); D. 672, *Un Souvenir de jeunesse* (A memory of youth), showing a couple revisiting a tree into which he had carved her name; D. 1176, *Une Nouvelle Connaissance* (A new acquaintance), depicting a couple in their sixties; and D. 1177, *Un Retour de jeunesse* (A return of youth), an old couple walking hand in hand. Daumier, unlike his contemporaries and predecessors, depicts some old women as attractive. (He was perhaps the only caricaturist to remain happily married.)

Daumier is critical of women who neglect their maternal and domestic duties, as in *Je me fiche bien de votre Mme SAND . . .,* from the series "Moeurs conjugales" (cat. 12). The same series represents a few unfaithful women such as those in cat. 6, D. 645 and 666, *Ma femme m'a dit: Attends-moi cinq minutes . . .* (My wife told me to wait five minutes . . .), as well as in occasional later prints such as cat. 26, where a husband enters the sitting room causing his wife, with another man, to retract: *Ma bonne amie, puis-je entrer! . . .*

Censorship laws determined whether Daumier worked predominantly in political or social caricature. By dividing his work into these two main categories, we can see when different types of women appear in his published lithographs. Daumier practiced political caricature when it was legally possible to do so.

In 1830–1835, a period of political caricatures, Daumier represented few women in any way. Of the 275 lithographs from this period, only 6, or 2 percent, include women. Two are political: D. 109 shows Louis-Philippe in bed with two tattooed savages, referring to his stay in the United States; D. 114 is a personification of France. There are four quotidian genre scenes.[5]

During a period of censorship from 1836 to 1848, Daumier turned to social caricature, recording the habits, customs, and manners of everyday life. Most of the caricatures in this period are divided into some 50 series. With this shift of focus to social circumstances comes a significant increase in the number of women represented, 440, or 33 percent of the total of 1,381 lithographs in those years. Clearly, for Daumier women are more part of the social sphere than of the political. In this period, 327 lithographs show women in traditional roles. There are 40 *bas-bleus,* 19 working women, 5 performers and professionals, and 49 miscellaneous types, including 12 foreigners and 5 concerned with class distinctions. Female emblematic figures representing Charity and a newspaper appear at this time.

From 1848 to 1852, a period free of censorship, 693 lithographs were published, of which 193, about 28 percent, are of women. There are 23 personifications of political entities or principles such as Liberty, France, the French Republic, Universal Suffrage, the Constitution, or the National Assembly; 20 on the subject of divorce and socialist women, and 2 other "independent" types; 114 quotidian subjects, 23 miscellaneous, 7 performers, 13 working women, and 1 professional.

Censorship was reinstituted from 1853 to 1865, and so Daumier worked primarily in social caricature. The instances of women increase to 39 percent of the 1,042 lithographs from this period. There are fewer series than before and more individual pieces under the category "Actualités" (Current events), dealing with the theater, art and artists, transportation and extremes of weather: 338 quotidian; 44 miscellaneous (including foreigners); 29 women performers; 11 workers; 5 *boursicotières* (women who dress as men to go to the stock market); and 8 allegorical/political figures.

Political caricatures reappear from 1866 to 1879 but now with an international scope: personifications of Diplomacy, Peace, Europe, Italy, Venice, Spain, Austria, Prussia, and the World's Fair appear, for a total of 99 allegorical figures. There are also 10 quotidian themes, 2 performers, and 1 worker. Caricatures for this period total 493; about 23 percent include women.

The Role of Women in Daumier's Series

Daumier's series on various Parisian types from the period 1835–1848 show women playing minor roles at best, a situation that reflects the limited educational opportunities and professional possibilities open to women.[6] Women predominate in two series: they appear in 52 of 60 plates of "Moeurs conjugales" (Married life, 1839–1842, D. 624–683; cat. 4, 6, 12, 13, and 14) with themes of domestic happiness, affection, parental pride, anger, disloyalty, boredom. Some 51 scenes with women appear in the 91 plates of "Les Bons Bourgeois" (The good bourgeois, 1846–1849, D. 1477–1567), which covers middle-class life at home, on outings, and in social encounters.

Otherwise, Daumier shows a clear preference for depicting men, whom he draws with greater physiognomic variety. "Galerie physionomique" with 25 plates (Physiognomic gallery, 1836, D. 326–350) focuses on men although the subjects could equally have included women: looking in a mirror, dressing, eating, drinking, reading a letter, writing, eavesdropping, going to the theater, attending a boring lecture.

"Types parisiens" comprises 48 plates (Parisian types, 1839–1843, D. 559–606, cat. 15). The editor of *Le Charivari* wrote that "Daumier is going to show the various types of physiognomy, the individual costumes, manners of the different classes in our society." Some 13 lithographs focus on women: shopping, coming from the market, riding a bus, having tea, gossiping, with children and husbands, and working as a concierge.

"Emotions parisiennes" (Parisian emotions, 51 plates, 1839–1842, D. 684–728, 754–759, see cat. 5) is largely about the discomforts and incursions into the private realm of city life: unwelcome encounters, being fleeced, barraged, caught in bad weather, and eating at bad restaurants. Only two scenes include women: a nursemaid talking with a doctor and men gawking at a passing woman.

"Coquetterie" contains 10 plates (Coquetry, 1839–1840, D. 736–745). Coquetry, a principal female trait according to the *Physiologie de la parisienne,* is shown by Daumier in its male guises. The three women who appear in this series are ancillary: a wife adjusts her husband's tie; another is strolling on the arm of a man who looks more vain than she; and an old man doffs his hat to a woman.

In "Les Bohémiens de Paris" (The Bohemians of Paris, 28 plates, 1840–1842, D. 822–849) there are three women: D. 823, *La Glaneuse* (The gleaner); D. 836, *La Marcheuse ou la garde malade* (The walker or nursemaid); and the third is the owner of the dog being scrubbed by the *tondeur de chiens* (the animal clipper, D. 842).

"Les Beaux Jours de la vie" (The good days in life; 101 plates, 1843–1846, D. 1088–1188) presents 3 women in central roles. In 23 they play a role more or less equal with men, often in scenes of family outings, and in 8 they are secondary at best.

The contemporary publication *Les Français peints par eux-mêmes,*[7] published in English as *Pictures of the French: A Series of Literary and Graphic Delineations of French Caricature,* presents a broader spectrum of female types than does Daumier's repertory. It includes grandes dames, courtesans, nuns, and a greater range of workers and professions, such as a teacher, a *restauratrice,* and a milkmaid.

Gender and Gesture

À LA FEMME LA MAISON, À L'HOMME LA PLACE PUBLIQUE.
Proudhon

Daumier appears to follow the accepted distinction between the roles of husbands and wives. As a contemporary observed: "Happiness in marriage is not possible unless each keeps perfectly within his role and confines himself to the virtues of his sex, without encroaching on the prerogatives of the opposite sex." The function of the husband is to "represent the family or to direct it in its relations with the external world and to ensure its preservation and its development. The wife, so well endowed with grace, intuition and a ready emotional sympathy, has as her mission to preside over the internal life of the house."[8] Daumier contrasts the public role of men and the private role of women through their gestures and bearing. By employing characteristic poses and gestural signs he indicates patterns of behavior typical of each sex.

Men assume public stances, staking their ground, standing with legs apart, feet parallel or perpendicular, in the conventional gentleman's stance. Their gestures tend to be expansive and often declamatory. With arms stretched out from the body, their fingers point in accusation, or palms are held out to indicate or demonstrate, signaling power and authority.

Traditional women occupy less space than men (except when they wear crinolines). Their stance is modest and less affected than that of men, their feet close together, arms generally held close to the torso. They often clasp their hands before them. When women raise their hands to express surprise, dismay, or shock, their arms bend at the elbow and their hands stay below shoulder level. They keep to themselves. Their gestures tend to be responsive. Women's facial expressions are generally less individuated and articulated than those of men. For example, in D. 1090, *Premier Rendez-Vous* (The first date), a veiled woman looks down, the man's eyes open wide, eyebrows raised. Working-class women, on the other hand, are shown as more expressive, as in D. 1151, in which two of them argue before a judge.

Women are shown walking submissively either alongside their husbands or two steps behind, as in D. 1275, 1407, 1416, 1737, 1764, and 2949. Daumier indicates that their appearance is consciously constructed, as in D. 2216 in 1852, where two women walk with self-confident strides, gesticulating. The caption explains: "When bluestockings have a dignified bearing they are always respected . . . no man would allow me to follow behind him in the street! . . . My dear, nor I!" (Quand des femmes savent avoir de la dignité dans la démarche, elles se font toujours respecter . . . ce n'est pas moi qu'un homme se permettrait jamais de suivre dans la rue! . . . Ma chère, ni moi!).

Daumier contrasts extroverted male poses with the female supporting role in D. 2599 from the series "Le Bon Bourgeois" in the figure of Joseph Prud'homme, the quintessential bourgeois, inscribing his name on a rock. He arches back, stomach protruding. His wife, standing behind him, props him up. The caption echoes the pompous pose: "I intend to leave an imperishable monument of our visit to this cliff . . . I shall add your name too, Adelaide; the respect that I profess for the fair sex obliges me" (Je veux laisser un monument impérissable de notre visite à cette falaise . . . j'ajouterai aussi votre nom, Adelaide, le respect que je professe pour le beau sexe m'en fait un devoir).[9]

On city buses men spread out, sitting with legs apart; women are cramped. In *Intérieur d'un omnibus* (cat. 15) a drunk slouches in the direction of a slender woman who retreats from him only to be wedged behind a bovine butcher, who holds his arms akimbo. The men are oblivious, the woman is compromised and distressed. Daumier seems to sympathize with women beleaguered by boorish men.

En chemin de fer . . . un voisin agréable (cat. 16) shows a man and woman seated side by side in a railway car. He puffs away at his cigar, filling the car with smoke. Looking straight ahead, legs apart, arms crossed, he appears stubborn and oblivious. The woman retracts, looking back in his direction, hands folded passively in her lap. As a contemporary memoir noted, "Timidity was long considered a virtue."[10]

Je t'ai épousée pour charmer mon existence . . . (I married you to please me and nothing suits me better than thinking nothing of it; D. 624) from "Moeurs conjugales" depicts a man, one hand on his smoking pipe, the other in his pocket, walking several steps ahead of his wife who carries the bundles.

The contrast of powerful men and powerless women is evident in *Vous avez perdu votre procès c'est vrai . . .* (cat. 17) from the series "Les Gens de justice," in which a pompous lawyer struts belly forward, nose up. His client, a widow bent over crying, is led forward by her small son.

Another image, *Mossieu le Directeur* (D. 2899), set backstage, contrasts the arrogant theater director, in the classic exaggerated gentleman's pose, weight on the forward leg, leaning back, hand in vest Napoleonic style, looking down his nose, and a young woman in an angel costume, who assumes a modest stance, hands clasped in front of her.

Conventions

Caricature draws on various conventions for representing types and emotions. There are precedents in painting, theatrical and rhetorical gesture, and manuals of deportment. Some gestures are recorded in all three categories.[11]

There is, for example, the pose and gesture of surprise or shock. The figure is taken aback, weight on the back leg, arms bent at the elbow, hands upraised. One sees this gesture throughout the history of art, for example in Giotto's frescoes of *The Death of St. Francis,* Leonardo da Vinci's *Last Supper,* Caravaggio's *Martyrdom of St. Matthew,* David's *Belisarius,* and even today in cartoons where Bugs Bunny or Mickey Mouse do what is called "the take." Charles Darwin used a photograph of

a man in this position to illustrate his argument that body gestures are universal.[12] Today we still recognize this stance and gesture though it would be exceptional to find someone actually doing it spontaneously. Daumier uses the take repeatedly for men and women. For example, a man being shaved at the barber's sees his wife walking down the street on the arm of another man and cries out: "That's my wife! Outrageous! While the barber gives me a shave, she gives me the slip" (C'est ma femme!! Oh! Scélérate . . .; from "Moeurs conjugales," D. 645). Women visiting the Salon are shocked and dismayed by all the nudes and respond with a take: "More Venuses this year . . . always Venuses! . . . as if there were any women who look like that!" (Cette année encore des Vénus . . . toujours des Vénus! . . . comme s'il y avait des femmes faites comme ça! . . .; from "Croquis pris au Salon" [Sketches from the Salon], D. 3440).

In some cases Daumier adopts a pose from painting and uses it for satiric purposes, using a male pose for a woman. The "heroic" poses of the three women in *L'Insurrection contre les maris* from "Les Femmes socialistes" of 1849 (cat. 28) puns on David's *Oath of the Horatii.*[13] In *La Patrie,* D. 2107 from 1851, Daumier quotes the pose of David's *Belisarius* and puns on its contents in his *Un Nouveau Bélisaire* with an impoverished elderly woman as the personification of the conservative Bonapartist journal *La Patrie,* which was supported by General Gérôme Bonaparte whose hat she proffers to solicit alms in front of the National Assembly.

Daumier employs theatrical gesture in his series "Physionomies tragiques," which is about classical drama. In D. 2178 Ophelia performs "the gesture of painful recollection," and in D. 2180 Andromache "the gesture of feminine despair."[14] The contrast of theatrical and spontaneous gesture is shown in D. 2897 from "Croquis dramatiques" (Dramatic sketches), *Une Reine se préparant à une grande tirade* (A queen preparing an especially demanding speech). Onstage the actor is shown in the traditional aristocratic stance, leaning back, weight on the forward leg, with the back leg extended, toes touching the ground. The "queen" in the wings blows her nose.[15]

Sometimes Daumier plays two conventional poses against each other, often in a situation of action and reaction (cat. 6). A husband returns home unexpectedly. His wife confronts him, stepping forward, one arm outstretched behind her, covering her lover hidden under the table, and in so doing signaling his presence to the viewer. The husband retracts in shock and does a variation of the take. The piece is perfectly choreographed, her step forward is matched by his step back. "Malheureux! tu veux donc tuer le père de tes enfants?"

Daumier refers to codified gesture in D. 3035, *La Leçon du professeur* from the series "Les Comédiens de société" (Amateur actors). A woman is being taught a dramatic gesture: "Madame, always have dignity in the gesture; in saying your sentence, take good care to imitate me, combine it with this gesture of contempt" (Madame, ayez toujours de la dignité dans le geste . . . en prononçant votre phrase, ayez soin de bien m'imiter . . . joignez-y ce geste de mépris . . .). The professor stretches his arm out across his body, hand raised, in the same gesture illustrated in Siddons's guide to rhetorical gesture for the theater.

Daumier plays on decorum, representing it, exaggerating it, breaching it. Certain situations, such as men and women at the swimming pool, call for poses beyond or beneath decorum. Women's bodies are more revealed in their swimsuits, and the women themselves tend to appear awkward, whether gawky or fat. *A la buvette* (At the refreshment bar, D. 1641), from the series "Les Baigneuses," shows women at the bathhouse smoking, slouched in chairs, arms outstretched. This is one of the few occasions in which Daumier shows a woman with her legs crossed, a definite breach of proper conduct for a lady. Crossed legs were considered a mark of disrespect, even among men.[16] Other instances of breaches of decorum include people yawning, as in the young couple in *Six Mois de mariage* (cat. 4).[17]

Women Activists

Daumier's series "Les Femmes socialistes" from 1849 was done in response to the feminist clubs and newspapers that resulted from the Revolution of 1848.[18] His series "Les Divorceuses" from 1848 was probably occasioned by an attempt by the minister of justice, Adolphe Crémieux, that year to reestablish the divorce law, which had been abolished in 1816 and was not restored until 1884.

Daumier represented female ambition and assertiveness in such series as "Les Divorceuses," "Les Femmes socialistes," and "Les Bas-Bleus" by women's appropriation of male gesture to proclaim, indicate, accuse, and hold their ground. Their body language signals a break with traditional roles. These women stand with arms crossed and legs apart, in poses of defiance in D. 2032 and cat. 32. They assume broad stances in D. 1930 and cat. 28 and walk with big strides, as in D. 1223: *Adieu, mon cher, je vais chez mes éditeurs* (Goodbye, my dear, I am going to my publisher). These women arch backward like men in D. 1254, 1255, and cat. 32. Some put their hands in their pockets, bad manners even for a man.[19] They sit with legs apart (D. 1239 and cat. 30), with hands clasped under their knees (D. 1774), with legs outstretched (D. 1926), or crossed as in D. 1794, in the scene where women are discussing being left out of the socialist dinners. Women are shown reaching out to get what they want, as for a book in a library in cat. 20. They are represented absorbed in work and ignoring their children in D. 1234 and cat. 23 and 24. Some smoke (D. 1229, 1253, and 1928).

Politically active women gesticulate emphatically while delivering a speech (D. 1245, 1923, and cat. 31). From the "Bas-Bleus" series *La Présidente criant à tue-tête . . .* (The president yelling at the top of her voice, 1844, D. 1245) shows women's broad oratorical gestures like those of male lawyers in the courtroom. Similar gestures are found in theatrical illustrations and in political prints at the time of the French Revolution, such as Chérieux's *Club de femmes patriotes dans une église* (Club of patriotic women in a church).[20]

Allegorical Figures

Daumier's allegorical women from around 1850 personify France, the Press, the Republic, Universal Suffrage, the National Assembly, and the Constitution, as in D. 2002, 2008, 2010, 2014, 2079, 2080, 2112, 2131, 2150, and cat. 18. Barefoot and dressed in loose shifts, rather classical and timeless, they are generally more noble, grand, and graceful than their human counterparts. These figures are not to be confused with real women; they serve a symbolic or emblematic function. For the most part their bearing reflects the conventions of decorum and theatrical presentation. Daumier, like other nineteenth-century French artists and illustrators, could portray the allegorical figure of France and the Republic with stances and gestures signifying moral purpose, courage, and determination not accorded to mortal women. Daumier fosters the myth of the female heroine in the allegory of the Republic but satirizes activist women.

Le Dernier Conseil des ex-ministres from 1848 (cat. 47) shows the personification of the Republic striding into the council chamber confronting Louis-Philippe's ministers who flee in panic. The historian Jules Michelet

commented on the pose in a letter to Daumier liken-
ing the Republic to one returning home and finding
"thieves at the table, who fall back in disarray."[21] Daumier's allegorical version of republican France follows
the model of Marianne, the personification of the Republic, first devised during the period of the French
Revolution. She is a "live allegory," striding into the
room, hair loose, wearing a Phrygian cap, and otherwise bearing no attributes.[22]

The irony of this image is that Daumier had used
the pose earlier for an irate, unfaithful wife (cat. 6).
Using a similar pose for two radically different types
and meanings shows the importance that context plays
in the reading of bearing and gesture. As sociologists
and anthropologists like R. L. Birdwhistell and Macdonald Critchley have shown, there are few absolute
universal gestures, Darwin's contention to the
contrary.[23]

Many of Daumier's allegorical figures are shown
threatened or victimized, depicted passively and with a
traditional female bearing and demeanor. Personifying
the press, a woman writing sits alone in a modest pose.
Thiers creeps up behind her with a club, about to
attack (1850, D. 2002). The figure of France retracts
fearfully, threatened by a man with an immense syringe
(D. 2008). A doctor is shown taking the pulse of a
woman personifying the National Assembly, who sits
with feet and knees together, one arm at her side holding a shield: "Doctor, I assure you that I am not as sick
as you say" (Docteur, je vous assure que je ne suis pas
aussi malade que vous me le dites!; 1851, D. 2131).

Where the allegorical figure is ascendant or victo-
rious, the pose is more assertive and male. The personification of the Constitution sits with legs apart, one
hand on her hip, in D. 2112. In D. 2150 from 1851 the
personification of France is dumping small men (politicians) from the basket on her back. She is remarkably
robust, with large arm muscles, as in Daumier's paintings of the Republic and as befits the inscription, "I've
been carrying you on my shoulders for too long!" (La
France. Il y a assez longtemps que je vous porte sur mes
épaules!").

After the censorship laws were lifted by Napoléon
III in 1866 and Daumier returned to the political caricature, the artist's focus was primarily on international
conflict. There are many more female personifications
in this period than there were around 1850. France was
engaged militarily with Italy, Russia, Austria, Prussia,
and Turkey, unsettling the balance of power. All these
countries are personified as women. For the most part

they are shown as old and ugly; Italy is thin, Prussia an
obese woman with a military hat. Peace is emaciated,
Diplomacy an old hag. Europe is in a state of disequi-
librium, balancing on a lit bomb (D. 3566), and in
another print (D. 3688) is threatened by a Turk as a
jack-in-the-box; in D. 3688, Europe does the take. By
1869 there are a few more positive images of noble
France, such as D. 3708, *La France se préparant à passer
ses candidats sous la toise* (France prepares to measure her
candidates). In D. 3712, Liberty is shown standing
erect, head up, holding back obsequious men (politicians): "Excuse me, but I don't embrace everyone"
(Pardon, je n'embrasse pas tout le monde). Liberty, accompanying herself on the piano, sings out in D. 3717,
while the jester, Daumier's personification of the caricaturist as witness and recorder, looks on approvingly:
"She definitely has a stronger voice" (Elle a décidément
plus de voix). In D. 3724, Liberty, standing fast, with
arm outstretched in a gesture of rejection, holds back a
male personification of war, who does the take: "Excuse
me, my dear, ascertain my powers before yours" (Pardon mon cher . . . Vérifions mes pouvoirs avant les
vôtres").

The Constitution and France were once again en-
dangered. A personified France is tied up and placed
between two cannons in D. 3808. France wounded,
arm in a sling, is forced by a soldier to the electoral box
in D. 3823. The National Assembly as a flattered and
acquiescent woman, bowing forward, eyes lowered, is
being escorted by a military officer (D. 3825). In the
aftermath of the Franco-Prussian War in 1871, France
personified is shown dead on the battlefield (cat. 53).
A powerful female figure, in robes, barefoot, hair loose
and straggly, stands on the battlefield, striding forward, reminiscent of the Republic at the ex-ministers,
and points one hand to the dead, the other to the electoral box: "This one has killed that one" (Ceci a tué
cela; D. 3845). This figure is one of the most powerful
of Daumier's women, not an explicit personification,
but a witness, like himself.

Conclusion

For the most part, Daumier confirms what has been
described by Lucette Czyba as the cardinal feminine
virtues for the time: "fidelity, submission, patience,
economy, generosity, devotion, self-sacrifice." He rarely
shows the other stereotypical image of bourgeois
women as "vindictive, weak, nervous, fragile, frivo-

lous, rivalrous," women as ornaments and consumers preoccupied with appearance.[24]

His women are less venal than those in the literary and pictorial renderings of most of his contemporaries, such as Gavarni's representations of the demimonde or Delord's satirical picture of the *parisienne*. Daumier shows little fear of women, nor does he mythologize them. For example, Daumier depicts actresses who were regarded as particularly seductive, in the nitty-gritty of their profession, on stage or preparing to make an entrance, fellow professionals contending with life and work.

Unlike most of the contemporary caricaturists, Daumier did not die mad or in despair. His well-tempered life, his basic affection for his fellow beings, both men and women, are reflected in his work. Daumier's contemporary, the poet Charles Baudelaire, observed that Daumier's caricatures convey no "rancor or bitterness."

A number of questions remain that cannot be addressed in this paper. Are the signs of body language in Daumier's caricatures faithful representations of how people actually behaved? If the characterizations are not naturalistic, how did and do they communicate convincingly? Was Daumier's preference for depicting men and the choice of conventional bourgeois women in part affected by the editor and the audience for *Le Charivari* and the other publications in which his caricatures appeared? Baudelaire described Daumier's audience as "honest burgher, businessman, youngster, fine lady." According to Baudelaire, Daumier's

figures . . . are faithfully portrayed in movement. His gift of observation is so sure that it would be quite impossible to find in his drawings a single head that does not seem to fit on to the body that carries it. . . . It is all the logic of the scholar transplanted into a light and fleeting art, which competes with the mobility of life itself.[25]

Daumier brought together the conventions of bearing and gesture with acute observation of actual behavior to render the fault lines between men and women.

NOTES

1 This figure is derived from the catalogue raisonné by Loys Delteil, *Le Peintre-Graveur illustré, XIXᵉ et XXᵉ siècles: Honoré Daumier,* 10 vols. (Paris, 1926; reprint, New York, 1969). The total of 3,959 includes the five lithographs listed in the addenda.

2 I wish to thank Claire Jones and Miranda Robbins for their assistance in calculating the various categories and Ms. Jones for translating a number of the captions.

3 See Heather McPherson, "Les Femmes de Gavarni": Gavarni's *Images of Women,* exh. cat. (Birmingham, 1985).

4 Taxile Delord, *Physiologie de la parisienne* (Paris: Aubert Lavigne, 1841).

5 D. 254, *La Bonne Gran'mère* (The good grandmother); D. 255, *Le Malade* (The sick person), tended by a young woman; D. 256, *La Lecture du journal* (Reading the newspaper); and D. 257, *Cavalerie légère* (Light cavalry), a mother helping her small child onto a donkey. The scenes are reminiscent of genre scenes in the style of Greuze.

6 Theodore Zeldin, *Ambition, Love, and Politics,* vol. 1 of *France: 1848–1945* (Oxford, 1973), pp. 344–45.

7 Published in Paris, 1842. The one-volume 1860 edition includes 136 types, of which just under one-third, or 46, are women.

8 Dr. Louis Seraine, *De la santé des gens mariés,* 2d ed. (Paris, 1865), pp. 112–16, cited in Zeldin, *Ambition, Love,* p. 300.

9 Daumier's men are shown on other occasions as more modestly sentimental and romantic, as in D. 1480 from "Les Bons Bourgeois," *C'est demain la fête de sa femme* (Tomorrow is his wife's birthday), which shows a man laden with plants and packages; smelling flowers in D. 594; looking up from a solitary bed at the picture of a woman on the wall in fig. 6.2; or the tender old couples mentioned above.

10 Madame E. Garnier in her memoirs of *A Parisian University Family in the Nineteenth Century,* cited in Zeldin, *Ambition, Love,* p. 355.

11 For painting, see Charles Le Brun's treatise on depicting emotions, *Conférence sur l'expression générale et particulière des passions* (Amsterdam, 1698). For theater, see Henry Siddons, *Practical Illustration of Rhetorical Gesture and Actions Adopted to the English Drama from a Work on the Subject by J. J. Engel* (London, 1822). And for guides to daily deportment, see Edward B. Warman, *Gestures and Attitudes: An Exposition of the Delsarte Philosophy of Expression, Practical and Theoretical* (Boston, 1892).

    For a further discussion of these traditions, see Judith Wechsler, *A Human Comedy: Physiognomy and Caricature in Nineteenth-Century Paris* (London and Chicago, 1982).

12 Charles Darwin, *The Expression of Emotions of Man and Animals* (London, 1872).

13 Daumier also uses the pose of the Horatii for men in D. 2029, Ratapoil and two workers; D. 2095, three ministers and Thiers; D. 2105, *Les Horaces de l'Elysée;* D. 2937, landlords; and D. 3561, armed soldiers.

14 Siddons, *Practical Illustration,* pp. 52 and 346.

15 One of the clearest examples contrasting acquired and natural poses takes place in the photographer's studio. Daumier contrasts *Pose de l'homme de la nature et pose de l'homme civilisé* in D. 2445, or natural man with civilized man. The former sits straight forward, legs apart, hands on thighs; the latter twists his body in an affected manner, legs crossed.

16 L. C. D., *Manuel de politesse française* (Paris, 1863), p. 23. Cited in Elizabeth Anne McCauley, *Disderi and the Carte-de-Visite Portrait Photograph* (New Haven, 1985), p. 142.

17 Yawning also appears in D. 797, *Oncle et neveu: Il faut semer pour*

recueillir (One must sow to harvest), in which a dapper young man emits a big yawn as he walks his old uncle. Orchestra musicians are shown yawning in D. 2243.

18 The issue of the vote for women was current in 1848–1851 when the first bill for women's right to vote was introduced. Around the same time the utopianist Charles Fourier advocated full educational equality and radical marriage reform. The Saint-Simonists actually practiced equality. Zeldin has written that feminism in the nineteenth century was principally supported by the socialists, but that there was no mass feminist movement. "The early feminists were isolated individuals and their activity was at first purely literary or journalistic." Feminists behaved like other "moderate societies." It was a "definitely bourgeois and upper-class movement" (*Love, Ambition,* pp. 346, 348). This is reflected in Daumier's caricatures in the "Bas-Bleus" series of women writers who demand equality. Daumier might have agreed with Xavier de Maistre, who wrote to his daughter: "The great defect in a woman is to want to be a man" (quoted in Zeldin, *Love, Ambition,* p. 356).

19 Marc Constantin, *Almanach du savoir-vivre* (Paris, 1859), p. 44; cited in McCauley, *Disdéri,* p. 142.

20 Madelyn Gutwirth brought this print to my attention.

21 Roger Passeron, *Daumier* (New York, 1981), pp. 157–58.

22 Maurice Agulhon, *Marianne into Battle: Republican Imagery and Symbolism in France, 1789–1880,* trans. Janet Lloyd (Cambridge, 1981), p. 88.

23 R. L. Birdwhistell, *Kinesics and Context* (London, 1971) and Macdonald Critchley, *The Language of Gesture* (London, 1939).

24 Lucette Czyba, *Mythes et idéologie de la femme dans les romans de Flaubert* (Lyon, 1983), pp. 15–16.

25 Charles Baudelaire, "Some French Caricaturists," in *Baudelaire: Selected Writings on Art and Artists,* trans. P. E. Charvet (London, 1972), pp. 215, 223.

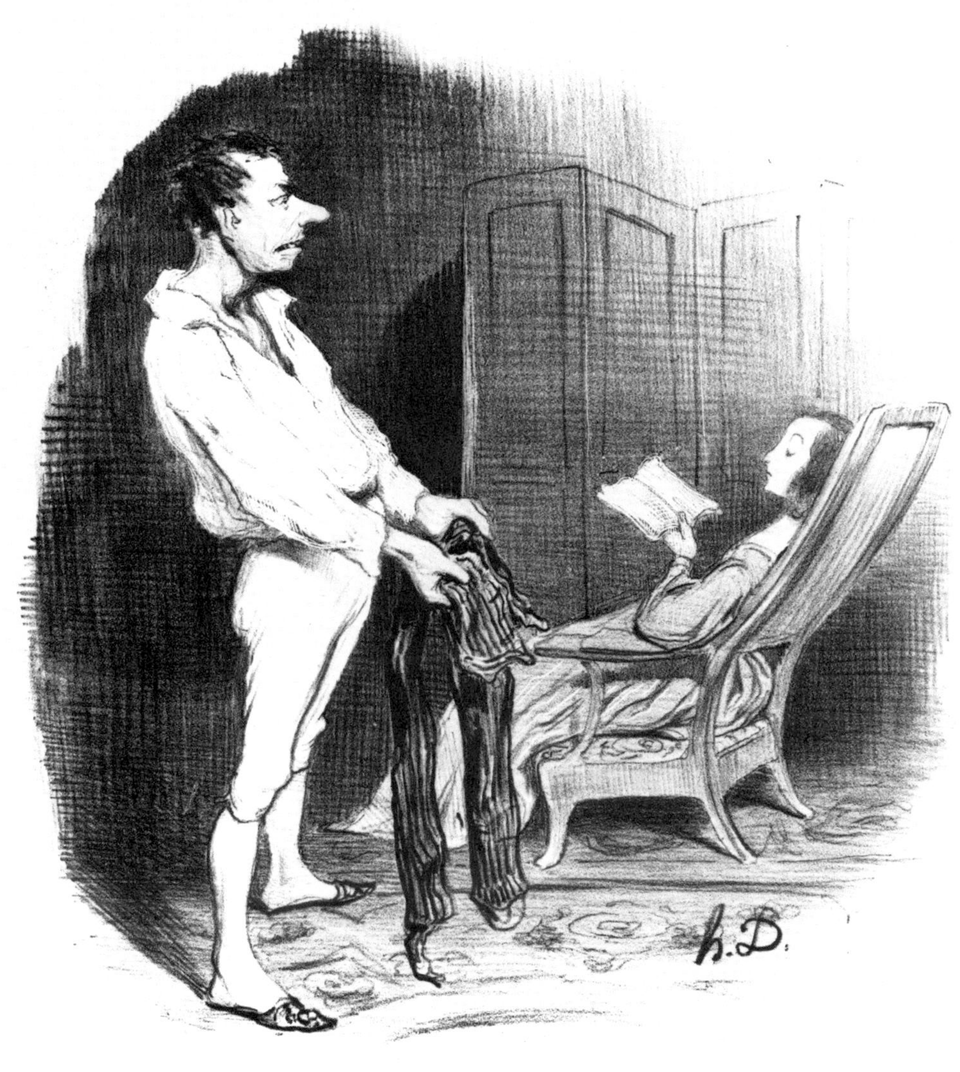

Cat. 12

*Je me fiche bien de votre Mme SAND qui empêche les femmes de
raccommoder les pantalons et qui est cause que les dessous de pied
sont décousus! . . . Il faut rétablir le divorce ou supprimer ces
auteurs-là!*

I don't give a damn about your Mme SAND who prevents
women from mending pants and darning socks! . . . We
must reestablish divorce or suppress those authors!

"Moeurs conjugales" (Married life), no. 6; published in
Le Charivari, June 30, 1839 (D. 629).

LENDER: PNY Fine Prints and Drawings, New York.

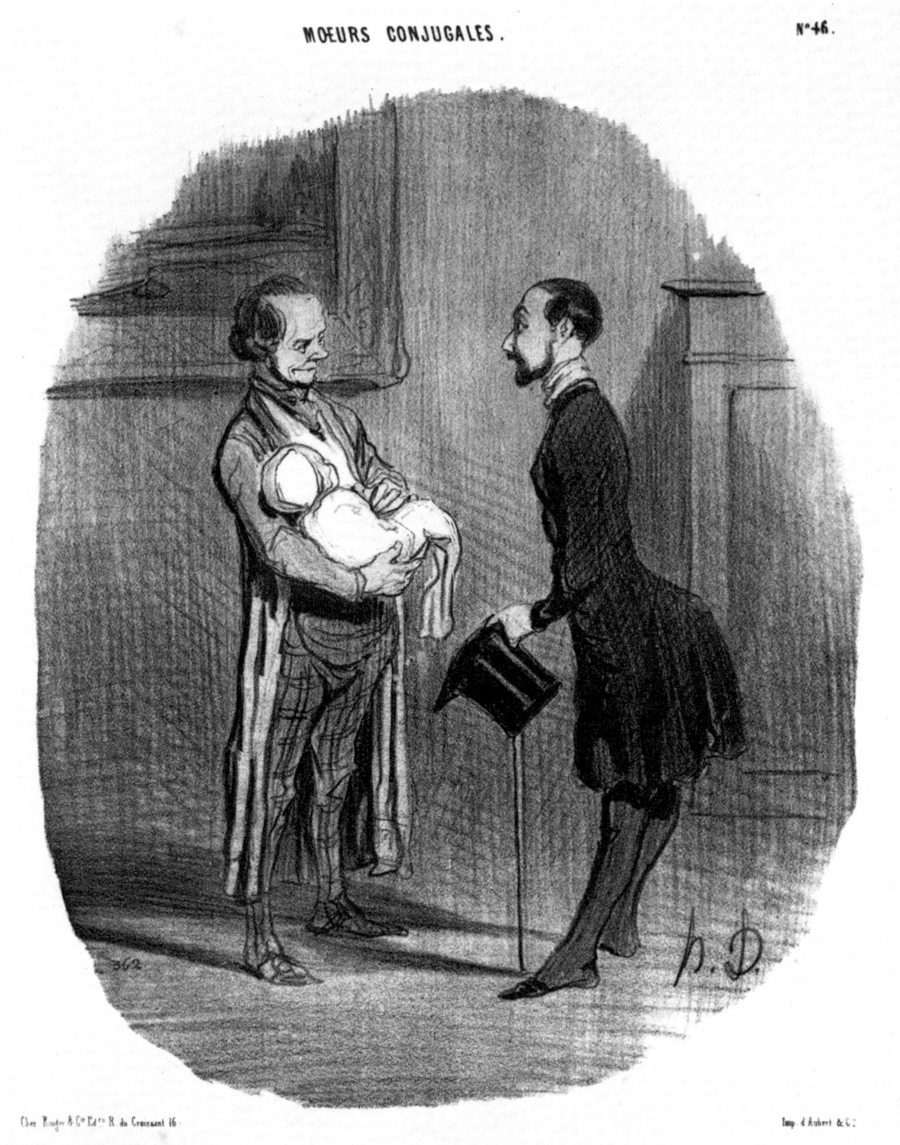

Cat. 13

LE MARI DU BAS-BLEU

Monsieur, ma femme est inspirée depuis ce matin: impossible de la voir; je suis comme vous voyez obligé de prodiguer mes soins au dernier ouvrage, que nous avons fait en collaboration!

THE BLUESTOCKING'S HUSBAND

Monsieur, my wife has been inspired since this morning: it is impossible to see her. As you see, I have to give my attention to our most recent collaborative work!

"Moeurs conjugales" (Married life), no. 46; published in *Le Charivari,* April 10, 1842 (D. 669).

LENDER: Print Collection, Miriam and Ira D. Wallach Division of Art, Prints and Photographs. The New York Public Library, Astor, Lenox, and Tilden Foundations.

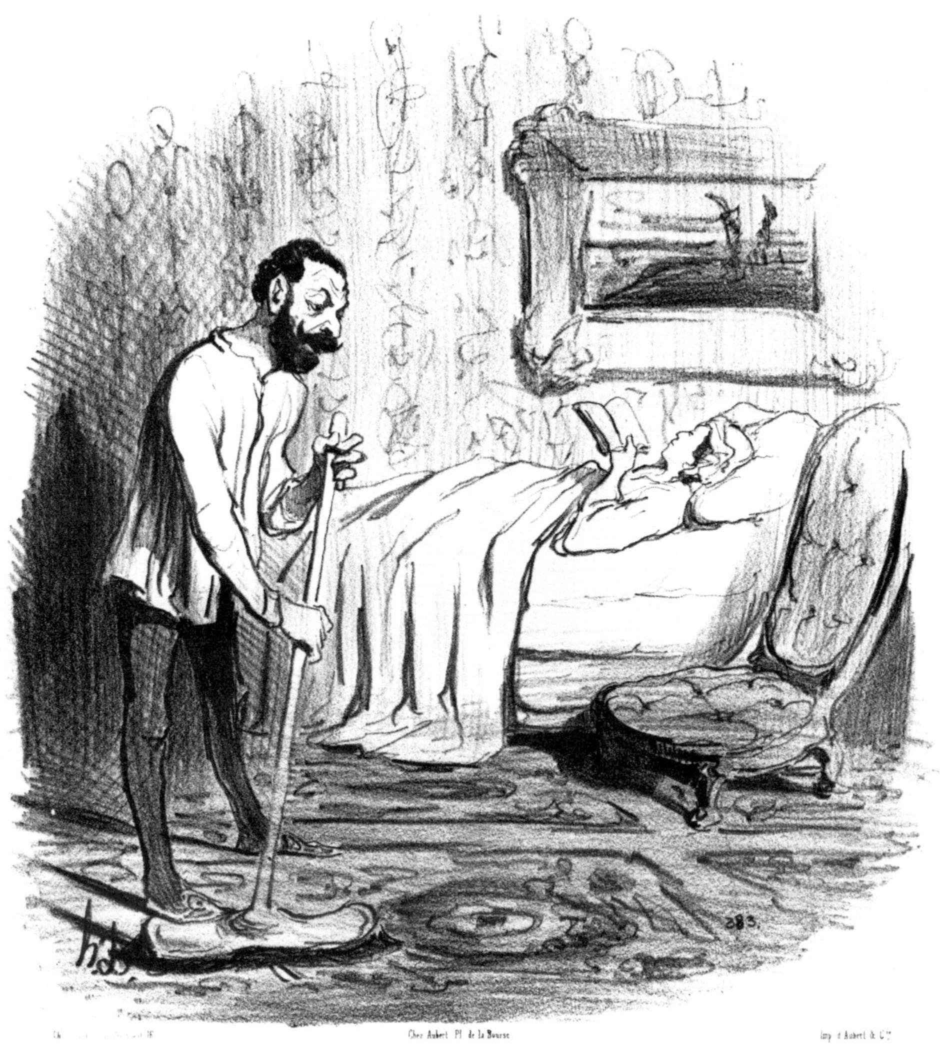

UN INTÉRIEUR PARISIEN.

Monsieur fait le ménage , Madame songe a le défaire.

Cat. 14

*Un Intérieur parisien. Monsieur fait le ménage; Madame songe à
le défaire.*

A Parisian home. Monsieur is the homemaker; Madame
is thinking of being the homewrecker.

"Moeurs conjugales" (Married life), no. 55; published in
La Caricature, May 15, 1842 (D. 678).

LENDER: PNY Fine Prints and Drawings, New York.

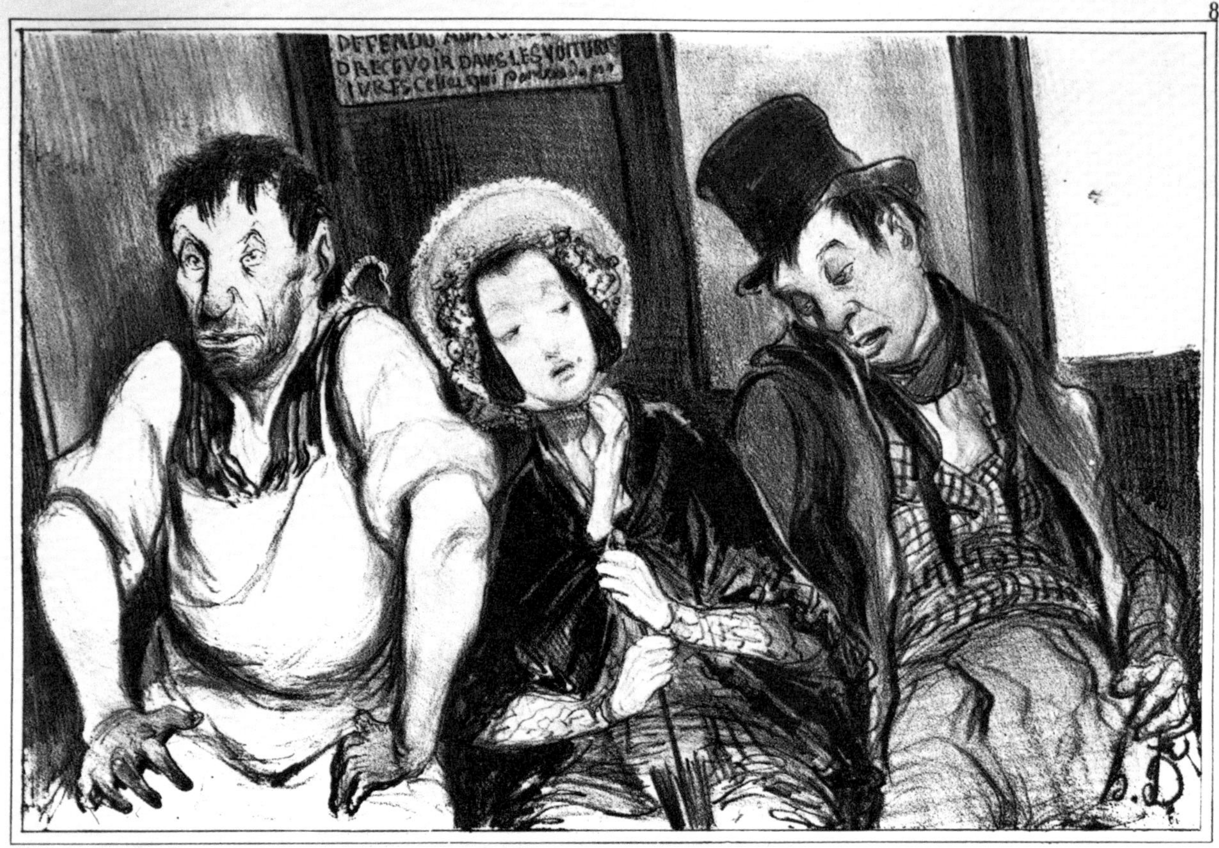

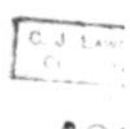

Cat. 15

Intérieur d'un omnibus. Entre un homme ivre et un charcutier.

Interior of an omnibus. Between a drunk man and a pork-butcher.

"Types parisiens" (Parisian types), no. 8; published in
La Caricature, November 13, 1839 (D. 566).

LENDER: Print Collection, Miriam and Ira D. Wallach
Division of Art, Prints and Photographs. The New York
Public Library, Astor, Lenox, and Tilden Foundations.

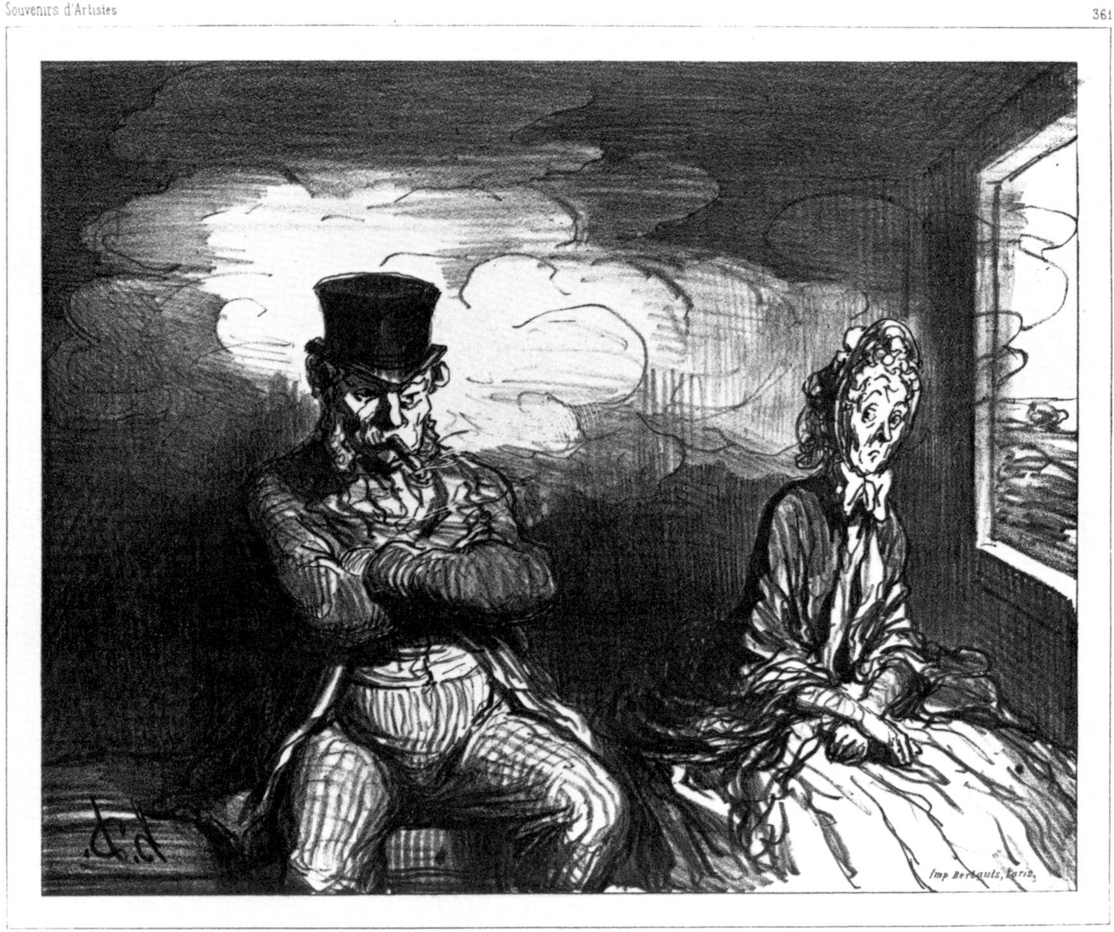

Cat. 16

En chemin de fer . . . un voisin agréable.

In the train . . . a pleasant neighbor.

"Souvenirs d'artistes" (Artists' recollections), no. 361;
published in *Le Boulevard,* September 21, 1862 (D. 3252).

LENDER: PNY Fine Prints and Drawings, New York.

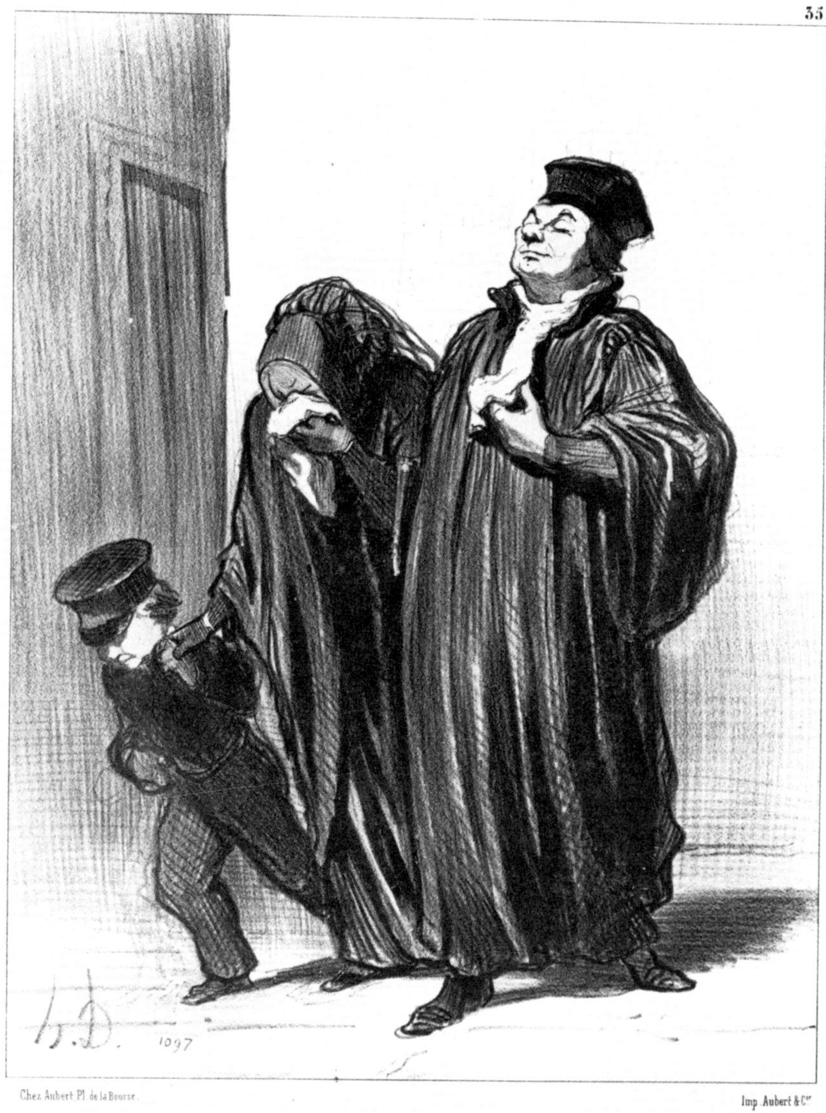

— Vous avez perdu votre procès c'est vrai......mais vous avez du éprouver bien du plaisir à m'entendre plaider.

Cat. 17

Vous avez perdu votre procès c'est vrai . . . mais vous avez du éprouver bien du plaisir à m'entendre plaider.

You lost your suit, it's true . . . but you must have taken great pleasure in hearing me plead the case.

"Les Gens de justice" (The people of justice), no. 35; published in *Le Charivari,* April 27, 1848 (D. 1371).

LENDER: The Rose Art Museum, Brandeis University, Waltham, Massachusetts, The Benjamin A. and Julia M. Trustman Collection.

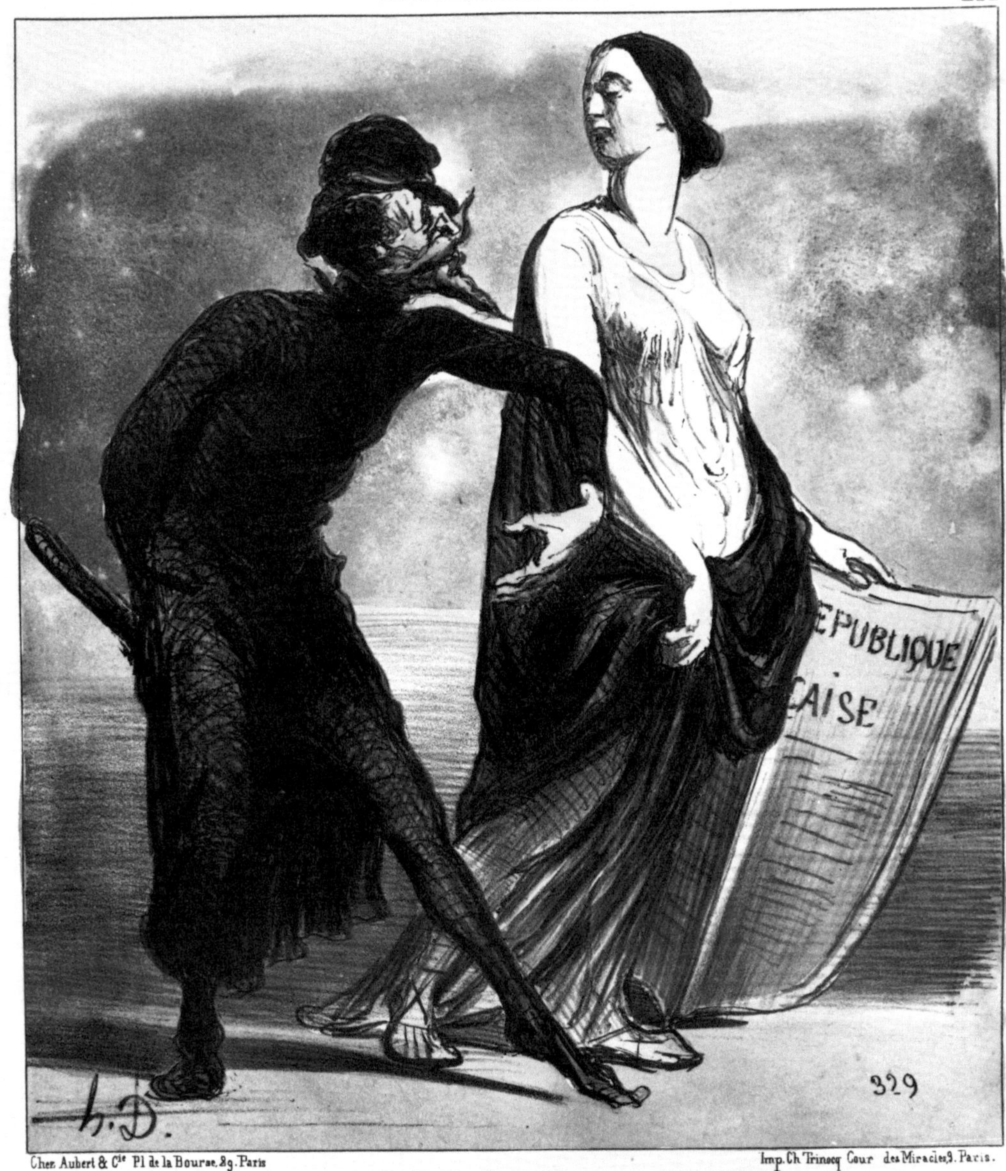

Cat. 18

—*Belle dame, voulez-vous bien accepter mon bras?*
—*Votre passion est trop subite pour que je puisse y croire!*

—Beautiful lady, would you take my arm?
—Your passion is too sudden to be believed!

"Actualités" (Current events), no. 212; published in *Le Charivari*, September 25, 1851 (D. 2153).

LENDER: Print Collection, Miriam and Ira D. Wallach Division of Art, Prints and Photographs. The New York Public Library, Astor, Lenox, and Tilden Foundations.

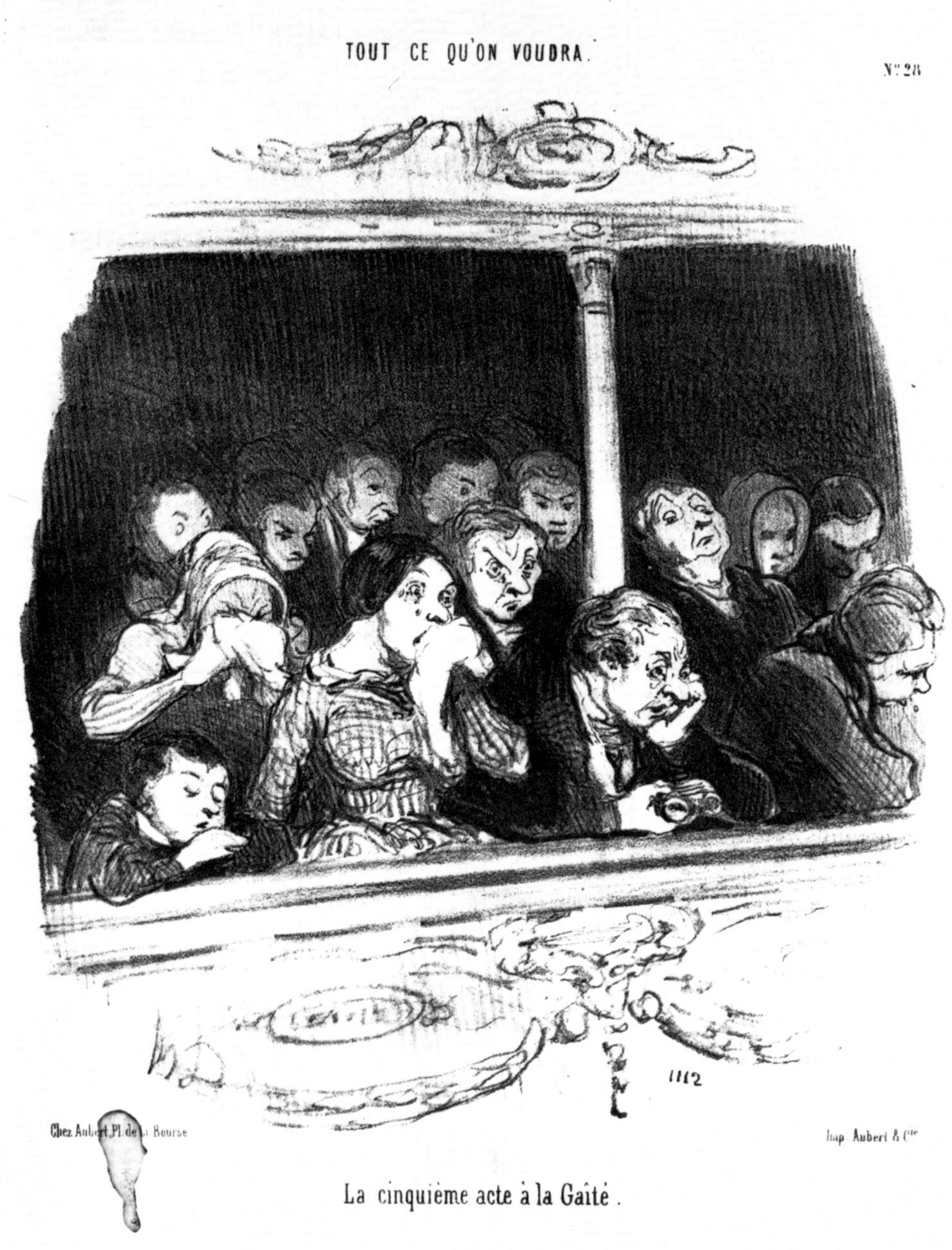

Cat. 19

La {sic} Cinquième Acte à la Gaité.

The fifth act at the Gaîté Theater.

"Tout ce qu'on voudra" (All that one would like), no. 28;
published in *Le Charivari,* February 7, 1848 (D. 1674).

LENDER: Museum of Fine Arts, Boston.

Conduct Unbecoming:
Daumier and "Les Bas-Bleus"

JANIS BERGMAN-CARTON

THE DECADES OF the 1970s and 1980s have produced numerous iconographical studies of female typological imagery in nineteenth-century French caricature and painting. Dominated by accounts of courtesans and women victimized into prostitution by social or economic constraints, these studies have usefully called attention to the obsession with the urban reality of French working-class women. But their focus on victimized women has perpetuated this single model of female identity at the expense of other more complex and equally historical ones. This essay resurrects an alternative model, prevalent in nineteenth-century art and life yet ignored in twentieth-century critical literature—that of the intellectual or political woman, the woman of ideas.

Though the concept of the woman of ideas in France is centuries old, the classification is not. More commonly and derogatorily labeled *le bas-bleu, la femme-homme,* or *l'amazone littéraire,* the woman of ideas is a female type born of the success and notoriety of such figures as Christine de Pisan and Mme de Staël, whose published works were viewed by many as invasions of the traditionally masculine public realms of literature and politics. The phrase "woman of ideas" refers to a figure principally identified by her nineteenth-century contemporaries (satirically or not) as an intellectual being who recognizes and utilizes the power of words to influence public opinion. It does not refer to the scores of talented women with careers in painting or music, areas in which women were able to function without challenging male assessments of the feminine nature. Rather, the label is intended exclusively to describe women operating in the fields of literature and politics—two highly visible and valued aspects of French public life for which women were considered ill-suited.

In the nineteenth century the woman of ideas became an increasingly popular target for visual and literary satires. One of the most extensive caricatural treatments of the subject is found in the oeuvre of Honoré Daumier. Between 1837 and 1849 Daumier devoted over seventy lithographs to the subject. The one or two paragraphs by previous Daumier scholars who discussed these images at all ranged from unselfconscious restatements of Daumier's antifeminist sentiments to assurances that Daumier was offended not by feminist theory but by the feminists themselves. Arsène Alexandre's 1888 characterization of Daumier's "Bas-Bleus" concludes simply that these are "women who do not want to resign themselves to being women"

(femmes qui ne veulent pas se résigner à être femmes).[1] Almost a century later, the criticism of these series is barely more substantive. In *Daumier and His World,* Howard Vincent writes that Daumier's attitude reflects nothing more than "dislike of the anti-feminine woman, the enthusiast . . .who is, after all, . . . a natural target for the satirist's laughter."[2] Oliver Larkin explains in *Daumier: Man of His Time* that "Daumier's ridicule is directed not at the notion of reform but at its sententious high priestesses and camp followers."[3]

Only two essays are devoted exclusively to Daumier's caricatures of the woman of ideas. They were written, not surprisingly, in the mid-1970s, the period in which the impact of feminism on art history and criticism was first registered.[4] Françoise Parturier's *Intellectuelles ("Les Bas-Bleus" et "Femmes socialistes")* and Cäcilia Rentmeister's more scholarly "Daumier und das hässliche Geschlect" provide contextual enrichment essential to the reading of Daumier's imagery. But these texts are principally concerned with elucidating the present through the resurrection of a comparable historical moment. Neither analyzes the lithographs in any detail nor examines their power to reinforce and generate social mythologies of gender.

During the July Monarchy the avenues of expression for women had expanded, owing, in part, to opportunities generated by industrialization in France. Not only traditional gender distinctions but class boundaries as well were rendered more fluid by the new outlets for female self-expression and the material and political rewards they entailed. Daumier's caricatures of the woman of ideas deny or discredit this fluidity by reducing the female form to the dichotomous alternatives of angelic mother or demonic whore.[5] This essay examines Daumier's largest series on the subject, "Les Bas-Bleus," which formed part of the social mechanism that undermined the literary and political achievements of women after 1830. It analyzes the way in which Daumier trivialized what was genuinely powerful about the woman of ideas by figuring her as a deviant, a creature who disrupts households, neglects children, and uses her fame to satisfy unnatural sexual appetites.

The developments in French social and cultural life to which Daumier was reacting are enumerated in the introductory essay to this catalogue. The principal arenas for the intellectual woman in the July Monarchy of concern here are the women's emancipation movement that had reemerged in the context of utopian socialist reform rhetoric and the popular press. The impetus for feminist activities during the July Monarchy derived from the male leaders of the emerging French socialist movements, who tended to associate women's rights with workers' rights and general political reform. Charles Fourier and the Saint-Simonist leader Prosper Enfantin, for example, viewed female liberation as the natural measure of the humanist ideal of general emancipation, as a part of the larger struggle to achieve a communal society free of inequities.[6]

The woman of ideas also flourished within the rapid growth of the popular press. Middle- and working-class women to whom most respectable professional careers had been closed because of legal, economic, or educational restrictions were able to claim a career in letters after 1830 thanks to fundamental changes taking place within what became known as the "French literary industry." As a serialized novelist, a *chroniqueuse,* an editor or publisher of literary and political magazines, and the targeted reader of the numerous *modiste* journals, during the July Monarchy the woman of ideas became a fashionable female model and favorite subject for caricatural attack. The activities of women like George Sand, Marie d'Agoult, and Flora Tristan inspired hundreds of caricatures by Daumier, Gavarni, Cham, de Beaumont, and others.

While Daumier's series "Les Bas-Bleus" must be seen as part of the general response in the popular press to the increased visibility of the woman of ideas, its fundamental context remains the antifeminist policies of *Le Charivari,* the journal in which all of the lithographs appeared, and its forerunner, *La Caricature.*[7] The first textual references to the woman of ideas in these publications appeared in nonsatirical book reviews that were descriptive and promotional rather than analytical. In fact, many titles of books reviewed reappear on page four, in the section devoted to advertisements.[8]

Although accounts of books by women were friendly in the early thirties, they were supplanted later in the decade by hostile, satirical articles on the woman of ideas. The change is due, in part, to Louis-Philippe's censorial September Laws of 1835 that forced the journal's editor, Charles Philipon, to redirect the satirical focus of *Le Charivari* from the *juste-milieu* government to less overtly political subject matter.[9] Following the imposition of these restrictions, Philipon found it necessary to alter the focus of *Le Charivari* to include art and literary criticism and social caricature. Daumier's series on the woman of ideas, like most of his lithographic work produced between 1835 and 1848, has been relegated to this so-called lesser aspect of his

oeuvre, to the period when the artist was forced to suppress his political concerns in favor of benign scenes of everyday life.

The number of articles on the woman of ideas in *Le Charivari* increased dramatically after 1835. The legally mandated shift in editorial focus from the government of Louis-Philippe to such subjects as the plays of Virginie Ancelot must have foregrounded an inequitable situation: the avenues for women writers to publicize women's issues were growing just as the opportunities for Philipon and his staff to exercise their own political agenda were waning. Unable to express their anger at the source of their disempowerment, Louis-Philippe, male journalists redirected a portion of their wrath toward a figure they saw as the female usurper of the male place, the newly professionalized *femme-auteur.* The most offensive of these usurpers was the increasingly successful bourgeois *femme de lettres.*[10]

A female literary tradition had existed in France since the fifteenth century, but, until the nineteenth century, it had been aristocratic and tied principally to the institution of the salon. The hostility toward the nineteenth-century woman of ideas derived from her increasing enjoyment of the financial and critical rewards once reserved exclusively for men. It also reflected her evolution in this period from mere *femme-auteur* to what the nineteenth-century playwright and essayist Frédéric Soulié labeled *le bas-bleu militant.*[11]

The personality who appears to have emblematized the bourgeois *bas-bleu militant* and whose activities prompted the first sustained attack on the woman of ideas in *Le Charivari* was Mme Marie-Madeleine Poutret de Mauchamp, who in 1836 established a moderate republican "Journal de législation et de jurisprudence" called *Gazette des femmes.* The model for the *Gazette des femmes* was Desirée Véret and Reine Guindorf's Saint-Simonist newspaper *La Femme libre* (1832–1834). Although the writers for *La Femme libre* were harangued constantly in the legitimist and *juste-milieu* press in the early thirties, they barely received mention in Philipon's publications. Their working-class origins seem to have ensured the benign neglect if not sympathy of Philipon, who reserved his contempt for the bourgeois women whom he accused of arrogating the feminist rhetoric of Véret and Guindorf and capitalizing on the vogue of *la femme émancipée.*[12]

Mme Poutret de Mauchamp's purpose, articulated in the first issue of the *Gazette des femmes,* was to educate women about legal issues and provide a platform to agitate for reform in the areas of political and civil rights. Her journal flourished between 1836 and 1838 until she, like the Saint-Simonist guru Père Enfantin, was officially silenced after being tried and convicted on fabricated morals charges.[13]

Gazette des femmes was prominent during the years when *Le Charivari* first began to assault the woman of ideas. One of the earliest attacks appears in a review of Théodore Muret's comedy *Les Droits de la femme,* which opened at the Théâtre français in May 1837. The reviewer analyzes the female protagonist's development, under the influence of Marie-Madeleine Poutret de Mauchamp, from innocent to *bas-bleu militant:* "Madame read the novels of George Sand, she cried at performances of *Marie,*[14] she is up-to-date on all of the demonstrations and insurrections recently publicized by women through the press and the popular theater"[15] (Madame a lu les romans de George Sand, elle a pleuré aux représentations de *Marie,* elle est au courant de toutes les protestations et de toutes les motions insurrectionelles que les femmes, depuis quelques temps, publient par la voie de la presse et du théâtre). The paradigm to which the play and its review conforms—the impressionable victim manipulated by an evil female mentor—is reproduced often in the pages of *Le Charivari* to account for the evolution of the woman of ideas.[16]

The review of Muret's play is followed, several issues later, by a lengthy article, "Curiosités littéraires: Les Demoiselles de lettres," which describes the phenomenon of the provincial woman of ideas.[17] In a scenario that bears a striking resemblance to the sad tale of Daumier's father, she is said to discover one morning that life in the provinces is too limited.[18] She flees to Paris where she makes the ritualistic visits to George Sand, who does not receive her, and Mme Poutret de Mauchamp, who welcomes her with open arms. A week later, *la demoiselle de lettres* is no longer recognizable, having become the myth, "preaching the liberation of woman and the enslavement of man" (préchânt la liberté de la femme et l'asservissement de l'homme).[19]

Throughout 1837 the invectives in *Le Charivari* against the woman of ideas intensify. The journal features mock petitions from Poutret de Mauchamp to Louis-Philippe and expands the rubric of the woman of ideas to include current female heads of state like Queen Victoria of England and Queen Marie-Christine of Spain. In diatribes that give thanks for the French *lois saliques* as they ridicule Victoria's and Marie-Christine's incompetence and unnatural relations with men, articles in *Le Charivari* warn of the fate of France

should Poutret de Mauchamp's efforts to empower women succeed.[20] The journal uses the same rhetorical formulae to describe women as different in stature and responsibility as Mme Poutret de Mauchamp and Queen Victoria, demonstrating how during the July Monarchy the woman of ideas evolved as the typological evocation of female deviance.

The impulse to diminish the reality of the woman of ideas by casting her as a type antithetical and dangerous to a female ideal is nowhere more explicit than in the work of Honoré Daumier.[21] Daumier's first representation of the intellectual woman appeared in 1839 as part of the "Moeurs conjugales" series. It images the threat posed by the woman of ideas rather than the writer herself, including her as an objectified concept rather than a physical entity. *Je me fiche bien de votre Mme SAND* (cat. 12) focuses on the impotent husband of a wife who has fallen under the spell of the unscrupulous George Sand, who here exists only as a disembodied presence. In the lithograph a man holding a pair of trousers stands before his wife who is seated in an easy chair absorbed in a novel. Their torsos incline backward, his in a gesture of indignant disbelief and hers slovenly conforming to the angle of her chair, punctuating the physical and psychic distance between them. His unmended pants are held in front of his genitals and appear in the center of the composition in counterpoint to the book. With disheveled hair, grimacing mouth, and protruding nose, he is the emasculated, ineffectual fool. She is individuated only by her dress and posture, her blurred and undistinguished facial features likened to the white pages of the text that consumes and becomes her identity.

"I don't give a damn about your Mme SAND," the husband declares in the legend, "who prevents women from mending pants and darning socks! . . . We must reestablish divorce or suppress those authors!" As Philippe Roberts-Jones notes, this image was published on June 28, 1839, around the same time that George Sand's new novel *Spiridion* was published, the same year that her portrait by Auguste Charpentier was hung at the Salon (and, in fact, reproduced in *Le Charivari* just two and a half weeks earlier), and the same year that her most provocative book, *Lélia,* was rereleased[22]—a book that incited critics like Capo de Feuillades to advise his readers to lock it away so that it could contaminate no one, especially young girls whose virgin souls need protection from a text as perverse in places as the works of the marquis de Sade.[23]

A similar marital encounter is the subject of *Un*

Intérieur parisien (cat. 14), a lithograph from the lengthy "Moeurs conjugales" series published in May 1842, a full three years later. Like the first, it reenacts a scene of domestic disorder engendered by a woman who has been corrupted by novels. What is different, however, is that the husband no longer complains; he, too, appears bloodless and inanimate. Furthermore, the legend in this later work is descriptive rather than dialogic: "Monsieur is the homemaker; Madame is thinking of being the homewrecker." The husband quietly mops the floor and attempts to maintain the very domestic order that the wife's novel inspires her to disrupt.

By 1842 the association of women reading and writing with domestic disarray had become a commonplace. Neither the text nor the author needs identification, nor is a description of the husband's misfortune necessary. The scenario would have been instantly recognized by an audience in 1842 that had been inundated since 1840 with similar parables in the popular theater and press concerning the French version of the British bluestocking.[24]

The *bas-bleu* was the subject of a number of plays in the early 1840s that include Ferdinand Langlé and F. de Villeneuve's *Le Bas-Bleu* at the Théâtre des Variétés, Pacini's opéra-séria *Saffo* ("the celebrated *bas-bleu* from the island of Lesbos") at the Théâtre des Italiens, and de Veau and Brisson's *La Fille aux bas-bleus* at the Théâtre français. Most were variations on the theme of misguided women who, after having followed the example of an unethical *bas-bleu,* were saved from humiliation and destitution by a wise man. And, most ended in marriage—the institution usually maligned by the female protagonists in the early moments of the play— with a promise, like that made by Athenais in the Langlé and de Villeneuve comedy, that from now on pants will be worn only by husbands and "I will use my quill only for my hats."[25]

Daumier's caricatural series, the content of which appears to have been in large part dictated by the editorial board of *Le Charivari,* often capitalized on well-received themes from the popular theater. But the decision to develop "Les Bas-Bleus" seems to have been a response principally to the success of several *physiologies* published between 1840 and 1842. "Les Bas-Bleus," Daumier's first and largest series on the woman of ideas, consists of forty lithographs issued intermittently in *Le Charivari* between January 30 and August 7, 1844. The series draws extensively from Frédéric Soulié's *Physiologie du bas-bleu* (1841–1842), Edmond Texier's *Physiologie du poète* (1841), and Jules Janin's "Un

Bas-Bleu," a typological essay included in Louis Curmer's *Les Français peints par eux-mêmes* (1842).[26]

Almost all of the lithographs in Daumier's "Les Bas-Bleus" visualize and embellish clichés or anecdotes from one of these three sources. The first plate of the series, for instance, *C'est singulier comme ce miroir m'applatit . . .* (fig. 4.1), concretizes Frédéric Soulié's description of *le bas-bleu véritable* "who floats between forty-five and fifty-five years old, . . . [who has] a skinny body, . . . a sad smile, . . . [and] an emaciated bosom" (qui flotte entre quarante-cinq et cinquante-cinq ans . . . [qui a] un corps maigre, . . . le sourire douloureux, . . . [et] une poitrine décharnée).[27] The lithograph features a woman examining herself in a

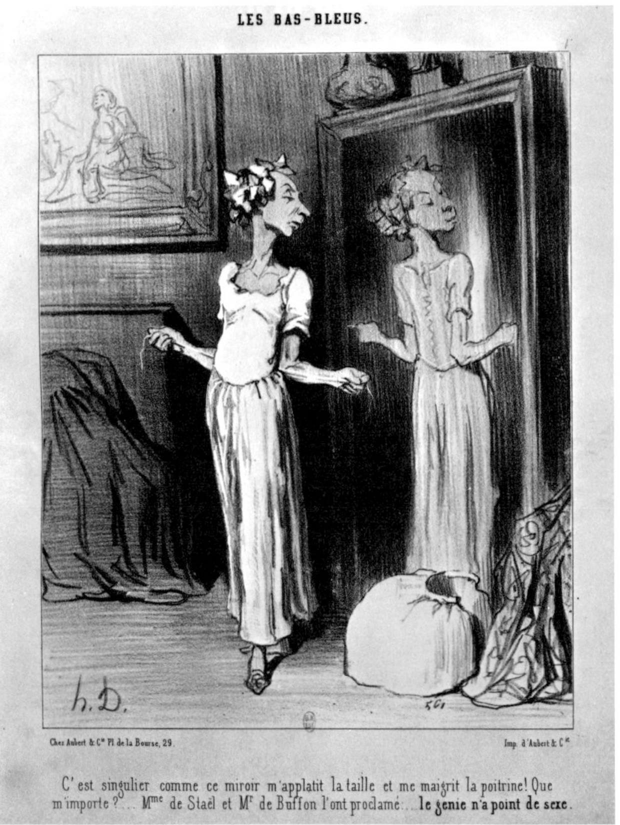

Fig. 4.1 Honoré Daumier.
C'est singulier comme ce miroir m'applatit la taille et me maigrit la poitrine! Que m'importe? . . . Mme de Staël et Mr de Buffon l'ont proclamé . . . le génie n'a point de sexe.

It's curious how this mirror flatters my height and slims my chest. What does it mean? Mme de Staël and Mr. de Buffon proclaimed it. . . genius has no sex.

"Les Bas-Bleus" (The bluestockings), no. 1; published in *Le Charivari,* January 30, 1844 (D. 1221).
Bibliothèque nationale, Paris, Cabinet des estampes.

full-length mirror. Behind her hangs a painting that invokes Daumier's engraving of *la dixième muse* (the name assigned female poets during the Restoration and July Monarchy) published three years earlier as the frontispiece to Texier's *Physiologie du poète.* She is surrounded by discarded clothing that had padded her straight silhouette to make it appear curvaceous and conventionally female. Having removed the false garments, she is shown to be vainly and foolishly attributing her sexlessness to the mirror's inadequacies rather than her own. She stands facing us, glancing over her left shoulder to see the "distorted" reflection of her curveless back. A literal embodiment of the popular phrase *la femme-homme de lettres,* this long-nosed, weak-chinned figure marvels at the "distortions" of her mirror: "How strange the way this mirror makes my figure appear straight and my bosom meager! What do I care anyway? Mme de Staël and M. de Buffon have proclaimed that genius has no sex" (C'est singulier, comme ce miroir m'applatit la taille et me maigrit la poitrine! Que m'importe? Mme de Staël et M. de Buffon l'ont proclamé le génie n'a point de sexe!). We, who are given a direct frontal view of the *bas-bleu,* are privy to the visual joke that her chest is a mirror image of her curveless back—in or out of the reflection. Daumier and his legend writer pun on the famous phrase "genius has no sex"—intended by Mme de Staël to assert the intellectual equality of women—to shift focus from the *bas-bleu's* success as a thinker to her failures as a woman. The lithograph offers its audience a moral lesson: women who substitute the life of the mind for the life of the home are no longer women.

Over half of Daumier's *bas-bleus* are berated for their dearth of sexual and intellectual powers. Within that genre, most are also maligned for their role in denigrating the literary arts. During the July Monarchy the literary establishment debated the merits of the growing commercialization of literature. The success of the woman of ideas was often made part of this debate. For instance, in Daumier's *Monsieur, pardon si je vous gêne un peu . . .* (cat. 20) a foolish old woman consumed by her desire for fame fails to recognize the inappropriateness of her aggressive behavior. She dominates the table of a library reading room. Her right elbow intrudes on one neighbor's space as her other arm reaches out unselfconsciously toward a stack of books, blocking the man to her left. The tidy arrangement of the volumes on the shelves behind the readers echoes the self-contained dignity of the men just as the only book that is askew, disrupting the order, is the one behind the *bas-bleu's*

head. Its irregularity underscores hers, the only woman and presumably the only nonintellect in the library.

In the early 1840s, prior to Daumier's series, *Le Charivari* published many articles on the women with whom male writers had to compete for jobs and government subsidies. The most venomous attacks focused on the phenomenon of journalistic nepotism—the practice of giving women undeserved publishing opportunities that they abused by sentimentalizing and cheapening literature.[28]

The identification of the *bas-bleu* with the bourgeois *femme-auteur,* who subverts the concept of the family and corrupts the conventions of literature, pervades the typological studies of Texier, Soulié, and Janin. Texier's *Physiologie du poète,* for example, a project to which Daumier contributed forty-one woodcut illustrations, classifies the various types of poets writing in Paris. The range of male poets from aristocratic gentlemen to members of the proletariat is striking in its social and economic diversity. Furthermore, though each is vulnerable to charges of vanity and self-absorption, none is accused of subverting the social order. Conversely, the discussion of female poets is relegated to the final two chapters and makes no such class distinction. Texier's representation of *la dixième muse* is uniformly bourgeois. Moreover, when the charges of self-centeredness are levied against her rather than her male counterpart, the tone is harsh and moralizing: "the tenth muse has multiplied at a terrifying rate. She has grown without cultivation like a fungus, . . . in the pages of serialized novels and on page four of the daily newspapers" (la dixième muse s'est multipliée dans une proportion effrayante; elle a poussé sans culture, comme les champignons, . . . dans les colonnes des feuilletons, et à la quatrième page des journaux).[29]

Soulié's pseudohistorical survey, *Physiologie du bas-bleu,* also focuses on the dangers of the bourgeois *femme-auteur* whose ascendancy he dates to the Revolution of 1830.[30] Like most *physiologies,* Soulié's disguises an idiosyncratic choice of content with a veneer of scientific classification and the rhetoric of social truism. The arbitrariness of what purports to be a legitimate categorization of the contemporary bourgeois *bas-bleu* is revealed in chapter six, "Bas-Bleu mariée, deuxième espèce," a figure who is, according to Soulié, "the most evil of all" (la plus méchante de toutes).[31] In this chapter claiming to describe a type of *bas-bleu,* there is only the story of an ambitious wife who offers herself to a cabinet minister to obtain a position for her husband as consul of state. Absolutely nothing in the chapter beyond its title would prompt the identification of the woman as a *bas-bleu*.

The label *bas-bleu* often was used indiscriminately in journalism and popular literature during the July Monarchy as a synonym for the aggressive female. It signified the freedom and confidence with which many women were operating in the public arena more than their involvement per se in literary activities. Soulié makes explicit this opposition of "le bas-bleu contemporain" to her aristocratic ancestors whose influence was restricted to the private sphere of the salon. He asserts that the contemporary bourgeois *bas-bleu* is contemptible "like everything that falls in the public domain" (comme tout ce qui tombe dans le domaine public).[32]

Jules Janin also cites the Revolution of 1830 as marking the sudden glorification of the written and spoken word and the hideous metamorphosis of the once-charming *salonnière* into an obsessive, fame-hungry *bas-bleu*. In "Un Bas-Bleu" Janin charges that modern journalism, the progeny of the French Revolution, has cheapened and corrupted literature. His essay alternates between a fiery assault on the preoccupation of the modern writer with issues of salability and an unfocused description of the bourgeois *bas-bleu* whom he implicitly holds responsible for this situation.

Male writers, angered at the greater freedom, notoriety, and often financial rewards enjoyed by some of their female competition, maligned the literary achievements of the woman of ideas as tainted and artistically bankrupt. To ensure the success of this strategy, they reinforced it with a more conventional but more damaging accusation: that the woman of ideas is both a literary whore and a sexual deviant responsible for the corruption of art and the dissolution of the bourgeois household.

The self-absorbed creatures who opt for the life of the spirit instead of the joys of marriage and maternity are merely foolish in Daumier's classification of *les bas-bleus*. Those who try to have it all are insidious. When Daumier's earlier depictions of the woman of ideas in the "Moeurs conjugales" series (see cat. 12 and 14) presage the theme of family ruin, they invoke the *bas-bleu* only as a sinister offstage presence manipulating female puppets. By 1844, however, the corruption is complete. Women are no longer passively absorbing lessons from novels. They have put down their books and are out of their chairs acting out the once-fictive scenarios of the sexual revolution.

Daumier's first allusion to the monstrous *bas-bleu*

who violates the integrity of both family and literature occurs in his final woodcut for Texier's *Physiologie du poète. Le Papa donnant la bouillie à son enfant* (The father feeding gruel to his child; fig. 4.2) depicts a husband in his dressing gown feeding his child. The wife is nowhere to be seen, but we are to presume from Texier's prose that she is out cavorting with publishers while her husband fulfills her domestic responsibilities: "The muse's husband, the same husband who devotes himself to the care of the household while his wife engages in adulterous business with Apollo, must resign himself to the complete loss of his individuality . . . he is only an object to his wife, . . . her number one domestic" (Le mari de la muse, ce même mari qui vaque aux soins du ménage pendant que sa femme entretient un commerce adultère avec Apollon, doit se résigner à perdre tout à fait sa personnalité . . . il n'est que la chose de sa femme, . . . c'est-à-dire son premier domestique).[33]

The degeneration of the family forms the subject of nineteen of Daumier's forty representations in "Les Bas-Bleus." Several draw directly on the emasculated figure of "le mari de la muse." In *Depuis que Virginie a obtenu le septième accessit . . .* (cat. 21), for example, the husband is shown sorting through mounds of dirty linen while his wife, hand to her chin, stands absorbed in a book. Not only has Virginia's literary award made her husband a domestic slave but the prize itself—as Daumier's audience would have instantly recognized—comes from an unworthy imitation of the Académie française, the Académie des femmes, founded by Louis-Joseph-Alphonse-Jules de Castellane in 1843.[34]

Another lithograph from "Les Bas-Bleus" engages the popular metaphorical question of Who wears the pants? In *Une femme comme moi . . .* (cat. 22) an incredulous wife, having just flung her husband's pants in his face, shouts, "A woman like me . . . sew on a button? . . . you're crazy!" Her torso, arms, and dress—curved and animated as if by a wind of fury—contrast with the stable vertical of her husband's humbled and pantless figure. His fingertips touch embarrassedly before his genitals in a gesture of shame while his pants, which in tonality and animation of line appear to belong more appropriately to the wife, seem to wear him. The pants hovering about his head read at once as a controlling vise and a ridiculous woman's bonnet.

Daumier's most damning critiques of the bourgeois *bas-bleu* extend her domestic crimes to include maternal irresponsibility. Eight of the lithographs in the series feature some variation on this subject: women giving

l'être si longtemps rêvé qui saura la comprendre,
et qui l'emportera enfin loin du contact des
hommes, dans le désert du divin sentiment et
dans la Thébaïde des émotions saisissantes.

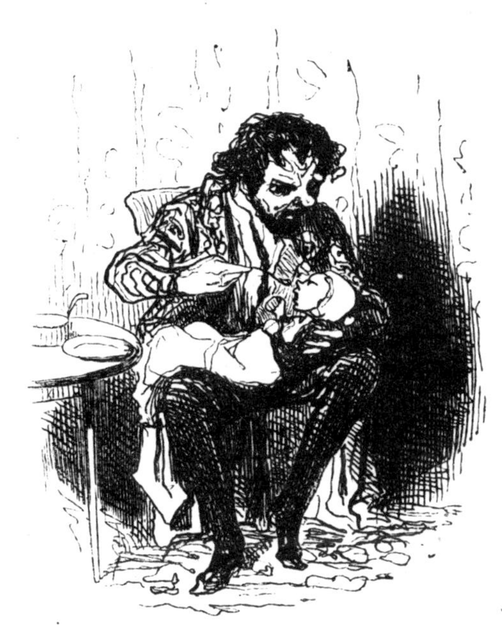

Fig. 4.2 Honoré Daumier.
Le Papa donnant la bouillie à son enfant.

The father feeding gruel to his child.

Published in Edmond Texier, *Physiologie du poète,* 1841. Bibliothèque
nationale, Paris.

daughters the wrong kind of education; children
drowning in bathtubs as their mothers sit absorbed in
thought (cat. 23); or shrews screaming at husbands to
take their children elsewhere so they can finish their
odes to maternity. In an image of the last type, *Emportez donc ça plus loin . . .* (cat. 24), a husband stands
with baby in arms behind the lyre-backed chair in
which his wife sits. The chair-lyre emasculates him as
does his willingness to stay at home in his dressing
gown and care for his child (who even appears to nurse
at his breast). The wife, seated amid the clutter she

calls her work (though there is more paper crumpled up
in the trash than there is on the desk before her), shouts
for her husband to take that thing away. She threatens
in the legend, "It's your first child, but I swear it will
be your last!"

Daumier's most cynical figuration of the unfit
mother features a pregnant woman blowing smoke
rings in the face of her husband *cum* house servant. In
Dis donc . . . mon mari . . . (cat. 25) a husband polishes
a bowl as his wife pontificates about her various creative
projects. In a reversal of conventional gender signs, his
body is self-contained and likened to the rounded vessel
shape usually associated with the female form; the *bas-
bleu,* meanwhile, is a pastiche of extrusions: her left
hand, her cigarette, her profile features, and her enormous belly that points accusingly toward her husband.
"Say, husband," she informs him dispassionately, "I
have a mind to call my play *Arthur* and to entitle my
child Oscar! . . . but no . . . all things considered, I
will decide nothing before consulting my collaborator."
Punning on the idea of a collaborator who is insinuated
to have spawned both the play and the child, the lithograph demeans the woman of ideas as both untalented
and unfaithful. Her husband stands passively by, symbolically robbed of his virility by the dust rag arranged
to suggest impotence juxtaposed with the huge protru-
sion of his wife's belly for which he clearly can claim no
responsibility.

The association of the woman of ideas with domestic disarray and sexual promiscuity is common in caricatures and textual descriptions during the July
Monarchy. The duped husband and provocative verb
"collaborate" are staple features of such prints. In *Ma
bonne amie . . .* (cat. 26), for instance, a woman writer
and a male companion are startled and appear to
recover from a compromising position as the husband
tentatively pokes his head in the room. He asks, "My
dear, may I come in? . . . Have you finished collaborating with Monsieur?"[35]

Within the genre of the *physiologie* Jules Janin's "Un
Bas-Bleu" most strikingly and viciously literalizes this
equation of literary and sexual transgression. The
woman of ideas is paid handsomely, Janin complains,
"to write the most abominable invectives that offend
principles of grammar and common sense" (à écrire les
plus abominables invectives contre la grammaire et les
sens commun).[36] If the public wants dramas, he con-
tinues, she writes a drama, choosing her subject carefully to maximize opportunities for blood and violence.
She is, in other words, a literary whore, who in the

name of providing bread and a good education for her beloved children will write a story of infanticide.[37] It is bearable, he explains, when male writers sell out because they are not the ones charged with the moral education of our next generation. The danger is when those who are the teachers of our children prostitute themselves as they write of virtue, when "what she has sold all her life in bedrooms and taverns she will even sell in books" (ce qu'elle a vendu toute sa vie dans les boudoirs ou dans les tavernes, elle le vendra encore dans les livres).[38]

Representing women writers not as women who write but as sexless hags and promiscuous shrews is not a neutral act. To ignore the cultural and political content of these images by studying them as benign scenes of everyday life is not a neutral act either. Daumier's figurations of the woman of ideas were far more complex and politically damaging than his renderings of Louis-Philippe as Gargantua precisely because they appeared so conventional, so "everyday." The lithographs of "Les Bas-Bleus" deny individual achievement and censor the details of a new female reality with which others might identify; they transmute an arena of power into a tired and destructive paradigm of female deviance.

As I have tried to suggest, Daumier did not work in isolation. If his antipathy toward the woman of ideas is consistent with the few details of his biography that we have,[39] it seems to have been encouraged and shaped by the policies and sensibilities of those for whom he worked in the offices of *Le Charivari* at La Maison Aubert. La Maison Aubert, which by 1841 had become the premier lithographic printer-publisher in Paris,[40] played a dominant role in the enormously lucrative *physiologie* trade that spawned Daumier's series "Les Bas-Bleus." The development of "Les Bas-Bleus" was consistent with Philipon's shrewd rethinking of his financial and editorial position after 1835 and the redirection of his business toward its natural audience, the haute bourgeoisie, the class that produced most of the women writers.

Like all good entrepreneurs, Philipon had it both ways; he at once denigrated and cultivated the bourgeois woman of ideas who composed a significant portion of his audience. He published texts and images that trivialized their achievements and flattered them with attention. Philipon's awareness of the need to balance ridicule with flattery is suggested by one of *Le Charivari*'s rare serious essays that appeared midway through Daumier's series. "Salon de 1844" is an article whose ostensible purpose was to call for Salon criticism devoted exclusively to women artists but whose real agenda seems to have been to appease an audience unsettled by Daumier's treatment of the woman of ideas. Its subtext differentiates the woman of ideas from other women with professional identities; it elucidates the differences between women of real talent and *bas-bleus.*

"Salon de 1844" contrasts Daumier's unfaithful wives and irresponsible mothers who "scribble poems and novels" with women who exercise more appropriate and conventional talents. "A woman painting or singing" tends to be attractive, the article explains, whereas "a drinker of ink . . . is as disagreeable to the sight as to the mind."[41] This is true, we are told, because women are by nature creatures of feeling rather than knowledge. Therefore, since being a *savante* requires learning and thought and being an artist above all requires emotion, women are more suited to be the latter. Logically, we are attracted to *la femme-artiste* because she "seems to obey her nature," unlike "la femme-homme de lettres" who repulses us and appears as "a sort of monster."[42]

"Salon de 1844" is a conciliatory effort on Philipon's part to suggest an alternative and acceptable type with whom his female readership might safely identify. It signals the desire of *Le Charivari* to participate in the vogue of ridiculing *la femme pensée* without risking the loss of her subscription fees. But to target the woman of ideas for satirical attack after 1835 was logical for another reason as well. *Le Charivari,* like La Maison Aubert, was an organization composed of male writers who were at once ambivalent about their own complicity in *la littérature industrielle* and threatened by their female competition. To identify the woman of ideas with the prostitution of literature allowed them to deflect anxiety about their own role in the commodification of literary culture. Jules Janin's significant comparison, in its very imperiousness, betrays this anxiety. The French man of letters, compliant with the September Laws and suppliant to a degraded popular taste, may have sold out. But, compared with his new women colleagues and competitors, he might not seem so diminished in moral, literary, and sexual stature. For even if both men and women writers were working the same market, it could not so easily be said of the former that they "sell in books what they may have sold all their lives in bedrooms and taverns."

NOTES

Research for this article was financed, in part, by fellowships from the Swann Foundation for the Study of Caricature and Cartoon and the Woodrow Wilson Foundation.

1   Arsène Alexandre, *Honoré Daumier: L'Homme et l'oeuvre* (Paris: H. Laurens, 1888), p. 263. Champfleury provides another contemporary account of the series in his *Exposition des peintures et dessins de Honoré Daumier* (Paris: Gauthiers-Villars, 1878). Though he, too, reaffirms Daumier's prejudices against *les femmes pensées,* he is the first to attempt to contextualize the imagery.

2   Howard Vincent, *Daumier and His World* (Evanston, Ill.: Northwestern University Press, 1968), p. 125.

3   Oliver Larkin, *Daumier: Man of His Time* (New York: McGraw-Hill, 1966), p. 50.

4   See Françoise Parturier and Jacqueline Armingeat, *Daumier: Intellectuelles ("Les Bas-Bleus" et "Femmes socialistes")* (Paris: Editions Vilo-Paris, 1974); and Cäcilia Rentmeister, "Daumier und das hässliche Geschlect," in *Honoré Daumier und die ungelösten Probleme der bürgerlichen Gesellschaft,* exh. cat. (Berlin: Neue Gesellschaft für bildende Kunst for the Schloss Charlottenburg, 1974), pp. 57–79. Lucette Czyba read an unpublished paper on *les bas-bleus* at the Daumier symposium held in Bielefeld, Germany, in December 1984, a revised version of which is included in the present volume.

5   This phenomenon is explored in Walter Benjamin, "Paris of the Second Empire in Baudelaire," in his *Charles Baudelaire: A Lyric Poet in the Era of High Capitalism,* trans. Harry Zohn (London: N. L. B., 1973), p. 12.

6   For a complete discussion, see Claire Moses, *French Feminism in the Nineteenth Century* (Albany, N.Y.: S.U.N.Y. Press, 1984), chap. four.

7   In any discussion of caricature it is essential to understand the collaborative nature of the process and the many different hands involved in the conception and elaboration of an image. In the case of Daumier, the most cogent discussion can be found in Elizabeth C. Childs, "Honoré Daumier and the Exotic Vision: Studies in French Caricature and Culture, 1830–1870," Ph.D. diss., Columbia University, 1989, chap. one.

8   See, for example, Eugène Morisseau, "'Indiana' par George Sand," *La Caricature* (May 31, 1832): 663, and "Bulletin bibliographique," *La Caricature* (May 23, 1833): 1062.

9   For an examination of the repercussions of the September Laws, see Edwin de T. Bechtel, *Freedom of the Press and L'Association Mensuelle—Philipon Versus Louis-Philippe* (New York: The Grolier Club, 1952). One must also take into consideration a change in personnel after 1835. In part, because of economic problems that were inevitably related to Louis-Philippe's restrictive policies, *Le Charivari* was sold in 1835 and again in 1836. See the discussion of changes in *Le Charivari's* editorial board and editorship in Jules Brisson and Félix Ribèyre, *Grands Journaux de France* (Paris: Jouast Père, 1862).

10   The hostility of male journalists toward the bourgeois *femme de lettres* is most explicit in Grandville and Travies's caricature *Les FeuILLES PUBLIQUES,* published in *La Caricature* (September 26, 1833). The image personifies the newspapers that market serialized novels as whores.

11   Frédéric Soulié, *Physiologie du bas-bleu* (Paris: Aubert et Cie, 1841–1842), p. 19.

12   See Laure Adler, *A l'aube du féminisme: Les Premières Journalistes, 1830–1850* (Paris: Payot, 1979). The trendiness of *la femme émancipée* in the mid-nineteenth century is suggested by her frequent characterization in fiction. Flaubert's La Vatnaz in *L'Education sentimentale,* for example, is based on Eugénie Niboyet and Jeanne Deroin, two prominent feminist activists of the 1840s. Many of Balzac's novels also feature a *femme-auteur.* In *Béatrix* (1840), for example, Félicité des Touches is modeled after George Sand and the marquise de Rochefide after Marie d'Agoult. Mme de la Baudraye in Balzac's *La Muse du département* was also inspired by George Sand.

13   The details of Poutret de Mauchamp's activities are discussed by Marie-Louise Puesch, "Une Supercherie littéraire: Le Véritable Rédacteur de la *Gazette des femmes, 1836–1838,*" *La Révolution de 1848* 32 (June–August 1935): 303–12, and Evelyne Sullerot, *Histoire de la presse féminine en France, des origines à 1848* (Paris: Armand Colin, 1966). For a discussion of Père Enfantin's leadership of the Saint-Simonist community and his imprisonment for corruption of public morals, see Moses, *French Feminism,* chap. three.

14   *Marie* was a highly publicized play by Virginie Ancelot, a female playwright often maligned in the popular press for the state subsidies she received. The play opened at the Théâtre français in October 1836.

15   *Le Charivari,* no. 136 (May 17, 1836): 2.

16   This paradigm is also used during the July Monarchy to explain aberrant male behavior, especially that of Louis-Philippe. Between 1839 and 1848, for instance, a sequence of articles in the legitimist journal *La Mode* assigned blame for the sins of Louis-Philippe alternately to his much despised sister Adelaide and to his former governess (the poet) Stéphanie de Genlis. See *La Mode* (February 1848): 449.

17   "Curiosités littéraires: Les Demoiselles de lettres," *Le Charivari* (May 30, 1837): 1–2.

18   Jean-Baptiste Daumier was an artisan with artistic aspirations. A glazier and poet, Jean-Baptiste had little success in the Parisian literary community and was financially dependent on his son. For the details of his decline and commitment to an insane asylum, see B. Lehmann, "Daumier père et Daumier fils," *Gazette des Beaux-Arts* 1 (May 1945): 297–316. The literary and financial rewards received by such undeserving *demoiselles de provinces* as Delphine de Girardin must have been irritating to Daumier, who saw his father emasculated by loss of livelihood and inability to attain recognition as an artist.

19   "Curiosités littéraires," p. 2.

20   See, for example, "Les femmes ne peuvent pas avoir l'art de régner, puisqu'il n'a pas le moindre rapport avec l'art de plaire"; *Le Charivari* (September 8, 1837): 1.

21   Daumier never grants any female writer the exposure and authority of a portrait likeness. This is particularly striking given his talent for the genre exercised in such series as "Les Représentants représentés." Linda Nochlin's essay "Women, Art, and Power" of 1988, from her anthology of the same title,

identifies the two feminists in Daumier's image *V'la une femme* from the series "Les Divorceuses" as Eugénie Niboyet and probably Jeanne Deroin. Though other caricaturists do figure actual feminists, Daumier does not. In fact, I know of no caricature from any of his series that includes a portrait charge of a female celebrity. To individuate them would have been to grant them stature and legitimacy. Furthermore, by August 1848, when this lithograph was published, Eugénie Niboyet and Jeanne Deroin had already parted company in a fairly public manner. Articles such as "Banquet féminin de la Gaîté," in *Journal pour rire,* another Maison Aubert publication, celebrated the rift between the two feminists and delighted in the fact that Deroin excluded Niboyet from banquets sponsored by the organization she had helped found ([November 25, 1848]: 1).

22 Philippe Roberts-Jones, *Daumier: Humours of Married Life,* trans. Angus Malcolm (Boston: Boston Book and Art Shop, 1968), p. 150.

23 Capo de Feuillade, "Lélia," *L'Europe littéraire* (August 22, 1833): 3.

24 *Le Charivari* first appropriated the term *bas-bleu* as the standard referent for the woman of ideas in the late 1830s, the same period in which invectives against her intensified. "Bluestocking" is a British term, coined in the eighteenth century to describe a circle of women that gathered regularly in the home of Elizabeth Montague (1720–1800). One of the few males allowed, Benjamin Stillingfleet, always wore blue stockings. For *Le Charivari* to have used the label *femme de lettres* would have been to continue to associate women writers like Delphine de Girardin with the historic and esteemed tradition of the French *homme de lettres*. *Le Charivari's* sudden and widespread deployment of the term *bas-bleu* (a term that can only be seen as derogatory) in the late 1830s coincided with the ascendancy of the bourgeois *femme-auteur* with whom the label is most closely associated.

25 Ferdinand Langlé and F. de Villeneuve, *Un Bas-Bleu* (Paris: Marchant, 1844), p. 12. Athenais is a barmaid seeking to escape the constraints of her class through an unexpected inheritance. One avenue of class mobility for a woman in the July Monarchy appears to have been to become a *bas-bleu,* a female type identified principally with the haute bourgeoisie.

26 The *physiologie,* a genre popular in the late 1830s and 1840s, is an extended typological essay classifying Parisian professions, avocations, and types. One of the most successful publishers of the *physiologie* was Charles Philipon. The three that appear to have shaped Daumier's series on "Les Bas-Bleus" include Frédéric Soulié, *Physiologie du bas-bleu* (Paris: Aubert et Cie, 1841), Edmond Texier, *Physiologie du poète* (Paris: J. Laisne, 1841), and Jules Janin, "Un Bas-Bleu," *Les Français peints par eux-mêmes* (Paris: L. Curmer, 1842).

27 Soulié, *Physiologie du bas-bleu,* p. 68.

28 This practice is documented in such sources as *Physiologie de la presse* (Paris: Jules Laisne, 1841). In the staff listings it publishes for *Le Constitutionnel* and *La Presse,* for instance, it includes the editors' wives, Mmes Charles Reynaud and Delphine de Girardin, respectively. Sophie Gay, Emile de Girardin's mother-in-law, is also cited in the staff list of *La Presse.* Louise Bertin,

daughter of *Journal des débats* editor, Louis Bertin, was the target of the most biting satires. See, for example, "L'Ombre d'Euterpe," *Le Charivari* (January 13, 1842): 1.

29 Texier, *Physiologie du poète,* p. 118.

30 The editor of Soulié's *Physiologie du bas-bleu* was Charles Philipon. It is not surprising that the text recapitulates many of the characterizations of the bourgeois woman of ideas first explored in *Le Charivari* in the late 1830s. Though Philipon had sold *Le Charivari* in 1835, he remained a powerful presence at La Maison Aubert which continued to publish the journal.

31 Soulié, *Physiologie du bas-bleu,* p. 52.

32 Soulié, *Physiologie du bas-bleu,* p. 15.

33 Texier, *Physiologie du poète,* p. 118. A related image, *Le Mari du bas-bleu,* was also published on April 10, 1842, in *Le Charivari* as part of the "Moeurs conjugales" series. A husband holding an infant explains to a gentleman that his wife is in the middle of an inspiration and cannot see him.

34 The Académie des femmes was the focus of a great deal of attention in Maison Aubert publications and elsewhere. A lithograph by Daumier on the subject appeared in *Le Charivari* on August 2, 1843, four months before the "Bas-Bleus" series was launched. Jules de Castellane, in a powdered wig and self-important stance, is shown placing a crown of laurels on the head of a kneeling "Corinne." She is surrounded by an audience of skinny and awkward *bas-bleus* who observe the ritual in religious silence. The legend reads: "A new Richelieu founding an academy of another kind . . . a feminine kind." Jules de Castellane's efforts to affect the aristocratic dress and demeanor of Cardinal Richelieu (who founded the real French academy in 1635) are undermined by Daumier's positioning of a chair behind him. The chairback protrudes like a curvaceous tail from Castellane's jacket, instantly connecting him with conventional representations in the 1830s of the lechery and devilry of the Saint-Simonist patriarchy. Jules de Castellane was, in fact, a Saint-Simonist, and *Le Charivari's* interest in belittling him by exposing his ties to the utopian socialist movement are explicit in an essay entitled "Cancans de presse" (March 25, 1844). The article, which appeared midway through the run of Daumier's "Les Bas-Bleus," exposes the fact that instead of the newspaper paying its female writers, "as has been the practice since the invention of the printing press," the writers pay the newspaper (p. 1).

35 The caricature undoubtedly was inspired by an identical anecdote that concludes chapter five of Soulié's *Physiologie du bas-bleu,* p. 50.

36 Janin, "Un Bas-Bleu," p. 376.

37 Janin, "Un Bas-Bleu," p. 378.

38 Janin, "Un Bas-Bleu," p. 380.

39 In the meager available biographical material, the only descriptive detail repeatedly invoked by friends and admirers concerns Daumier's fierce commitment to privacy and family. Thus, his attack on women who argued in favor of the right to work and the right to divorce seems consistent with his personal ideals. Women such as these symbolized for Daumier societal degeneration and the dissolution of the family. For a complete discussion of this issue, see Janis Bergman-Carton, "Conduct Unbe-

coming: Representations of the *Woman of Ideas* in French Art,
1830–1848," Ph.D. diss., University of Texas at Austin, 1990,
chap. three.

40   See James Cuno, "Charles Philipon, La Maison Aubert, and the
Business of Caricature in Paris, 1829–1841," *Art Journal* 43,
no. 4 (Winter 1983): 352–53.

41   "Une femme peingnant ou chantant . . . une buveuse d'encre . . .
est désagréable à la vue comme à l'esprit"; "Salon de 1844,"
Le Charivari (May 10, 1844): 1.

42   "[S]emble obéir à sa nature . . . une sorte de monstre"; "Salon
de 1844," p. 1.

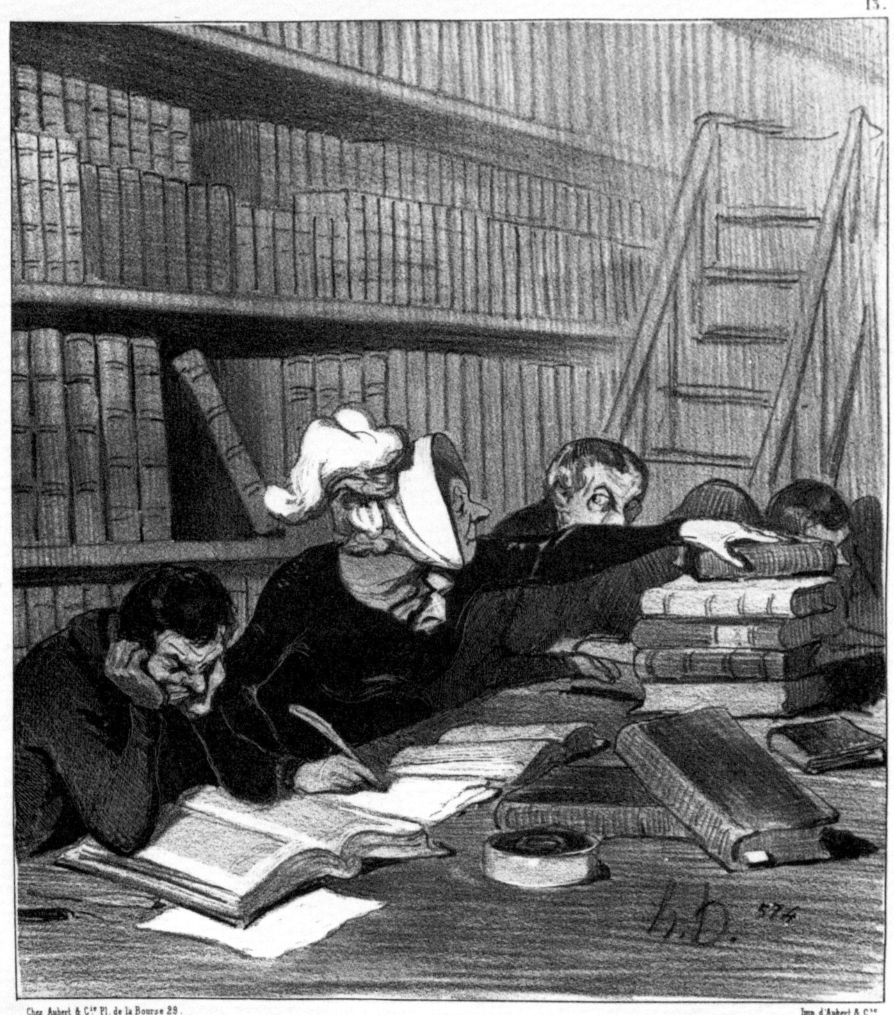

Cat. 20

—*Monsieur, pardon si je vous gêne un peu . . . mais vous comprenez qu'écrivant en ce moment un roman nouveau, je dois consulter une foule d'auteurs anciens! . . .*
—*(Le Monsieur à part) des auteurs anciens! . . . parbleu elle aurait bien dû les consulter de leur vivant, car elle a dû être leur contemporaine! . . .*

—Monsieur, excuse me if I get in your way a little . . . but you understand, writing a new novel, I have to consult a host of ancient writers! . . .
—(The gentleman in an aside) ancient writers! . . . she should have consulted them while they were alive, she must be their contemporary! . . .

"Les Bas-Bleus" (The bluestockings), no. 13; published in *Le Charivari,* March 8, 1844 (D. 1233).

LENDER: Print Collection, Miriam and Ira D. Wallach Division of Art, Prints and Photographs. The New York Public Library, Astor, Lenox, and Tilden Foundations.

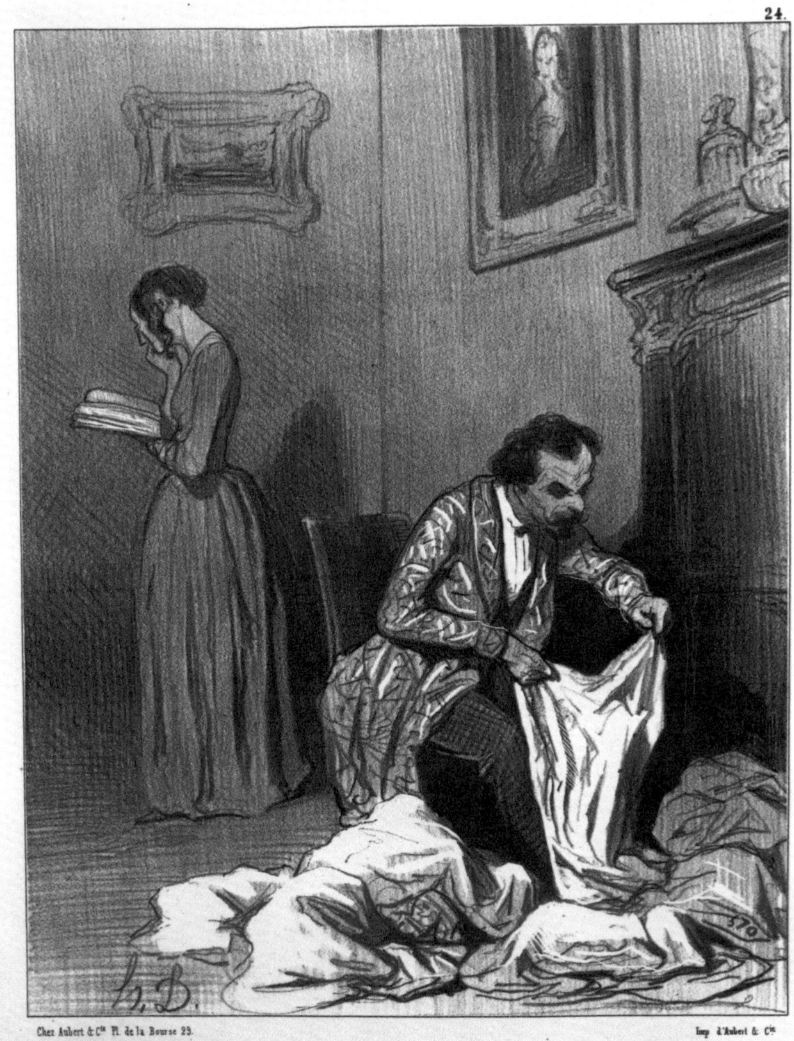

Cat. 21

*Depuis que Virginie a obtenu le septième accessit de poésie à
l'Académie française il faut que ce soit moi . . . moi capitaine de la
garde nationale . . . qui compte tous les samedis le linge à donner à
la blanchisseuse . . . et je le fais parce que sans cela ma femme me
laverait la tête! . . .*

Ever since Virginia got the seventh prize for poetry at the
Académie française it always has to be me . . . me, captain
in the National Guard . . . who counts the laundry to give
to the laundress every Saturday . . . and I do it because
otherwise my wife would give me a scrubbing! . . .

"Les Bas-Bleus" (The bluestockings), no. 24; published in
Le Charivari, April 18, 1844 (D. 1244).

LENDER: Print Collection, Miriam and Ira D. Wallach
Division of Art, Prints and Photographs. The New York
Public Library, Astor, Lenox, and Tilden Foundations.

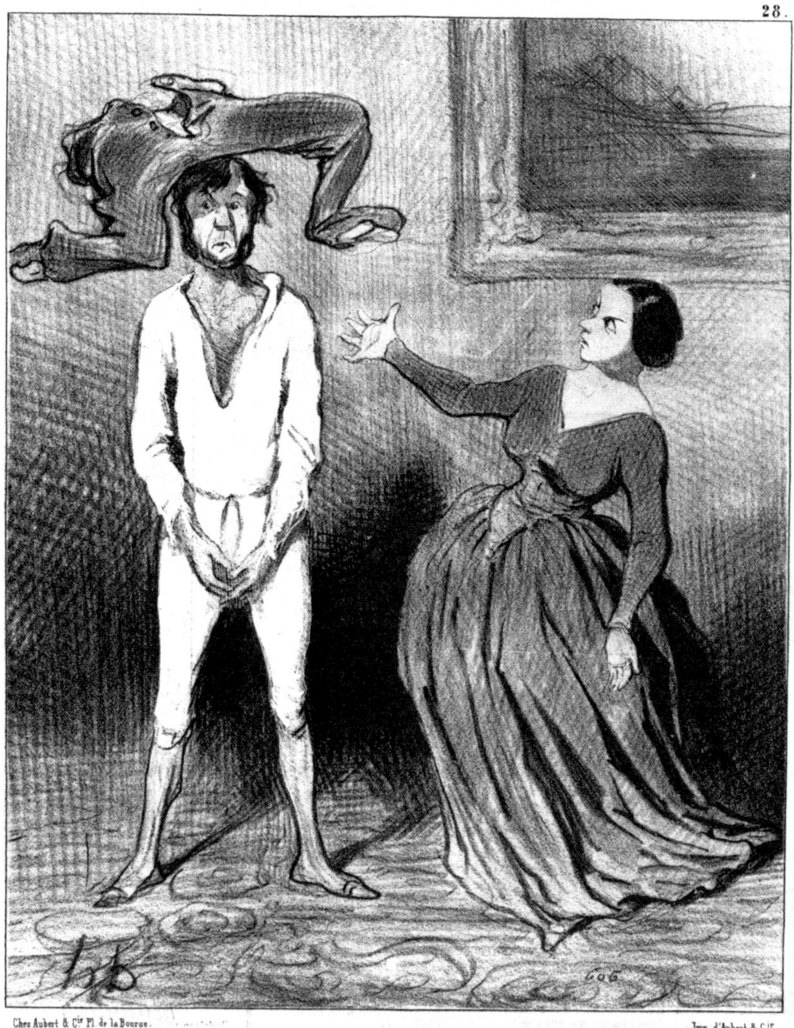

—Une femme comme moi . . . remettre un bouton ? . . . vous êtes fou ! . . . .
—Allons bon ! . . voila qu'elle ne se contente plus de porter les culottes . . . . il faut encore
qu'elle me les jette à la tête ! . . . .

Cat. 22

—Une femme comme moi . . . remettre un bouton? . . . vous êtes fou! . . .
—Allons bon! . . . voilà qu'elle ne se contente plus de porter les culottes . . . il faut encore qu'elle me les jette à la tête! . . .

—A woman like me . . . sew on a button? . . . you're crazy! . . .
—She is no longer satisfied with wearing the pants in the family . . . she needs to throw them in my face too! . . .

"Les Bas-Bleus" (The bluestockings), no. 28; published in *Le Charivari,* May 23, 1844 (D. 1248).

LENDER: The Rose Art Museum, Brandeis University, Waltham, Massachusetts, The Benjamin A. and Julia M. Trustman Collection.

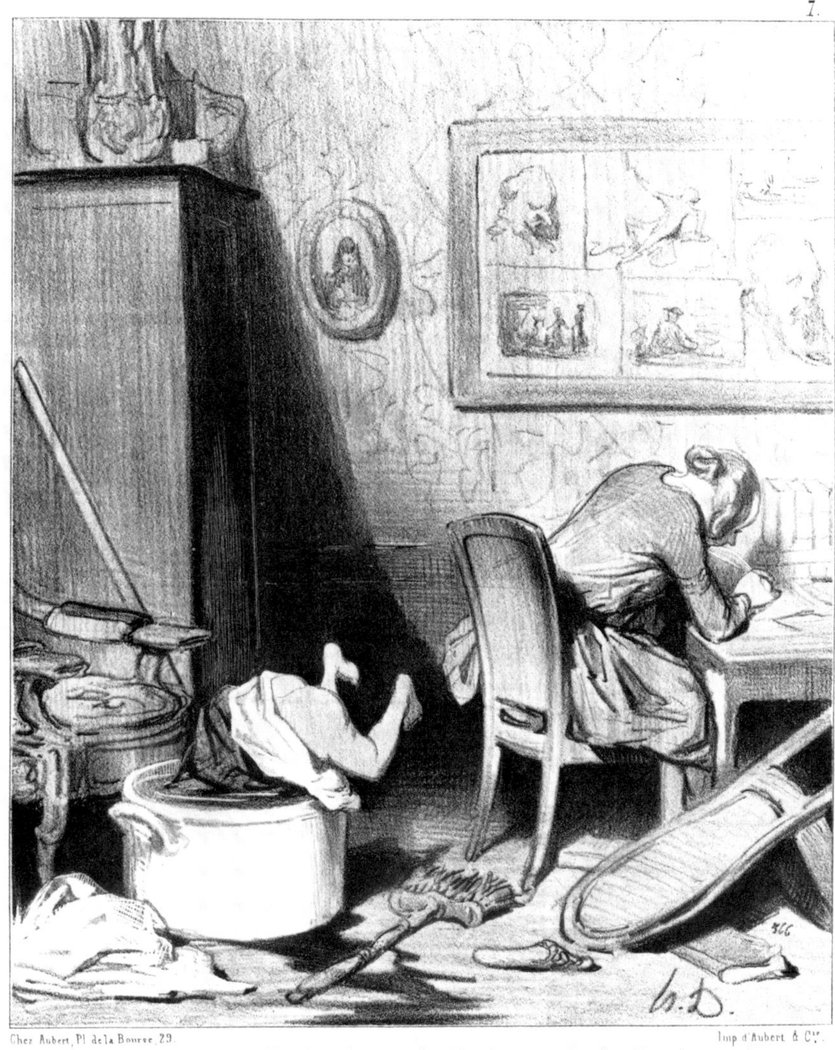

Cat. 23

La mère est dans le feu de la composition, l'enfant est dans l'eau de la baignoire!

The mother is in the fire of composition, the baby is in the bath water!

"Les Bas-Bleus" (The bluestockings), plate 7; published in *Le Charivari,* February 26, 1844 (D. 1227).

LENDER: The Rose Art Museum, Brandeis University, Waltham, Massachusetts, The Benjamin A. and Julia M. Trustman Collection.

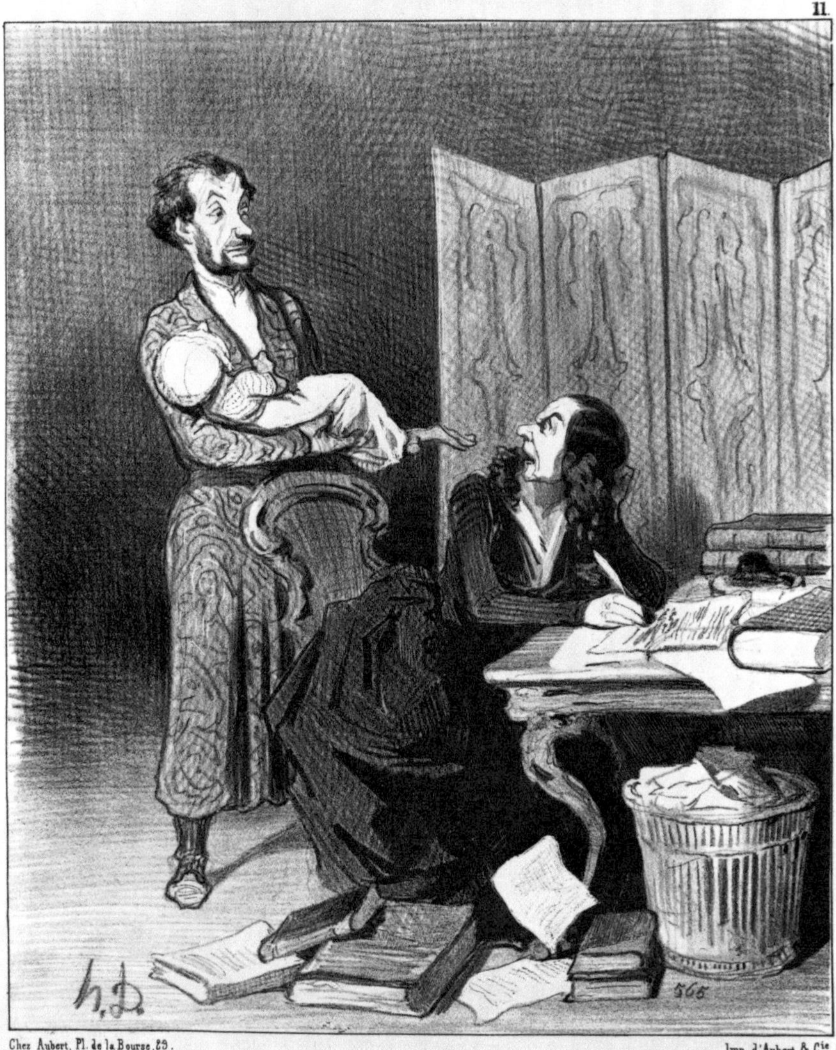

Emportez donc ça plus loin... il est impossible de travailler au milieu d'un vacarme pareil..
allez vous promener à la petite provence , et en revenant, achetez de nouveaux biberons passage Choiseul !... Ah! Mʳ Cabassol c'est votre premier enfant, mais je vous jure que ce sera votre dernier!

Cat. 24

Emportez donc ça plus loin . . . il est impossible de travailler au milieu d'un vacarme pareil . . . allez vous promener à la petite provence, et en revenant, achetez de nouveaux biberons passage Choiseul! . . . Ah! Mr Cabassol c'est votre premier enfant, mais je vous jure que ce sera votre dernier!

Take that farther away . . . it is impossible to work in the middle of such a racket . . . go take a walk and on the way back buy some new bottles in the Passage Choiseul! . . . Ah! Mr. Cabassol, it's your first child, but I swear it will be your last!

"Les Bas-Bleus" ("The bluestockings"), no. 11; published in *Le Charivari,* March 2, 1844 (D. 1231).

LENDER: Print Collection, Miriam and Ira D. Wallach Division of Art, Prints and Photographs. The New York Public Library, Astor, Lenox, and Tilden Foundations.

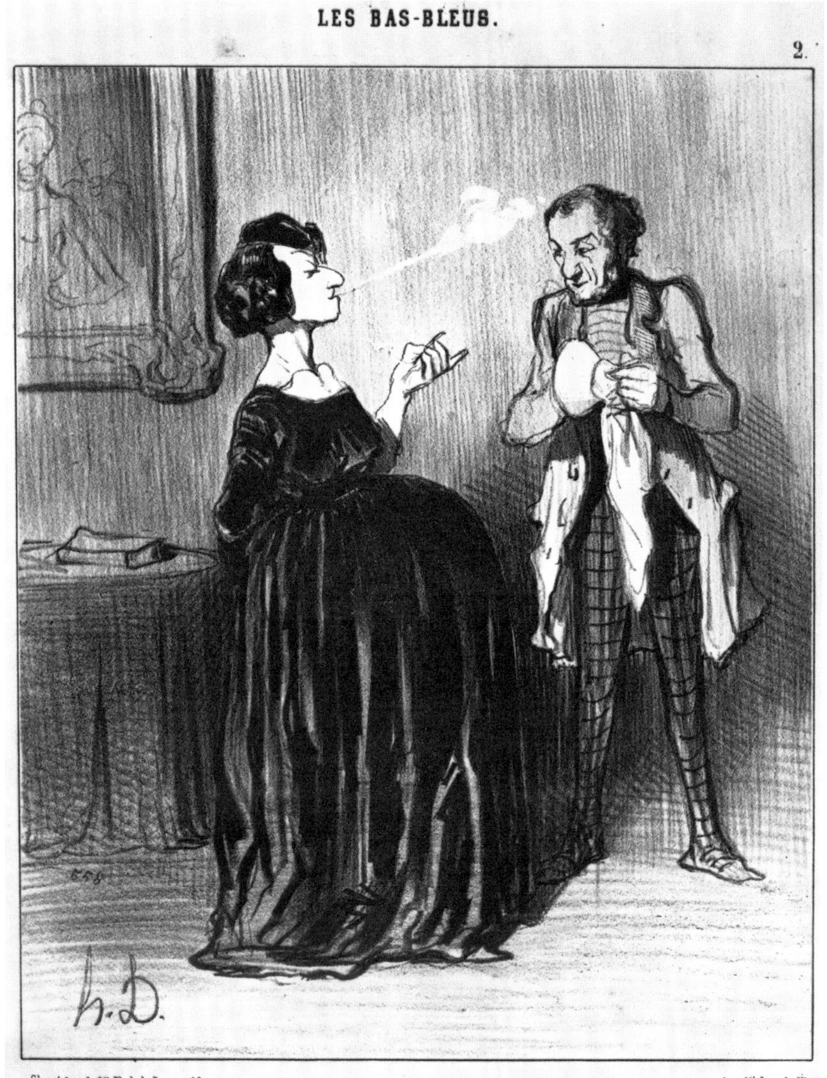

Cat. 25

*Dis donc . . . mon mari . . . j'ai bien envie d'appeler mon drame
"Arthur" et d'intituler mon enfant Oscar! . . . mais non . . . toute
réflexion faite, je ne déciderai rien avant d'avoir consulté mon
collaborateur! . . .*

Say, husband . . . I have a mind to call my play *Arthur* and
to entitle my child Oscar! . . . but no . . . all things
considered, I will decide nothing before consulting my
collaborator! . . .

"Les Bas-Bleus" (The bluestockings), no. 2; published in *Le
Charivari,* February 1, 1844 (D. 1222).

LENDER: Museum of Fine Arts, Boston.

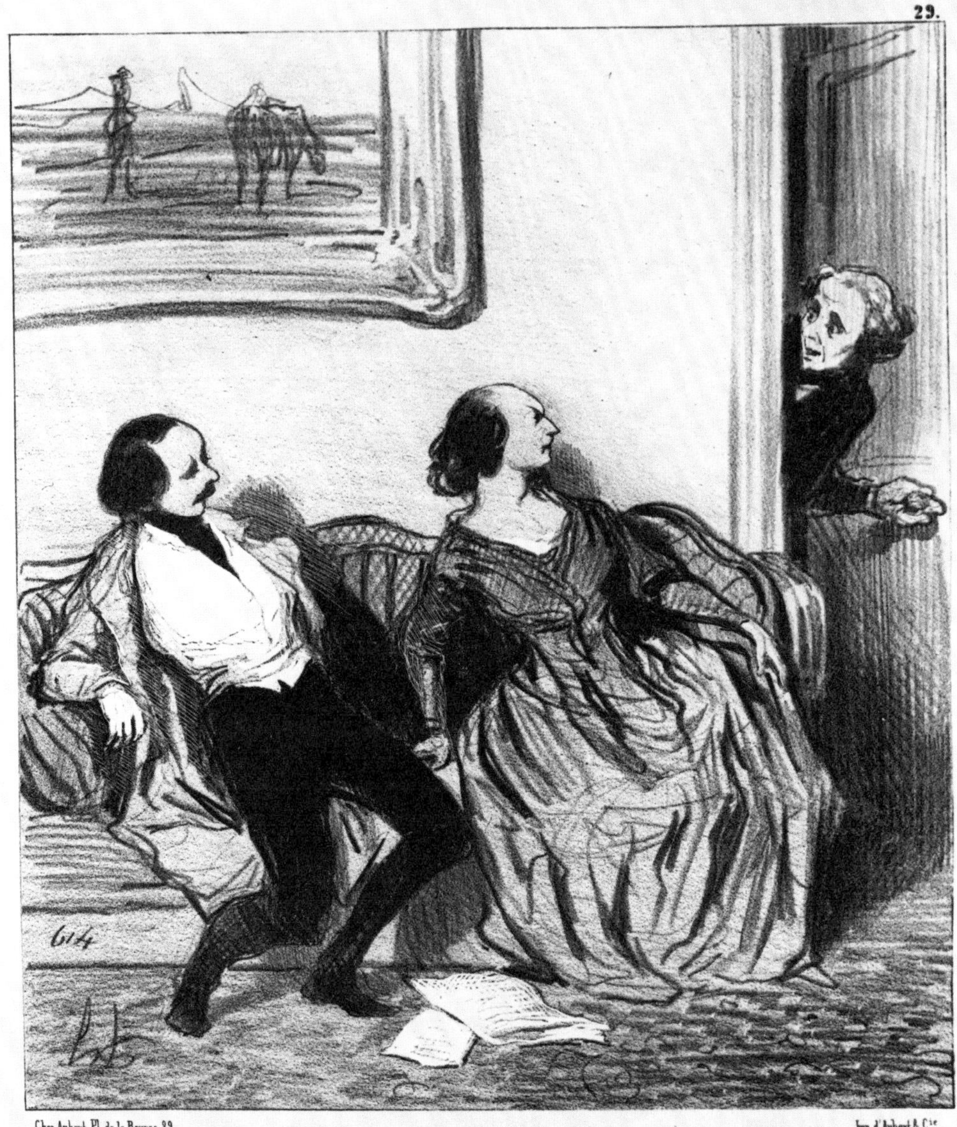

—Ma bonne amie, puis-je entrer!.... as-tu fini de collaborer avec monsieur?.......

Cat. 26

—*Ma bonne amie, puis-je entrer! . . . as-tu fini de collaborer avec monsieur? . . .*

—My dear, may I come in? . . . Have you finished collaborating with Monsieur? . . .

"Les Bas-Bleus" (The bluestockings), no. 29; published in *Le Charivari,* May 30, 1844 (D. 1249).

LENDER: Print Collection, Miriam and Ira D. Wallach Division of Art, Prints and Photographs. The New York Public Library, Astor, Lenox, and Tilden Foundations.

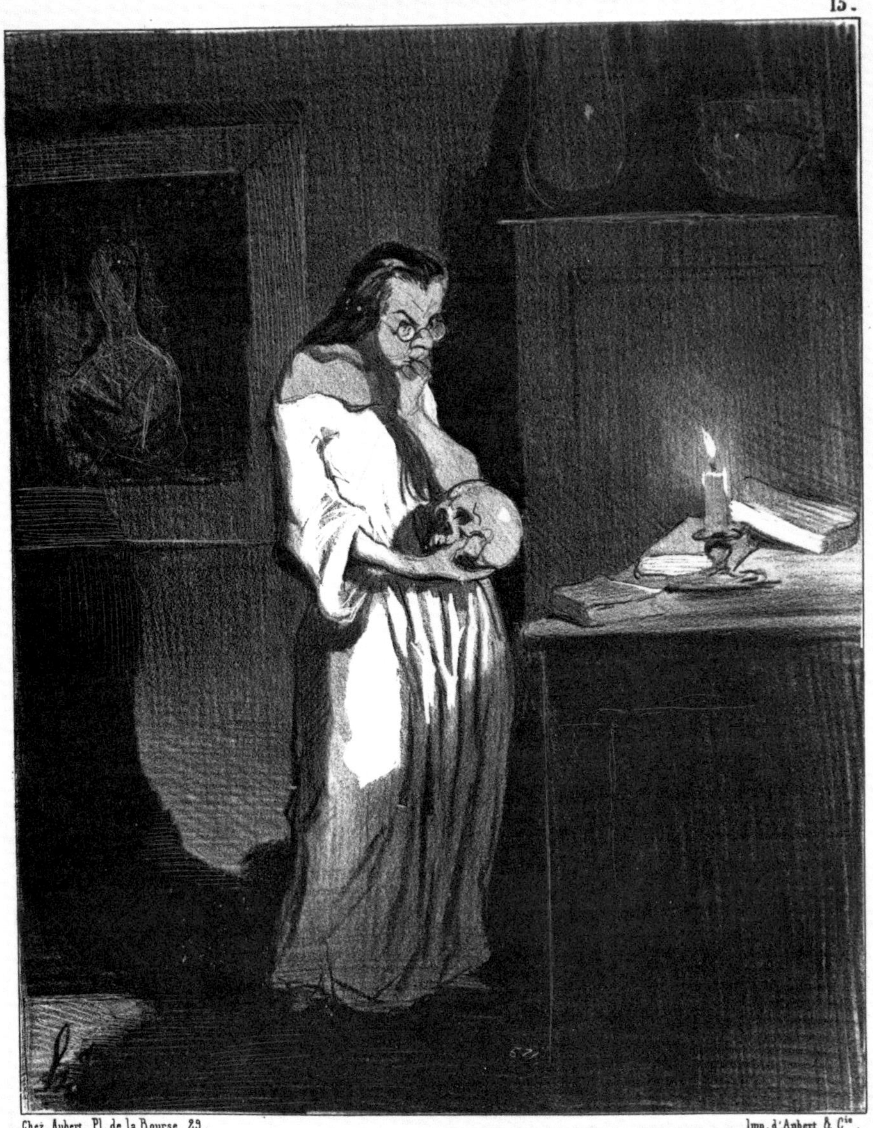

Femme de lettre humanitaire se livrant sur l'homme a des réflexions crânement philosophiques !

Cat. 27

Femme de lettre humanitaire se livrant sur l'homme à des réflexions crânement philosophiques!

Humanitarian woman of letters, taking up Man, has heady philosophical thoughts!

"Les Bas-Bleus" (The bluestockings), no. 15; published in *Le Charivari,* March 10, 1844 (D. 1235).

LENDER: Print Collection, Miriam and Ira D. Wallach Division of Art, Prints and Photographs. The New York Public Library, Astor, Lenox, and Tilden Foundations.

*From Daumier to Flaubert:
Caricatures of Feminism in the
1840s and in 1848*

LUCETTE CZYBA

BOTH THE PRINTS OF Honoré Daumier and Gustave Flaubert's novel *L'Education sentimentale*[1] feature caricatures of the feminist movement in France in the 1840s and particularly as the movement was affected by the events of 1848. Flaubert's satire is embodied in the figure of Mlle Vatnaz; he often reduces her to a caricature by calling her simply "Vatnaz" or "la Vatnaz," not using the title "Mlle." Two sets of prints by Daumier provide analogues to her character: "Les Bas-Bleus" (D. 1221–1260), a series of forty prints that make fun of women writers published in *Le Charivari* from January to August 1844; and "Les Femmes socialistes," a series of prints mocking the political activities of women, ten of which were published in *Le Charivari* from April to June 1849.[2] The legends accompanying the prints not only clarify the meanings of many images but also sum up the clichés and stereotypes of the journalistic and literary satire of feminism during the period. I will base my study on the complementarity of the legends and images in Daumier's prints and on their parallels with Flaubert's text, and will show how they both respond to the same set of social influences.

The period between 1830 and 1848 was a particularly rich one for feminism in France, owing not to the results gained, for none of the women's demands were met at that time, but to the public ferment these ideas generated. Women called for civil and political equality of the two sexes and the rights to education and participation in cultural activities, in addition to the rights to divorce and to organize work for women. The Republic of 1848 rapidly disappointed the hopes that women had held at its outset. Whereas universal suffrage was reestablished—that is to say, that the right to vote was again accorded to all men—it was still refused women. The civil, political, and cultural claims of women were consistently held up to ridicule. With the opposition of Pierre-Joseph Proudhon, the most influential social theorist of the time, who declared that socialism must free itself from any solidarity with feminism, the feminists of 1848 had practically all public opinion against them.

It should be understood that when Daumier began the "Bas-Bleus" series in 1844 he was not guided by misogynist principles but instead was following the directives of a newspaper editor whose publication was being censored by the government. As a subject, the *bas-bleu* was not risky.[3] In fact, it had proven to be highly successful with the literary and theatrical publics, as demonstrated by the publication of *La Physi-*

ologie du bas-bleu (1841–1842; The physiology of the bluestocking), the presentation of *Le Bas-Bleu,* a vaudeville by Ferdinand Langlé and F. de Villeneuve at the Théâtre des Variétés on January 24, 1842, and the appearance of Gavarni's numerous satirical prints published as "Hommes et femmes de plume" (Male and female writers).[4] Daumier's satirical drawings of 1844 were thus prompted by an established myth of the feminine based on stereotypes, that is, a representation that appealed to the imagination of the reader or viewer—male or female. Caricatures like Daumier's strengthened the myth through the impact of pictures, in which meanings are condensed in a visual code. As a contemporary critic noted:

Caricature enters through the eyes and stirs what is sensitive in us: imagination. Everybody can understand it. . . . The satirical tract leaves only ideas in the memory, and they are soon blotted out by new ones. A caricature engraves in the mind images whose forms and colors linger long after one has seen them.[5]

The mythic figure of the bluestocking depicted in Daumier's caricatures (supplanted in 1848 by the figures of the *femme-artiste*[6] and the socialist woman) does not reflect the actual demands made by women under the July Monarchy. Rather, since caricature during this period mirrored societal *moeurs,* or habits of thought, it also reflected the often irrational public reaction to the feminist claims. The preponderance of caricatures of feminism in the 1840s does not imply that feminist concepts of the status and role of women in society were ideas new to the decade: these ideas had appeared at the beginning of the July Monarchy, initiated by the double subversion of Saint-Simonist and Fourierist utopias.[7] The appearance in caricature of the different types of women—bluestocking, *femme-artiste,* and socialist—raises questions about the origins and functions of such restrictive and grotesque representations of feminism.

The *Charivari* caricatures presented only the stereotyped image of the feminists of the 1840s; no credence was given to the importance and seriousness of their claims. An article published in 1848 in the journal *La Voix des femmes* (The voice of women) makes this one-sidedness clear; it responds to an article in *Le Charivari* attacking a piece written by Eugénie Niboyet in favor of a petition sent to the provisional government. This petition called for official acknowledgment of citizenship for women and the granting of suffrage rights to widows who did not remarry, providing they had reached their majority. The negative reputation of the bluestockings, as expressed in *Le Charivari,* provoked a writer in *La Voix des femmes* to respond:

Would you take us, by chance, for bluestockings . . . , for old recalcitrant shrews, wearing both petticoats and moustaches? . . .

Far from being nameless, bristled, bloated characters with unkempt hair, ink-stained fingers, and quills in our ears, we are simply women. . . . We read Le Charivari *and we like it . . . just the same.*[8]

Similarly, in 1869 Amélie Bosquet, a feminist writer from Rouen, protested the caricature of feminism in 1848 as embodied in the character of the *femme-artiste* as portrayed in *L'Education sentimentale.* Writing in Léon Richer's newspaper, *Le Droit des femmes* (Women's rights), Bosquet objected to a commonly perceived stereotype for women: "The mouthpiece of the claim for women's rights is Mlle Vatnaz, the go-between, the thief."[9] Bosquet wrote as well to Flaubert: "You gave a rather humiliating role to the woman who stands up for her rights."[10]

Why were the feminists of 1848—as well as those prior to 1848—ridiculed through grotesque distortion by a systematic reduction to popular stereotypes? Public opinion in 1848 and 1849 suggested that laughter was an efficient weapon against the scandalous and dangerous political activities of women, whether that activity took the form of writing in newspapers or taking the floor in clubs,[11] and against their petition for the public recognition of their political rights when universal suffrage was restored. The women who rose to fame at that time—Eugénie Niboyet, Suzanne Voilquin, Elisa Lemonnier, Désirée Gay, and Jeanne Deroin—were all former Saint-Simonists and Fourierists, or sympathizers.[12] Accordingly, we can say that feminism in 1848 was socialistic and that the caricatural type of the socialist woman can be more easily understood when seen in this light.[13] It also indicates that by 1848 these feminists had been convinced of the necessity of women's emancipation for more than fifteen years. Among their demands for equality between the sexes in the name of social justice was a proposal for a new organization of work.[14]

These social and political claims, which are not unusual today given the norms of our society, were then considered abnormal. The typological caricature of the bluestocking and the socialist woman emphasizes the signs of this abnormality. Behind a successful caricature always lies an implicit reference to the norm, in this case, to women's status established by the Napoleonic Civil Code of 1804 as an expression of the ruling classes and as a foundation of family, society, and the nineteenth-century bourgeois order. Dedicated to marriage and maternity, women remained legally under age all their lives, submissive to their husbands' authority, and confined to the house.[15] Women's roles were limited to exercising their powers of physical attraction and the charm of their silence and sweetness. There was a strong tendency in nineteenth-century France to rationalize this cultural code of female status with the concept of a feminine "nature," in an attempt to retain the strictures on women by calling them something different. To highlight the abnormality of the feminists of 1848 caricature implicitly and invariably referred to this myth of female "nature." This was the ideological foundation of the press campaign against the Club des femmes, which flourished after the 1848 revolution as a place to discuss feminist ideas. This antifeminist perspective is demonstrated by an article from *La Liberté* written by Charles Hugo in 1848:

Until now women's meetings had three names: the house, the dance hall, and the church; we have just given them a fourth: the club. At home the women were pure, at the dance hall, beautiful, at church, holy; but at home, at the dance hall, at church they were women. . . . {Now} instead of comforting mankind, they rail against it. . . . They will turn their voices, which until now had been soft *like a song, tender like a piece of advice, or inspired like a prayer, into a sort of unnameable* cry. . . . *We shall see a red bonnet on a bluestocking {emphasis added}.*[16]

We find in caricatures of feminists a variety of metonymies, or visual codes, that suggest that bluestockings are not, or are no longer, women: women who dabble in writing forget their "natural" vocation. The ideology of the times restricting femininity to beauty, youth, and elegant clothes implied that bluestockings were invariably ugly, old, skinny women, dowdy and asexual. The woman who consults ancient authors at the library in Daumier's print *Monsieur, pardon, si je vous gêne un peu* (cat. 20) surely "must be their [the ancient authors'] contemporary," according to the print's legend.[17] The features seen in many (though not all) of Daumier's depictions of feminists—a "distressing" nose (D. 1243),[18] a flat chest, a deflated waist (D. 1260),[19] inevitably prominent cheekbones—are enough to epitomize ugliness. An extravagant hat sums up the bluestockings' lack of attractiveness, and their expressions are most often aggressive ones of peevishness, anger, revolt, and acrimony. It is significant that in the whole of the *bas-bleus* series only a few women have sweet and graceful features. One example is the traditional mother, busy with her needlework and providing a contrast to the appalling witch-like authoress in *Ah! ma chère, quelle singulière éducation vous donnez à votre fille?* . . . (Ah, my dear, what a singular education you are giving your daughter; D. 1255). In the same vein Flaubert's Mlle Vatnaz looks much older and "ugly": she is a "lean faded person," with "fat lips," a "bony" face, "gaunt" hands, "thin" arms, and "long" feet.[20] Once again Daumier (before Flaubert but like Flaubert) reproduces the common scenes of the satire of feminism.

Daumier's caricatures imply not only that writing is not a woman's job but when a woman does engage in it she does it badly. The artist systematically associates the verbosity of a bluestocking with her lack of talent: her unsold books overstock the bookshop (D. 1250); the reading of her play bores the audience to death (D. 1242); she is hissed off the stage (D. 1239); the journalists who "are busy with geese every morning"[21] never review her novel (D. 1230); or they find her book "painfully poor" (D. 1258). Her lack of talent is even more insidiously emphasized when the bluestocking is criticized by her colleagues (D. 1254) or when she expects their journalistic complacency "to make her soapy water lather" (D. 1241).[22] Daumier's bluestockings choose conventional themes, exemplified in the choice of a title such as *Soupirs de mon âme* (Sighs of my soul; D. 1250). The "jauntily philosophical" reflections of the "humanitarian woman" (cat. 27) are summed up in a grotesque pose: wearing spectacles, she holds a skull in her hand, forehead furrowed with lines; the scene takes place in the dark of night.[23]

Flaubert also ridiculed the posturings and literary pretensions of the *femme-artiste*.[24] Mlle Vatnaz's scruffy activity is stressed and, far from reaching the status of a woman of letters, she cannot even sell her productions.[25] Her works, including an "Ode to Poland," a hackneyed subject which is "heartfelt," are praised in *L'Education sentimentale* by Regimbart; his incompetence in literary taste had just been underlined by Flaubert to point out the inferiority of Mlle Vatnaz's writings. The narrator is equally ironic regarding Mlle Vatnaz's second book, *La Guirlande des jeunes personnes* (The young ladies' wreath), a "collection of literary and moral pieces." Mlle Vatnaz is not a true writer: she flatly follows the fashion of writing so-called educational books, a female specialty of the time. She is

compelled to ask the journalist Hussonnet to revise this "wreath" stylistically (p. 121): she prides herself on being a "superior" woman because she does not make the error of spelling *catégorie* with a *th* (p. 164). Furthermore, the narrator breaks in to explain that Mlle Vatnaz's feminism results from her resentment: she could not fulfill what was considered to be a woman's "natural" destiny, a husband, children, and a home:

She was one of these Parisian spinsters, *who, every evening, after tutoring, striving to sell little drawings or poor manuscripts, return home with mud-stained petticoats, cook their dinner, eat* alone, *and with their feet on a footwarmer by the light of an ill-fitted lamp, they* dream of a love story, a family, a home, a fortune, all that is lacking. *Accordingly, as many did, she had greeted* the advent of revenge *in the Revolution; and she dedicated herself to frantic socialist propaganda {emphasis added}.*[26]

Therefore, Mlle Vatnaz's feminism vanishes as soon as she hopes to marry Dussardier: "At her age such good fortune was unhoped for. She threw herself into the attack like a bird of prey; she renounced literature, socialism, 'comforting doctrines and generous utopias,' her lecture on *Woman's Dissubalternation,* everything" (emphasis added).[27]

Similarly, in Daumier's caricatures visual codes are chosen to indicate that the author betrays her "natural" roles of housewife and mother. The bluestocking is a bad mother who neglects her home. While she is "in the burning excitement of composing," her child drowns "in his bath water" among overturned pieces of furniture (cat. 23). A woman with a book in her hand does not fulfill her "natural" roles of preparing food or doing needlework: "Instead of milk, she pours out shoe polish" in her husband's chocolate (D. 1257); she refuses to knot his tie (D. 1236); to sew his pants or suspender buttons on again (cat. 22; see also D. 1922). On March 28, 1848, in *La Voix des femmes* Paulin Niboyet ironically denounces the use of these culinary and needlework metonymies as tokens of the abnormality of feminists. Addressing the feminists he wrote:

You claim your rights, you contribute to newspapers, you found clubs, and start people wondering. . . . Le Charivari goes even further, they are alarmed. According to them the destiny of braces buttons, of quince jelly, and backstitches seems seriously impaired by the creation of the Voice of Women. *They voted for a new rival paper, the* Voice of Men, *which would devote itself to the defense of braces buttons and quince jelly, threatened in their best interests.*[28]

A bad mother and a bad mistress of the house, the bluestocking is a wicked wife. Feminism implies the decay of husbands' authority, a point that Daumier makes clear when he shows bluestockings who not only are wives who "wear the pants in the family" but also "throw them in the face" of those who should be their undisputed masters (cat. 22). It is significant that the first print in the series "Femmes socialistes" should be *L'Insurrection contre les maris* (cat. 28): three termagants with angry faces vow on a top hat the "abolition of husbands." They use the hat as a symbol equally of their bourgeois husbands and the authority of which the women have been denied; it is a bare-headed woman who holds the hat in her hand. The wife in *Ah! vous êtes mon mari, ah! vous êtes le maître . . .* (cat. 29), inspired by a lecture by the feminist Jeanne Deroin, claims her right to throw her husband out of the house. The weakness, subjection, and foolishness of husbands are always emphasized, contrasting with their wives' physical violence and overbearing aggressiveness. Traditional roles are inverted, as the recurring visual code of smoking illustrates—bluestockings provocatively engage in this predominantly male activity (D. 1229, 1246, and 1253).[29] Armed with a whisk, the husband is "obliged every morning to dust the bust of his wife," a poetess with a laurel wreath (D. 1232); a captain of the National Guard is "doomed every Saturday to count" the linen for the washerwoman (cat. 21). Finally, the most significant tokens of this abnormal inversion of traditional roles are mothering fathers, taking care of babies, feeding them, and staying at home (D. 1223, 1234, and cat. 24), while mothers write or attend to business outside the home.

Both Daumier's and Flaubert's caricatures stigmatize women who abandon their "natural" place at home to encroach on male space—outdoors and in the street— where decent women are not allowed. By extension, female writers are characterized as having dubious manners and questionable morals. As connoted by her "mud-stained" petticoat, Mlle Vatnaz "does not amount to much."[30] Indeed, Flaubert bluntly calls her "Arnoux's procuress" in his rough draft for the novel.[31] Likewise, in Daumier's caricatures a woman's literary contribution is often synonymous with adultery (cat. 25 and 26). The bluestocking on horseback who posts in the Bois de Boulogne with M. Edouard is no longer "riding in the saddle of virtue" (D. 1247). For Daumier, feminism impairs social order because mothers no longer transmit the moral values of family respect, submission, and a female sense of decency: inducing a

young girl to write is encouraging her down the road to destruction (D. 1256). Writing constitutes an indecent public exposure forbidden to "decent" women: a *femme-artiste* "strips herself of her pure female garment."[32]

But what appears as a crowning profligacy and lewdness is, as Charles Hugo puts it, "un bonnet rouge sur un bas-bleu," a woman who figuratively dons the Phrygian liberty cap symbolic of the French Revolution to go up to the tribune, who claims the right to take the floor like a man in clubs or banquets, who demands equality in political rights. Delteil 1919 and 1921 in the "Femmes socialistes" series refer to two famous socialist banquets organized on behalf of women. The first one took place on November 25, 1848, at Dunoyer's restaurant at the Maine *barrière*,[33] presided over by Pierre Leroux, Martin Bernard, and Armand Barbès;[34] the second one took place on Christmas Day of the same year, presided over by Leroux and Félix Pyat. Daumier's prints disparage women's attendance at these banquets by suggesting that the events were strictly an opportunity to dress up (D. 1919), by playing on the ambiguous meaning of a "communion" with "eight hundred brethren," and by punning on the connotation of *barrière,* which was synonymous with mixed and questionable company. A woman who attended these banquets was likened to a woman who slept around, having left husband and children behind for "nearly forty-eight hours" (D. 1927). Feminists were aware of the force of these misconceptions that mistook the legitimate demands of women for debauchery. Eugénie Niboyet and her collaborators were thus forced to defend the moral purity of their actions and intentions.[35] Jeanne Deroin recalled that "she was happy to remain worthy, honorable and pure, a genuinely Christian mother, a devoted citizen."[36]

The creation of the myth of the Vesuvians brings further evidence to bear on the impact of these misconceptions.[37] The Vesuvians, who likened their feminist ideas to an explosion of lava that could not be contained, was one of the most radical women's clubs of their time. Their demands included total equality in marriage and wages, as well as female military service and unisex fashions.[38] The public tended to overlook the fact that the Vesuvians was an actual workers' association with common interests,[39] turning it into "a women's legion with doubtful habits."[40] The image that prevailed was that of assuming male costume, carrying bayonets, and performing military service. From May to November 1848 Edouard de Beaumont devoted a series of eighteen prints in *Le Charivari* to this theme. Daumier had only to quote the term *Vésuvienne* to the readers of *Le Charivari* to call this representation to mind (cat. 30).

The stereotyped metonymies of caricatures of women's clubs also point out the indecency of women making public and political speeches at all. The violent expressions and cries, the hysterical gestures, and the turmoil of women's meetings were opposed to the soft voices and restrained, harmonious female deportment called for by the sociocultural code of the time. As early as 1844 *Le Charivari* stated that women were incapable of proper decorum at meetings (D. 1245):[41] they do not debate, they "bicker" and "tear each other's hair."[42] In Daumier's caricatures (D. 1923, 1925, 1926, and cat. 29) the very name of Jeanne Deroin cited in the legends is sufficient to epitomize the grotesque character of feminist claims concerning equal rights for both sexes. The power of her name was the result of the scandal caused by Deroin's attempts to obtain these civil rights, which she expressed in *L'Opinion des femmes* (Women's opinions) from August 1848 onward and in the form of posters on the walls of Paris announcing her (symbolic) candidacy for the general election of May 1849.[43]

The journalistic campaign of satire to deride the women of 1848 in caricature ultimately reveals its conventionalism. The relentless attacks on the women's clubs and political claims mounted in *Le Charivari* expressed the conservative position of the majority of the population. This conservatism included that of the socialist Proudhon, who declared in two articles published in his paper *Le Peuple* that socialism must free itself from any fellowship with feminism. He also condemned Deroin's candidacy for the Legislative Assembly: "We understand a woman legislator no more than a nursing father. . . . Woman has her home, man his public life."[44] Although from 1830 to 1850 George Sand embodied the emancipated woman, she was spared from caricatural attack in 1848, since she clearly displayed her opposition to women's political rights and publicly withdrew her support from Eugénie Niboyet and her followers when they proposed her as a candidate to the assembly in *La Voix des femmes* on April 6, 1848.[45] In addition, while caricaturists likened feminists' actions to a threat against husbands' power, they glossed over what partly motivated this action—namely female labor, or the problem of the resources of women deprived of a husband or a protector.

Ultimately when caricaturists like Daumier re-peated the myth of female "nature," they played a large part in strengthening it, owing to the impact of the seemingly realistic picture, which fostered and maintained the illusion of reality for readers. Whether or not Daumier wrote his own captions, the little dramas he drew gave color and meaning to the accompanying words. These caricatures helped justify the role that the Napoleonic Code assigned to women in the nineteenth century in the name of "nature"—although it was only a matter of culture. Today we question this ideology of woman confined to the house and dedicated to her family, which we find implicitly expressed in satires of feminists of the 1840s. It explains why the drawings of the "Bas-Bleus" and "Femmes socialistes" cannot make us laugh now: parodying Henri Bergson's phrase, we can say that we do not belong to the parish any longer.

NOTES

An earlier version of this paper was presented at the International Daumier Symposium at the University of Bielefeld in 1984.

We wish to thank Professor Czyba for providing a preliminary translation of her essay and we thank Tracy Rangnow for her assistance in preparing the final version. [—Eds.]

1   Gustave Flaubert, *L'Education sentimentale* (1869; Paris: Garnier, 1964).
2   These fifty prints can be found in Françoise Parturier and Jacqueline Armingeat, *Daumier: Intellectuelles ("Les Bas-Bleus" et "Femmes socialistes")* (Paris: Editions Vilo-Paris, 1974).
3   Parturier, preface, in Parturier and Armingeat, *Intellectuelles,* p. 15.
4   Parturier, preface, in Parturier and Armingeat, *Intellectuelles,* p. 15, and Armingeat, in Parturier and Armingeat, *Intellectuelles,* cat. no. 1, p. 125. According to the Goncourt brothers Gavarni used to say about bluestockings, "Lyrisme et pot-au-feu; ça sentait le chou" (Lyricism and beef-broth; it would reek of cabbage). Moreover, Gavarni would reproach them for their extravagant clothes ("leurs toilettes incroyables").
5   "La caricature entre par les yeux et remue ce qu'il y a de plus sensible en nous, l'imagination. Elle est intelligible à tous. . . . Le pamphlet ne laisse dans la mémoire que les idées, et d'autres ont bien vite fait de les effacer. La caricature y grave des images dont les formes et les couleurs flottent dans le souvenir longtemps encore après qu'on les a vues"; F. Sarcey, *La Revue comique* (October 15, 1871), quoted in Philippe Roberts-Jones, *De Daumier à Lautrec* (Paris: Les Beaux-Arts, 1960), p. xi.
6   The woman who wrote or claimed to write qualified as a *femme-artiste.* The expression was a pejorative one; indeed, one did not say *homme-artiste* (man-artist) but simply *artiste.* What is suggested is a contradiction in terms, for at this time women were not thought capable of being true artists. See Flaubert, *L'Education sentimentale,* p. 133, where Mlle Vatnaz is described as a *femme-artiste.*

7 We know the subversive function of Saint-Simonist and Fourierist utopias: the former questions society's family foundations
established by the Napoleonic Code, that is, the respect of pro-
prietorship and monogamous marriage; the latter substitutes
love for money, love as a central factor of an ideal society, and
sets a relativistic skepticism against the absolute dogmatism of
the marital and family morals of the time.

8 "Nous prendriez-vous par hasard pour des bas-bleus . . . , pour
de vieilles mégères frondeuses, portant à la fois un jupon et des
moustaches? . . . Loin d'être des personnages sans nom, hé-
rissés, boursouflés, mal coiffés, ayant de l'encre aux doigts et
des plumes sur les oreilles, nous sommes tout simplement des
femmes. . . . Nous lisons *Le Charivari* et nous l'aimons . . .
quand même"; Marie Noémi, in *La Voix des femmes* (March–
June 1848).

9 "L'organe de la revendication des droits de la femme, c'est Mlle
Vatnaz, entremetteuse et voleuse"; Amélie Bosquet, "L'Education sentimentale," *Le Droit des femmes* (December 11–18,
1869), quoted in *Les Amis de Flaubert* 26 (May 1965): 22.

10 "Vous avez donné un rôle bien humilié à la femme qui défend ses
droits"; quoted in A. Dubuc, "Flaubert et la rouennaise Amélie
Bosquet," *Les Amis de Flaubert* 27 (December 1965): 29.
Flaubert did not deny having produced a parody in the person
of Mlle Vatnaz; on December 14, 1869, he wrote to A. Darcel,
"The bluestockings I met were the best of the bunch and they
had nothing in common with Mlle Vatnaz."

11 After the proclamation of the Republic in February 1848 male
revolutionary clubs multiplied. Some of them admitted
women, but soon the women founded their own clubs to have a
forum to discuss their specific problems. Among the most
famous of the women's clubs was the Société de la voix des
femmes, founded by Eugénie Niboyet, and whose organ was
the newspaper *La Voix des femmes*. The meetings of this club
were often disrupted by men who, finding the existence of a
women's club scandalous, met there to make noise, laugh, ridicule, and create havoc. Niboyet's club was the target of sarcasm
and mockery from the press. In *La Voix des femmes*, Niboyet and
her colleagues often deplored the absurd attacks directed
against them. For example, in an article called "Le Club des
femmes" readers were advised:

*We must well accept this appellation, since it has been given to us. . . .
Le Club des femmes . . . is the novelty of the day, the focal point of
much curiosity. . . . We listen, worrying little about it; one must
first attack what is new with absurdity.*

*We have come armed with our united courage, strong in our con-
viction, to speak to the crowd that mocks us. We have dared to leave
the obscurity of women to make everyone hear the words of justice, and
even those who have inspired us with this courage have misunderstood
us. . . . No matter, we accept their insults, we endure their mockery,
their sarcasm. God has given us strength in our undertakings, we will
accomplish them.*

*Il faut bien accepter cette dénomination, puisqu'on nous l'a donnée
. . . . Le Club des femmes . . . est la nouveauté du jour, le point de
mire de la curiosité générale. . . . Nous écoutons, peu s'en soucient; il
faut d'abord attaquer par le ridicule ce qui est nouveau.*

Nous sommes venues armées de notre seul courage, fortes de notre

*conviction, parler à la foule qui raille. Nous avons osé sortir de notre
obscurité de femmes pour faire entendre à tous des paroles de justice et
celles-là même qui nous inspiraient ce courage nous ont méconnues. . . .
N'importe, nous acceptons leurs outrages, nous subirons leurs railleries,
leurs sarcasmes. Dieu nous a donné la force de nos oeuvres, nous les
accomplirons* ("Le Club des femmes," La Voix des femmes 41 {June
6–8, 1848}, emphasis added).

On June 6, 1848, the prefect of police announced the dissolution of the club. Niboyet wrote on June 7:

*Eight days ago a decision was made to disrupt our meetings, to create
disorder to attain a goal: their dissolution. . . . The meetings forbidden to us, we have renounced ourselves. . . . We want to serve neither
as spectacle nor as plaything to anyone.*

*C'était, depuis huit jours, un parti pris de troubler nos séances, d'y
jeter le désordre pour arriver à un fait, leur dissolution. . . . Les
réunions qu'on nous interdit, nous y avions renoncé nous-mêmes. . . .
Nous ne voulons servir ni de spectacle ni de jouet à personne* (Eugénie
Niboyet, "La Liberté et l'égalité," La Voix des femmes 42 {June
8–10, 1848}).

That the Club des femmes was systematically held up to
ridicule is evidenced by a one-act vaudeville presented on June
4, 1848, entitled *Le Club des maris et le club des femmes*, written
by Louis F. N. Clairville and Jules Cordier. Completely apoliti-
cal, the play has a plot based on the effects of simple surprises,
following the most hackneyed clichés of conjugal infidelity. It
presents the woman's revenge and concludes: "If husbands are
gallant with their wives, the wives will not have lovers!" See
Louis F. N. Clairville and Jules Cordier, *Le Club des maris et le
club des femmes* (Paris: Beck, 1848).

12 It took all of the illogic of the utopian dreams of the Saint-
Simonists and of Charles Fourier to conceive of the emancipation of women by calling into question social structures and
their foundations (property and monogamous marriage). The
adherents of the movement claimed that the Saint-Simonist era
would be signaled by the complete enfranchisement of women.

For his part, in his radical critique of contemporary society
Fourier condemned bourgeois marriage based on wealth. He
affirmed that women's progress toward liberty is the condition
of social progress. He destroyed the myth that women have a
specific and eternal nature by showing that they are the product
of their education, an education that alienated them from society by smothering a woman's character so she would "submit to
the first man that her parents will give her as a husband." The
difficulties encountered by the Saint-Simonists (persecution,
trial in 1832, imprisonment) and the censure of which Fourier
(who died in 1837) and his disciples were the object signify
how intolerable these ideas were to the majority of the French.

13 See Maïté Albistur and Daniel Armogathe, *Histoire du féminisme*, vol. 2 (Paris: Editions des Femmes, 1977), p. 449.

14 Low salaries for women sometimes forced them to supplement
their income through prostitution. Female textile workers wove
on machines in large workshops for twelve to thirteen hours a
day; female needleworkers at home worked sixteen or seventeen
hours a day. The newspaper *La Voix des femmes* attributed the
women's low salaries to the action of intermediaries who sup-

plied the work to the women and took an exorbitant commission. Hence, the desire arose to set up a workers' organization of an autonomous production co-op, where orders would be given directly to the workers, work-day time would be reduced to nine and a half hours, and salaries would be increased.

15 The Revolution of 1789 had not established equality of the sexes in France. The Napoleonic Code explicitly confirmed a selective equality: "The persons deprived of juridical rights are minors, married women, criminals, and the mentally deficient" (Article 1124). The status of women in France was conditioned by the desire to ensure the transmission of inheritance to legitimate heirs by avoiding all risk of illegitimacy. This need to perpetuate the family and to keep the patrimony intact resulted in the oppression of women. Therefore the Napoleonic Code makes a woman the property of her husband: "Just as a pear tree belongs to its owner, the woman is the property of the man for whom she supplies children" (Article 1124).

16 "Les réunions de femmes avaient eu jusqu'ici trois noms: la maison, le bal et l'église; on vient de leur en appliquer un quatrième, le club. A la maison les femmes étaient pures, au bal belles, à l'église saintes; mais au foyer, au bal, à l'église, *elles étaient femmes.* . . . Au lieu de le consoler, elles crient contre le genre humain. . . . Elles feront de leur *voix,* qui avait été jusque-là *douce* comme un chant, tendre comme un conseil ou inspirée comme une prière, une sorte de *cri* sans nom. . . . On verra *un bonnet rouge sur un bas-bleu*"; Charles Hugo, "Le Club des femmes," *La Liberté* (May 29, 1848): 4, emphasis added.

17 Armingeat rightly reminds us that Eugénie Niboyet, in campaigning for education for women, had demanded the opening of a reading room for them at the Bibliothèque nationale. See Armingeat, in Parturier and Armingeat, *Intellectuelles,* p. 127.

18 The play on words in the caption can hardly be translated: the gentleman considers "distressing" the nose of the so-called "distressed woman."

19 *Le Génie n'est pas une affaire de sexe* (Genius is not a matter of sex); in this case, the "plump" and "lithe waist" are the metonymies of attractive women.

20 Mlle Vatnaz, who was already in her early thirties at the beginning of the novel (1840), had reached her forties by 1848; she was an "old lady" for Flaubert and his contemporaries. Also, see Flaubert, *L'Education sentimentale,* pp. 256, 26, 72, 312, and 134. See also the descriptions of the women who attend Mlle Vatnaz's party (p. 361). The rough drafts of *L'Education sentimentale* are even more explicit (Bibliothèque nationale, Paris, N.A.F. 17608, vol. 10, pp. 107–9): "A line of women stretched against the wall, some of them gray-haired, almost all of them with no collars and no cuffs . . . lined up against the wall there was a medley of faces of humanitarian bluestockings."

21 In French there is a play on the word *bécasse* (woodcock, but in slang "a little idiot"). It is not translatable, and therefore we suggest an equivalent with the word "goose."

22 Another untranslatable French phrase, "faire mousser ses bulles de savon," connotes flattery directed toward an unworthy object or person.

23 The play on the French words *crânement* (jauntily) and *crane* (skull) cannot be translated.

24 See the "oriental scarf" of Mlle Vatnaz, who aped Mme de

Staël's attitudes in the party mentioned above, n. 20. In the rough drafts we can read that Flaubert satirized Mlle Vatnaz as aspiring to look like Mme de Staël's heroine Corinne "at Cape Miseno."

25 "A former provincial schoolmistress, she was now tutoring and trying to contribute to minor newspapers"; Flaubert, *L'Education sentimentale,* p. 38. To augment her income she also organized a table d'hôte, saw to Rosanette's shopping (p. 133), and she used to "trade laces to women of loose morals" and "to contribute to fashion papers" (p. 396).

26 "Elle était *une de ces célibataires* parisiennes qui, chaque soir, quand elles ont donné leurs leçons, ou tâché de vendre de petits dessins, de placer de pauvres manuscrits, rentrent chez elles avec de la crotte à leurs jupons, font leur dîner, le mangent *toutes seules,* puis, les pieds sur une chaufferette, à la lueur d'une lampe malpropre, *rêvent un amour, une famille, un foyer, la fortune, tout ce qui leur manque.* Aussi, comme beaucoup d'autres, avait-elle salué dans la Révolution *l'avènement de la vengeance;* et elle se livrait à une propagande socialiste effrénée"; Flaubert, *L'Education sentimentale,* p. 299, emphasis added.

27 "Une pareille bonne fortune à son âge était inespérée. Elle se jeta dessus avec un appétit d'ogresse; et elle en avait abandonné la littérature, le socialisme, 'les doctrines consolantes et les utopies généreuses,' le cours qu'elle professait sur la *Désubalternisation de la femme,* tout"; Flaubert, *L'Education sentimentale,* p. 397, emphasis added.

28 "Vous réclamez vos droits, vous écrivez dans les journaux, vous fondez des clubs et l'on s'étonne. . . . *Le Charivari* va même plus loin, il s'effraie. Le sort des boutons de bretelles, de la gelée de coings et de l'arrière-point lui paraît gravement compromis par la création de la *Voix des femmes.* Il vote pour la fondation d'une feuille rivale, intitulée la *Voix des hommes,* laquelle feuille prendrait sérieusement en mains la défense des boutons de bretelles et de la gelée de coings, menacés dans leurs intérêts les plus chers"; Paulin Niboyet, in *La Voix des femmes* 8 (March 28, 1848): 3. Paulin Niboyet was Eugénie Niboyet's son and a contributor to *La Voix des femmes.*

29 The bluestocking in *Madame, comment trouvez-vous cette cigarette?* . . . (D. 1229) likes only the biggest cigars and composes a sonnet to the caporal brand of tobacco, which she eventually publishes in a book called *Smokes of My Pipe.* The bluestocking in *O plaisir de l'opium que tu me ravis* . . . (D. 1246) smokes an opium pipe.

30 This estimation is according to Dussardier, the "good guy" of the novel. The fiction multiplies the signs of carnality in the old spinster in love, who considers young men her prey, an attitude conveyed in her passionate love for the histrionic Delmar and her attitude toward Dussardier.

31 Drafts for *L'Education sentimentale* (Bibliothèque nationale, Paris, N.A.F. 17608, vol. 11, pt. 3, p. 110).

32 See Eugénie Niboyet's article on Anaïs Ségalas's compilation "La Femme" in *La Voix des femmes* 7 (March 27, 1848): 3.

> *Mme Ségalas sketched the portrait of the* femme-artiste *in fiery strokes. She indignantly casts the blame on this exaggerated muck, who, taking ridicule for truth, the profligate for the enthusiast, strips herself of her pure female garment to remain sexless and nameless. Many things could be said on this subject.*

*Mme Ségalas a crayonné en traits de feu le portrait de la femme-
artiste. Du haut de son indignation, elle jette le blâme sur cette tourbe
exagérée qui, prenant le ridicule pour le vrai, le dévergondé pour
l'enthousiaste, se dépouille de son chaste vêtement de femme pour n'avoir
ni sexe ni nom. Nous aurions beaucoup à dire à ce sujet.*

33 Since the creation of the city toll under Louis XIV, the *barrières*
were established at city entrances to collect tolls to regulate
traffic. Paris had sixty toll gates, twenty-two of which were at
the entrances to suburbs, among them the Maine *barrière*. It
was considered a disreputable place, frequented by the lowest
levels of society—thieves, drunks, prostitutes.

34 Armingeat, in Parturier and Armingeat, *Intellectuelles,*
pp. 132–33, rightly reports that Pierre Leroux promoted
women's emancipation, and that he vainly called for the fran-
chise for women in municipal elections. Leroux's feminist
socialism accounts for his contribution, with George Sand, to
La Revue indépendante, when they created its first issue on
November 1, 1841. Sand's novel *Consuelo* began publication in
La Revue indépendante in February 1842.

35 See articles in *La Voix des femmes* 3 (March 23, 1848) and 24
(April 15, 1848).

36 Jeanne Deroin, in *La Voix des femmes* 27 (April 19, 1848).

37 During the Revolution of 1848 jokes and caricatures in the
newspapers and popular songs contributed to the myth of the
Vesuvians. Thus their historic reality was completely over-
shadowed by their legend, which began with the scandal
caused by the female military service project conceived by the
Vesuvians. See *Les Vésuviennes ou la constitution politique des femmes
par une société de françaises* (Paris: Imprimerie de Edouard
Bautruche, 1848), p. 21.

38 Claire Moses, *French Feminism in the Nineteenth Century* (Albany,
N.Y.: S.U.N.Y. Press, 1984), pp. 128–30.

39 Albistur and Armogathe, *Histoire du féminisme,* p. 454. See also
p. 453: "the constitution of the Vesuvians was lavishly lampooned."

40 Daniel Stern [Mme d'Agoult], *Histoire de la Révolution de 1848,*
vol. 2 (Paris: Calmann-Lévy, 1878), pp. 158–61. See Albert
Montémont's song quoted by Alfred Delvau in the entry "Vésuvienne" [lewd woman], in *Dictionnaire de la langue verte, argots
parisiens comparés,* 2d ed. (Paris: Dentu, 1866).

*I am a Vesuvian
I am miles ahead
Anyone can come
And rumple my petticoat!*

*Je suis Vésuvienne
A moi le pompon
Que chacun me vienne
Fripper le jupon!*

41 *La Présidente criant à tue-tête* (The chairwoman yelling at the top
of her voice; D 1245) and waving her bell recalls that the rules
of procedure "specify that the academicians will not be allowed
to speak more than five at once." A caricature in 1848 by Mas-
son, *Club de femmes* (Women's club) came out with this caption:
"All that I can grant you is a maximum of twenty-five speakers

at once"; Armingeat, in Parturier and Armingeat, *Intellectuelles,*
p. 128.

42 Five years later *Le Charivari* (April 25, 1849) commented on
the vaudeville at the Théâtre Montansier, entitled *Femmes
saucialistes* [sic].

And now Théâtre Montansier competes with Charivari. . . . *Cham
and Daumier will stand up to M. Vautrin and M. Roger de Beau-
voir.* . . . *This vaudeville is nothing but a string of absurdities.* . . .
*The jokes might be a bit broad, but with socialist women, nothing is
far-fetched.*

Voici que le théâtre Montansier fait concurrence au Charivari. . . .
*Cham et Daumier tiendront tête à messieurs Vatrin et Roger de Beau-
voir.* . . . *Ce vaudeville ne se compose que d'un tissu d'extravagances
* . . . . *Les plaisanteries sont peut-être vives, mais, avec les femmes
socialistes, il n'y a rien de trop risqué.*

43 For the text of this proclamation, see Jules Tixerant, *Le Féminisme à l'époque de 1848 dans l'ordre politique et dans l'ordre écon-
omique* (Paris: Law Thesis, 1908), p. 82.

44 "Nous ne comprenons pas plus une femme législateur qu'un
homme nourrice. . . . A la femme la maison, à l'homme la
place publique"; Albistur and Armogathe, *Histoire du féminisme,* pp. 456–57. Proudhon refused to publish Deroin's reply
in *Le Peuple.* She then replied in *L'Opinion des femmes.* She was
not pardoned for being the instigator of a large federation plan
of all workers' associations. This scheme, which consisted of
giving to workers their means of production through a peaceful
process, resulted in severe repression from the government.
Contrary to what happened under the July Monarchy, the two
emancipated groups, women and workers, were no longer
linked; *Histoire du féminisme,* pp. 463–64. Deroin was forced
into exile in England at the outbreak of the coup d'état on
December 2, 1851, and the socialist feminist movement suf-
fered an eclipse for nearly twenty years; *Histoire du féminisme,*
p. 476.

45 Niboyet wrote: "The person who wins our praise is the he- and
she-type, a male being owing to manliness, a woman to divine
instinct, to poetry, namely G. Sand." In an open letter she sent
to *La Réforme* and not to *La Voix des femmes,* Sand termed this
position "a joke," "a ludicrous claim"; Albistur and
Armogathe, *Histoire du féminisme,* pp. 451–52. In the *Bulletin
de la république* she had already set herself against women's
political rights. See Albistur and Armogathe, *Histoire du
féminisme,* pp. 451–52.

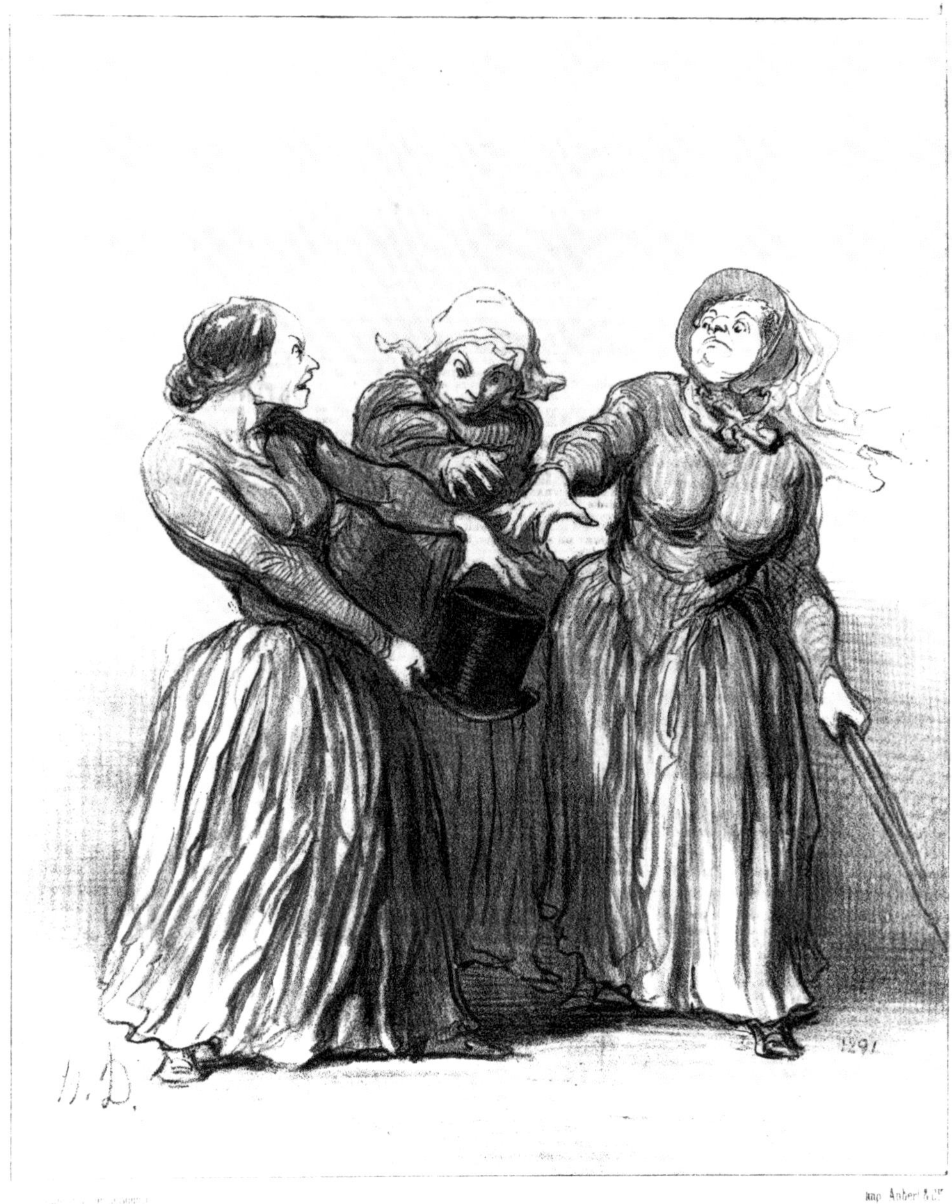

Cat. 28

L'Insurrection contre les maris est proclamée le plus saint des devoirs!

Insurrection against husbands is proclaimed the holiest of duties!

"Les Femmes socialistes" (Socialist women), no. 1; published in *Le Charivari,* April 20, 1849 (D. 1918).

LENDER: The Rose Art Museum, Brandeis University, Waltham, Massachusetts, The Benjamin A. and Julia M. Trustman Collection.

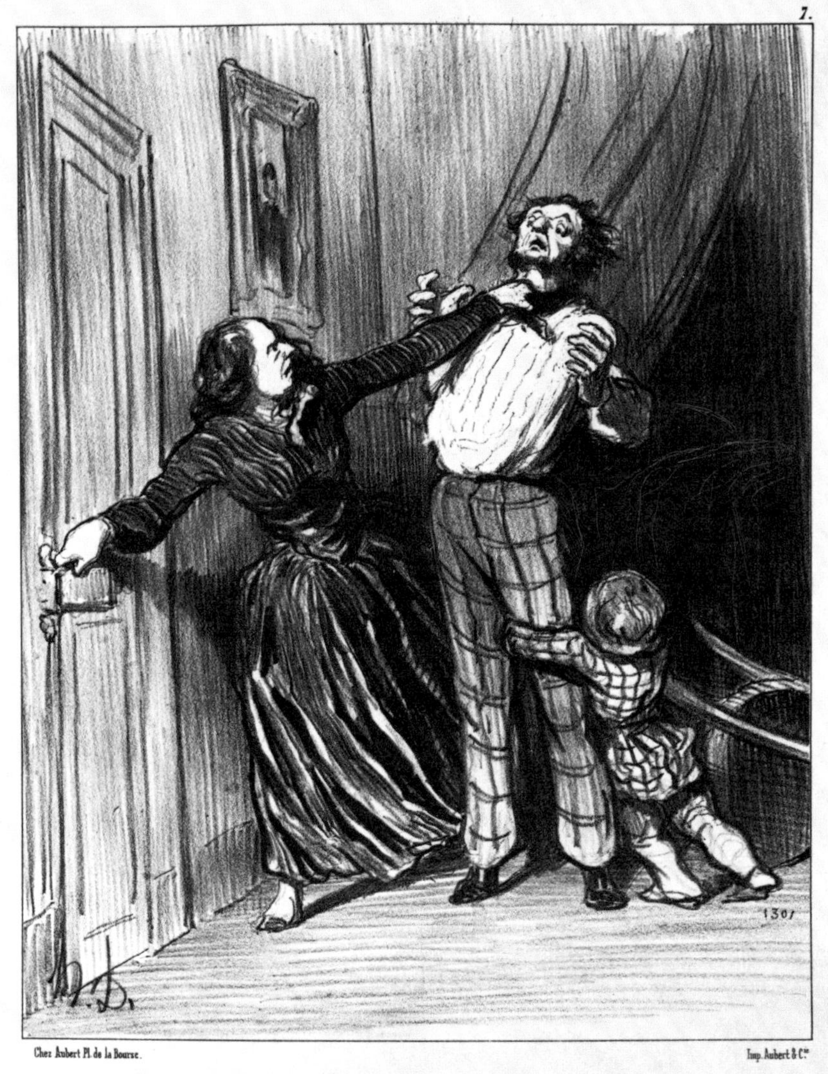

Cat. 29

Ah! vous êtes mon mari, ah! vous êtes le maître . . . eh! bien moi,
j'ai le droit de vous flanquer à la porte de chez vous. . . . Jeanne
Derouin me l'a prouvé hier soir!. . . . .allez vous expliquer avec
elle! . . .

Oh, so you're my husband, oh, you're the master? Well, I
have the right to throw you out of your house . . . . Jeanne
Derouin proved it to me last night! . . . Go take it up with
her! . . .

"Les Femmes socialistes" (Socialist women), no. 7; published
in *Le Charivari,* May 23, 1849 (D. 1924).

LENDER: Print Collection, Miriam and Ira D. Wallach
Division of Art, Prints and Photographs. The New York
Public Library, Astor, Lenox, and Tilden Foundations.

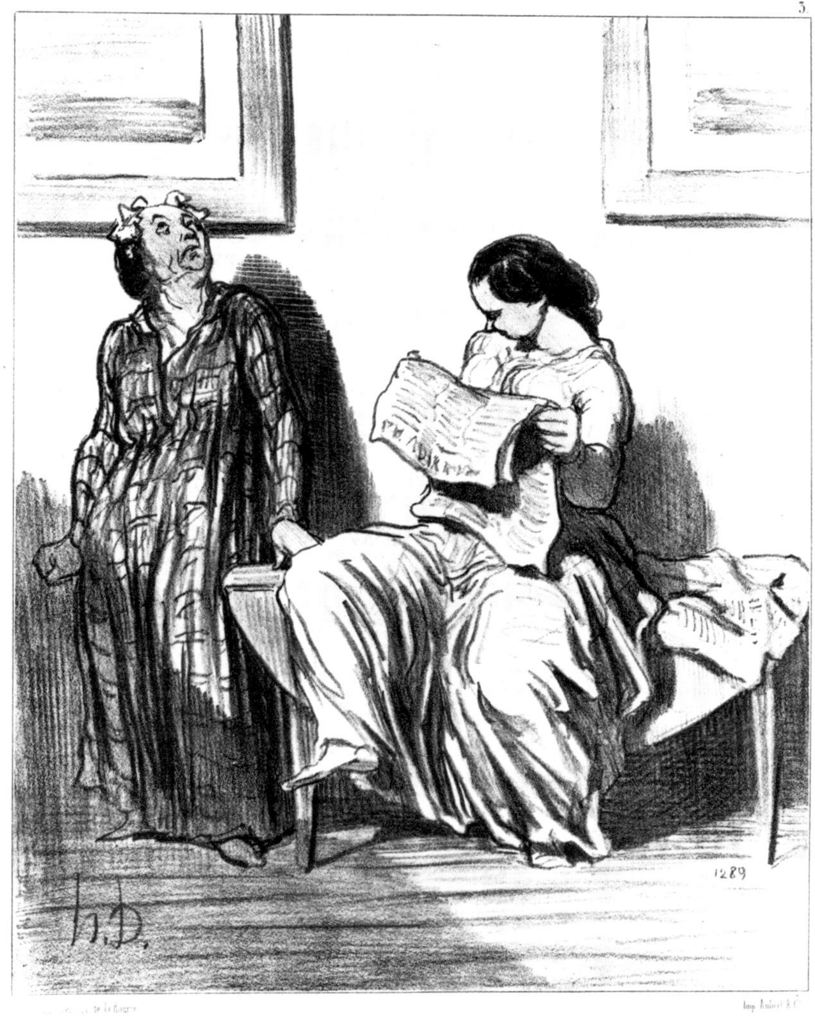

—Il paraît que les clubs vont être complétement fermés . . . . . .
—Les **réacs** . . . . . ils n'auraient jamais osé faire cela avant que la légion des **Vésuviennes**
fût dissoute! . . . . .

Cat. 30

—Il paraît que les clubs vont être complètement fermés. . . .
—Les réacs . . . ils n'auraient jamais osé faire cela avant que la
légion des Vésuviennes fut dissoute! . . .

—It appears that the clubs are going to be completely
closed. . . .
—The reactionaries! . . . they would never have dared to do
that before the Legion of Vesuvian Women was dissolved! . . .

"Les Femmes socialistes" (Socialist women), no. 3; published
in *Le Charivari,* April 25, 1849 (D. 1920).

LENDER: The Rose Art Museum, Brandeis University,
Waltham, Massachusetts, The Benjamin A. and Julia M.
Trustman Collection.

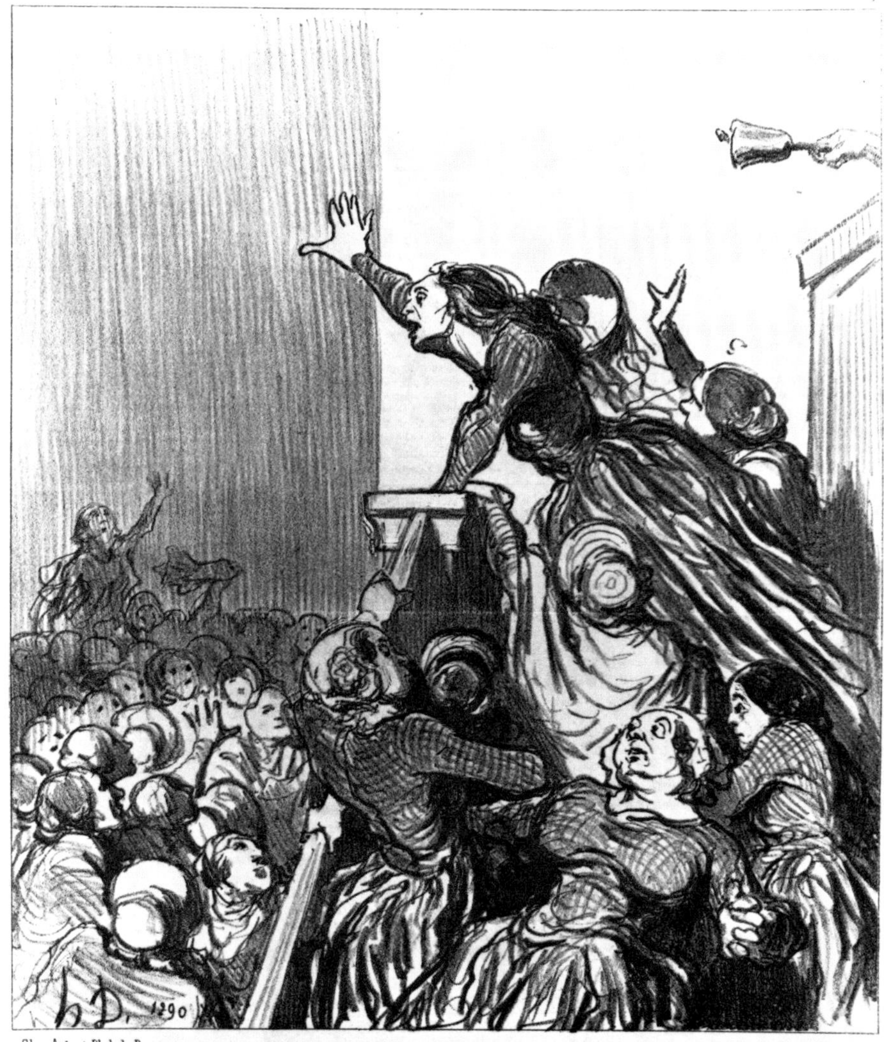

Cat. 31

*Citoyennes . . . on fait courir le bruit que le divorce est sur le point
de nous être refusé . . . constituons-nous ici en permanence et
déclarons que la patrie est en danger! . . .*

Women citizens . . . a report is spreading that soon we will
be refused a law for divorce . . . Let's organize ourselves here
permanently and declare that the nation is in danger! . . .

"Les Divorceuses" (Advocates of divorce), no. 1; published in
Le Charivari, August 4, 1848 (D. 1769).

LENDER: The Rose Art Museum, Brandeis University,
Waltham, Massachusetts, The Benjamin A. and Julia M.
Trustman Collection.

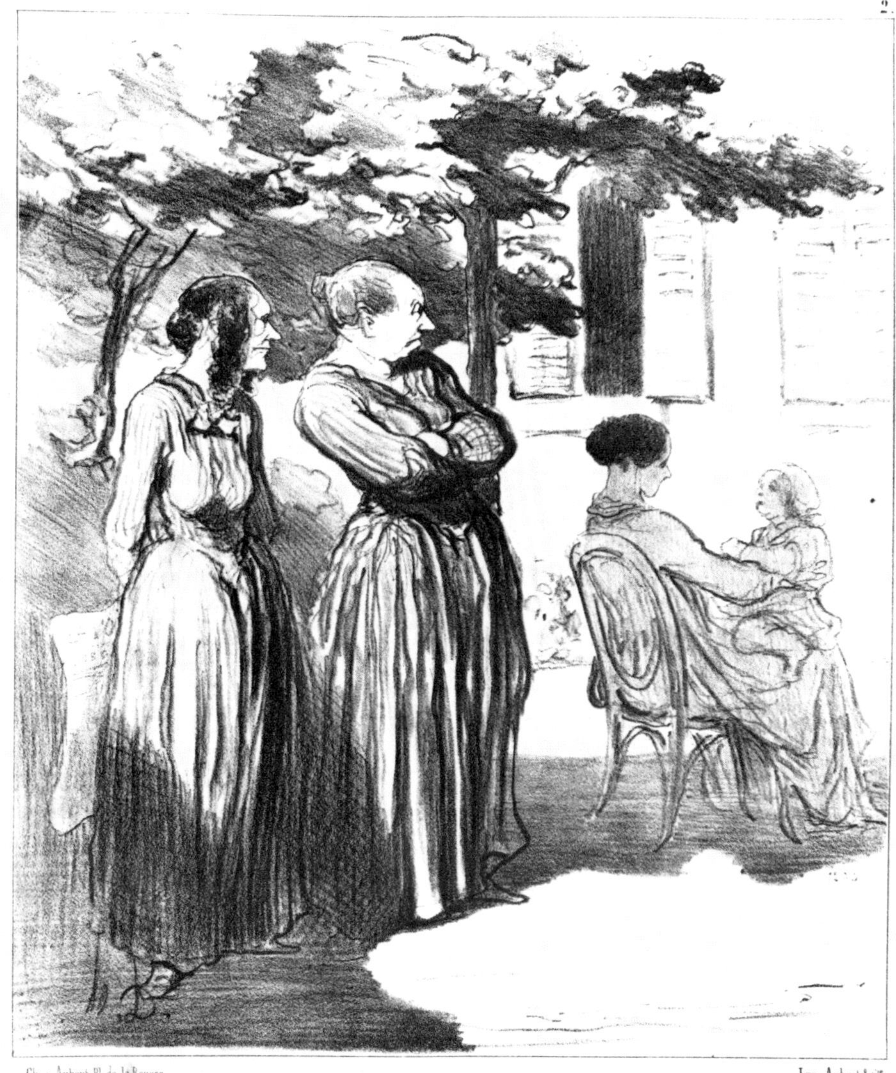

Cat. 32

*Voila une femme qui, à l'heure solennelle où nous sommes, s'occupe
bêtement de ses enfans . . . qu'il y a encore en France des êtres
abruptes et arrièrés!*

There goes a woman who, at our solemn hour, stupidly
occupies herself with her children . . . how can such narrow,
dull-witted creatures still exist in France!

"Les Divorceuses" (Advocates of divorce), no. 2; published in
Le Charivari, August 12, 1848 (D. 1770).

LENDER: The Rose Art Museum, Brandeis University,
Waltham, Massachusetts, The Benjamin A. and Julia M.
Trustman Collection.

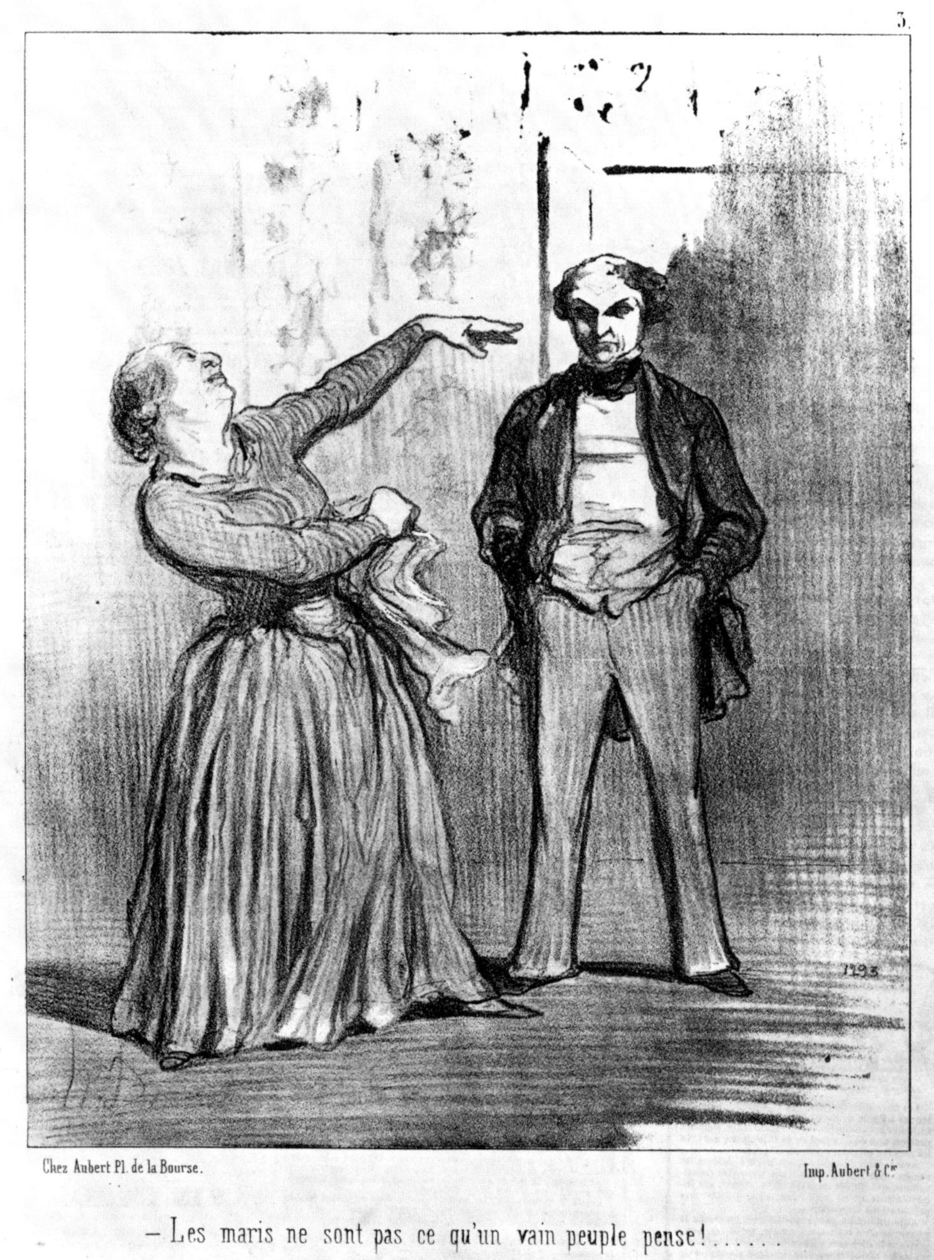

Cat. 33

Les maris ne sont pas ce qu'un vain peuple pense!

Husbands are not what people think!

"Les Divorceuses" (Advocates of divorce), no. 3; published in
Le Charivari, August 23, 1848 (D. 1771).

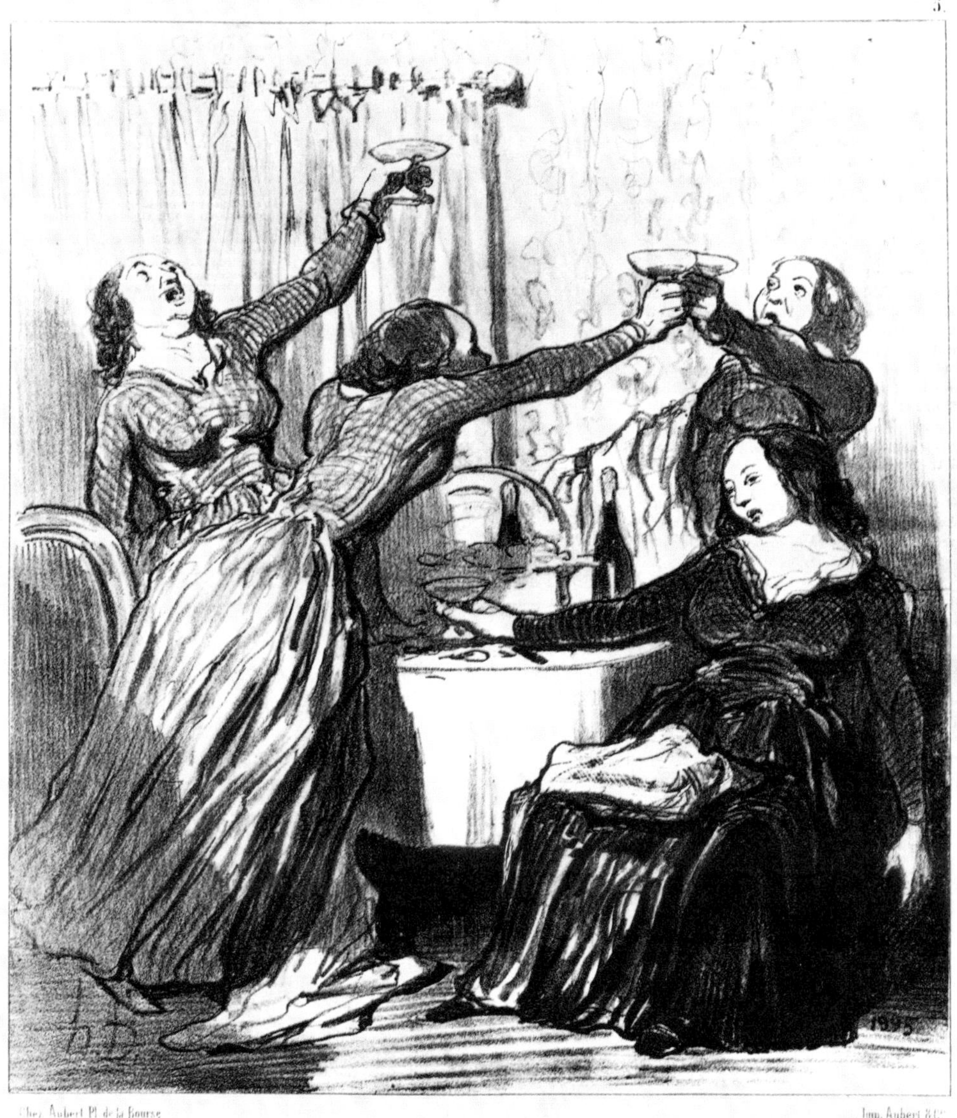

Cat. 34

Toast porté à l'émancipation des femmes, par des femmes déjà furieusement émancipées . . .

A toast made to the emancipation of women by women already amazingly emancipated . . .

"Les Divorceuses" (Advocates of divorce), no. 5; published in *Le Charivari,* October 12, 1848 (D. 1773).

LENDER: The Metropolitan Museum of Art, Bequest of Edwin De T. Bechtel, 1957 (57.650.453).

Parody and the Past: The Heroines of "Histoire ancienne"

KIRSTEN POWELL

BETWEEN December 22, 1841, and January 5, 1843, Daumier published the fifty lithographs of the series "Histoire ancienne" (Ancient history) for the editors of *Le Charivari.* Praised by Baudelaire as the best paraphrase of the famous lament, "Who will deliver us from the Greeks and the Romans,"[1] the series satirizes the heroes and heroines of ancient Greece and Rome through comic distortions of physiognomies and poses, through a refusal to idealize appearances, and through the inclusion of anachronistic references to contemporary life. Baudelaire found the series to be not only blasphemous but also useful—an assessment that suggests that Daumier's vision of antiquity is more than a gentle parody of revered classical heroes.[2] Rather, as Baudelaire suspected, the prints are an uncompromising manifesto of modernity that challenges a matrix of social, literary, and political authority structures through the body types, gestures, poses, and gender associations encoded in the prints' protagonists.

Caricature is an art that depends on shifting premises of power. What is assumed to be powerful is mocked, and that mockery reduces its power.[3] The artist who frames a joke and the viewer who participates in it are in cahoots. Their collusion diminishes a subject's stature: a king is reduced to a pear or an ancient hero is transformed into a buffoon.[4] This subversive disempowerment shared by artist and viewer is most obvious in political caricature, and it is easy to understand both the importance of this art form during the revolutions of 1789, 1830, and 1848 and its subsequent harsh censorship during the majority of the July Monarchy and Second Empire periods.[5] But this disempowerment is also evident, in subtler forms, in prints whose ostensible subjects are social and intellectual institutions rather than individuals, as seen in the "Histoire ancienne" lithographs.

The art historian Klaus Herding has shown that behind many of the "Histoire ancienne" prints, and perhaps even the series as a whole, lies a critique of controversial reforms proposed after 1830 for the French educational system.[6] On one side of the debate "humanist-idealist" educators urged studying the heroic themes of antiquity, while on the other side "scientific-realists" argued for studying the ways in which modernity diverged from the past. As Herding observes, not only do the lithographs parody the ancient texts commonly taught in schools, but several of the prints show teachers and pupils in mock-antique settings.[7] Moreover, many of the quotations in the legends are attributed to prominent academicians and scholars of classical literature, although these "quotations" are parodies that the authors undoubtedly would never have penned.[8]

It would have been easy for Daumier's male audience to make associations with contemporary educational practices; despite attempts at reform, the study of Latin and Greek language, literature, and history was a staple of the secondary education system for young men in France during the nineteenth century.[9] By contrast, women were generally denied a classical education, unless they came from a privileged family that could provide a tutor; most probably many of the jokes in these prints would have been lost on them.[10] Despite these restrictions, the world of antiquity was seen as a source of universal stability in a revolutionary world: François Guizot, then minister of public instruction, wrote to the duc de Broglie in 1832, "Greece and Rome are good company for the human spirit, and in the midst of the fall of all the aristocracies, one must make sure that it lives on."[11] And live on it did. In 1902 Ernest Lavisse recalled of his childhood: "I had the feeling of having been brought up in a noble setting, foreign and distant. I lived in Athens at the time of Pericles, in Rome at the time of Augustus, at Versailles at the time of Louis XIV."[12]

Antiquity ruled especially in academic settings, much to the dismay of Frenchmen who felt that the revolutions of 1789 and 1830 had ushered in a new, modern era. In particular, the generation of 1830, of which Daumier was a prominent member, chafed at the academy's insistence on maintaining the traditions of classicism.[13] In 1831 the *concours* in architecture for the Ecole des Beaux-Arts was a design competition for public baths on the lines of the great structures of ancient Rome. Commenting on this competition, an outraged author wrote in the journal *L'Artiste:* "Always Greece and ancient Rome:—never France! never the nineteenth century! What strange blindness! In our schools, the rhetoric students receive, as programs for their compositions, scenes of melodramas adjusted for the antique. There, always Greece and Rome:—of France, where these children must one day live, not a word."[14] The author suggested that a more appropriate architectural contest would have been to design a monument to the July Revolution of 1830, and he claimed that the academy should have been the first to inscribe on its building's pediment: "Let us be French, let us be of our own era."[15] Like Daumier's own rallying cry, "We must be of our own times,"[16] this plea for modernity was a direct challenge to the classical world and to those individuals and institutions whose own status depended on the public acceptance of its importance.

When *Ménélas vainqueur* (cat. 35), the first plate of the "Histoire ancienne" series, appeared in *Le Charivari* on December 22, 1841, it was accompanied by an article that jokingly paired Daumier and the paragon of academic painting, Jean-Dominique Ingres, as the Siamese twins of beauty.[17] As a painter of images of dominant males and supine, passive females, exemplified by his *Jupiter and Thetis* (1811, Aix-en-Provence, Musée Granet), Ingres and his cool, withdrawn classicism stood at the opposite end on the spectrum of attitudes about the past.[18] The son of an unsuccessful author of classical tragedies, Daumier himself had received academic instruction from Alexandre Lenoir, an amateur archaeologist who assigned his students the usual tasks of copying classical works of art. But, like many of his contemporaries in the 1830s and 1840s (and unlike Ingres), Daumier soon shifted his attention from the glories of the past to the realities of the present. Behind many of his drawings, paintings, and prints lies a devoted examination of the social details and political developments in nineteenth-century French daily life. In this regard, Ingres's art was the antithesis of Daumier's, and it is not surprising that in one of the "Histoire ancienne" prints—*Oedipe chez le Sphinx* (Oedipus and the Sphinx, D. 967) Daumier mocked a classical subject by producing a parody of one of Ingres's own paintings.[19]

The article in *Le Charivari* joked that Daumier had just returned from a sketching trip to Greece, where he had discovered the "primitive and pure sentiments" expressed in *Ménélas vainqueur.* In this lithograph, the king of Sparta leads his wife, Helen, whom Paris had abducted, from the smoking ramparts of Troy (in ancient accounts Menelaus had rushed at her with a raised sword, but at the sight of her beauty again fell deeply in love with her again and spared her). He prances over broken swords and fallen bodies, arching his leading foot like a ballerina. Behind his back, Helen mimics his exaggerated pose, and as the king lifts his nose so that it is almost level with the brim of his helmet, she thumbs her nose at him—a gesture, the article tells us, that the artist observed his contemporaries making before the king of Bavaria.[20] Menelaus's sagging potbelly adds to his image as a cuckold, while Helen's round face and sour expression belie her reputation for irresistibility. The effect is especially ironic when paired with the seemingly deadpan legend, which quotes the description of the blond Helen from

the *Iliad* as "more beautiful than ever with modesty and love."[21] In Daumier's rendition Helen is not beautiful, she shows an immodest amount of leg, and her crude gesture bespeaks contempt instead of love. She implies her own superiority as she mocks Menelaus's foppish pose, thumbing her nose in derision. Her scorn makes even the title ironic, since, through her mockery of him, it is Helen who conquers by reducing the stature of her rescuer. Daumier's Helen was not universally admired: Baudelaire later recalled, "I remember a lyric poet of the 'pagan school'[22] being deeply indignant at it. He called it sacrilege and spoke of the fair Helen as others speak of the Blessed Virgin. But those who have no great respect for Olympus, or for tragedy, were naturally beside themselves with delight."[23]

There were other reasons to be indignant at Daumier's version of this scene from ancient literature. Daumier's satires mocked more than a classical text: it mocked a king. The *Charivari* article pretended that Daumier derived Helen's gesture from his observation of people thumbing their noses at the king of Bavaria, but the target for Daumier's disrespect would more likely have been France's own portly Citizen King, Louis-Philippe. Even though the passage of the so-called September Laws of 1835 rendered direct caricature of the French king illegal (in 1842, when most of the "Histoire ancienne" prints appeared, *Charivari* writers still frequently complained about press censorship and suppression),[24] artists like Daumier devised a variety of clever ways to veil their attacks on the king and his policies.[25] Although Daumier's Helen lacks the dignity of later allegorical figures of the Republic (see, for example, cat. 18), she anticipates their role as uncompromising critics of monarchy and bureaucracy.

By using a classical subject to suggest that kings could be objects of scorn, Daumier and his collaborators at *Le Charivari* moreover implied a broader attack on French civilization. One of the main arguments of educators favoring the study of antiquity was the belief that the ancient world was, according to one spokesman, "an essential and almost indispensable element in the formation of the national spirit and the French genius. . . . Our destiny and our title of nobility is to be, by an uninterrupted succession, the sons and heirs of antiquity."[26] Through his relentless mockery of the ancient world, Daumier questioned this destiny.

In other "Histoire ancienne" prints, more exaggerated reversals of gender roles than that demonstrated by Helen are used to disempower the heroes of history and myth. *Socrate chez Aspasie* (cat. 36) shows the Greek philosopher with Aspasia, the mistress of Pericles, defined in the caption as a *lorette,* a nineteenth-century woman of loose morals. Under her instruction, Socrates rises on his toes to dance the cancan. The caption compares him to a *débardeur*—a modern male dancer familiar from the caricaturist Gavarni's scenes of carnival balls—although his pose is far more feminine than one would expect from the robust dockworkers caricatured by this artist (fig. 6.1). Socrates' stance is precarious, and, like that of Menelaus, his forward foot mimics the pointe of a ballerina. To underline the contrast further, Aspasia's pose is steady and secure, and even though her naked arm and leg are visible, her stance diffuses any hint of eroticism. Her feet are flat on the floor, her weight is low, and her arms are held close to her body. She leans away from Socrates while inclining her head toward him, a posture that balances her form and exaggerates the philosopher's instability.

Daumier's parody of Socrates is especially pointed when it is compared with the treatment of Aspasia in books intended for the gentle intellectual stimulation of women, such as Amable Tastu's *Le Livre des femmes, choix de morceaux extraits des meilleurs écrivains français sur le caractère, les moeurs, et l'esprit des femmes* (The lady's book, choice of extracts from the best French writers on the character, customs, and mind of women).[27] The author of an essay on women's character during different centuries observes that courtesans in Athens heard so much talk of philosophy, politics, and poetry that they developed a taste for these subjects. The reader is told that their conversation was therefore brilliant, in turn inspiring poets and philosophers, and she is reminded that, according to classical lore, Socrates and Pericles met with Aspasia, acquiring from her finesse and taste, and by honoring her with a visit they gave her a good name in exchange.[28] In Daumier's caricature, however, these lofty associations are lampooned, as the elements of finesse and taste imparted by the sturdy Aspasia make Socrates look undignified and foolish.

Daumier's comparison of a woman's grim strength with a man's passivity in *Socrate chez Aspasie* is taken even further in *L'Enlèvement d'Hélène* (cat. 37). According to the caption, while Paris recovers from lovemaking by smoking a cigar, Helen lifts him in her arms and carries him off. Although in Homer's epic Helen was a consenting party (neoclassicists like David, in his *Paris and Helen* [1788, Paris, Musée du Louvre], show her as a submissive, passive figure), Daumier endows her with masculine strength and gives her the

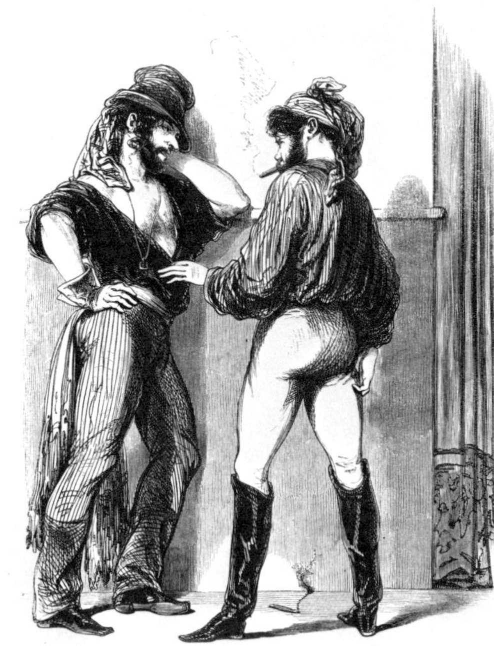

Fig. 6.1 Gavarni [Guillaume-Sulpice Chevalier].
J' te parie mon Alezan doré contre ta Vicomtesse, que j'emporte ce soir le petit rat du Baron . . .

I bet you my golden horse Alezan against your Viscountess that tonight I'll carry off the Baron's little ballet dancer . . .

Gavarni. Oeuvres choisies: Les Débardeurs (Paris: J. Hetzel, Garnier Frères, 1848), n.p.
Private collection.

male role of abductor. This technique of reversing gender roles was one Daumier often used in prints to satirize contemporary women. To attack the *bas-bleus,* he repeatedly placed men in traditional women's roles of caring for children (cat. 13 and 24) and performing domestic tasks (cat. 14 and 21), and to make the activities of political women seem ludicrous Daumier placed the women in positions associated with male actions: oath taking (cat. 28), toastmaking (cat. 34), and addressing a crowd (cat. 31). In the case of *L'Enlèvement d'Hélène,* however, the point of the role reversal is not so much to devalue Helen (although Daumier does render her as stocky and muscular—traits not associated with female beauty in nineteenth-century France) as to mock the veneration of the classics as a whole, and especially within the confines of the academy. This mockery is given a contemporary twist in the caption, whose text is attributed to a parody of the *Aeneid* by a Monsieur Patin. As a professor of Latin at the Sorbonne and a respected authority on classical literature, Henri-Joseph-Guillaume Patin would certainly not have tampered with the classics.[29] Thus, the supposed author's parody is really a parody of the author and, by extension, the academy. And, as in the *Ménélas vainqueur* print, the satire is especially powerful because, like the allegorical figures of the Republic (such as cat. 47), it is a woman who seizes the moment to challenge and revise the authority of the past.

If all of the women in the "Histoire ancienne" prints followed these patterns of gender and authority reversal, one could assume that Daumier's view of the women of antiquity paralleled his representations of allegorical women, who are characterized by strength and virtue. But women are not always elevated to positions of power in the "Histoire ancienne" series. In several lithographs they appear as loving wives and doting mothers—antique counterparts to the characters in Daumier's caricatures of contemporary life. In *Les Nuits de Pénélope* (cat. 38),[30] the faithful, aging Penelope rests from her nightly toil of unweaving Laertes' shroud (a ruse to prevent her from having to choose a new husband) to swoon erotically before the profile of her absent spouse, Ulysses, which, the caption tells us, always shone like a star for her.[31] Since the profile appears as naive graffiti on the wall beside her, the appeal ironically resides in the beholder's eye. In ancient literature Penelope represented strength of character and independence, qualities Daumier downplays. The same theme of love's blindness recurs in *Ulysse et Pénélope* (cat. 39), where Penelope gazes lovingly at the gaunt face of the elderly Ulysses, half hidden under his sleeping cap, a scene that parallels such tender moments as the embrace shared by a bourgeois couple in *Tendresse conjugale* of 1852 (D. 2224) and the reminiscence of youthful romance in *Souvenirs* (fig. 6.2).

In these representations of Penelope, Daumier sets

Fig. 6.2 Honoré Daumier. *Souvenirs* (Recollections). "Types parisiens" (Parisian types), no. 23; published in *Le Charivari,* January 5, 1842 (D. 579). Collection of John McWilliams, Middlebury, Vermont.

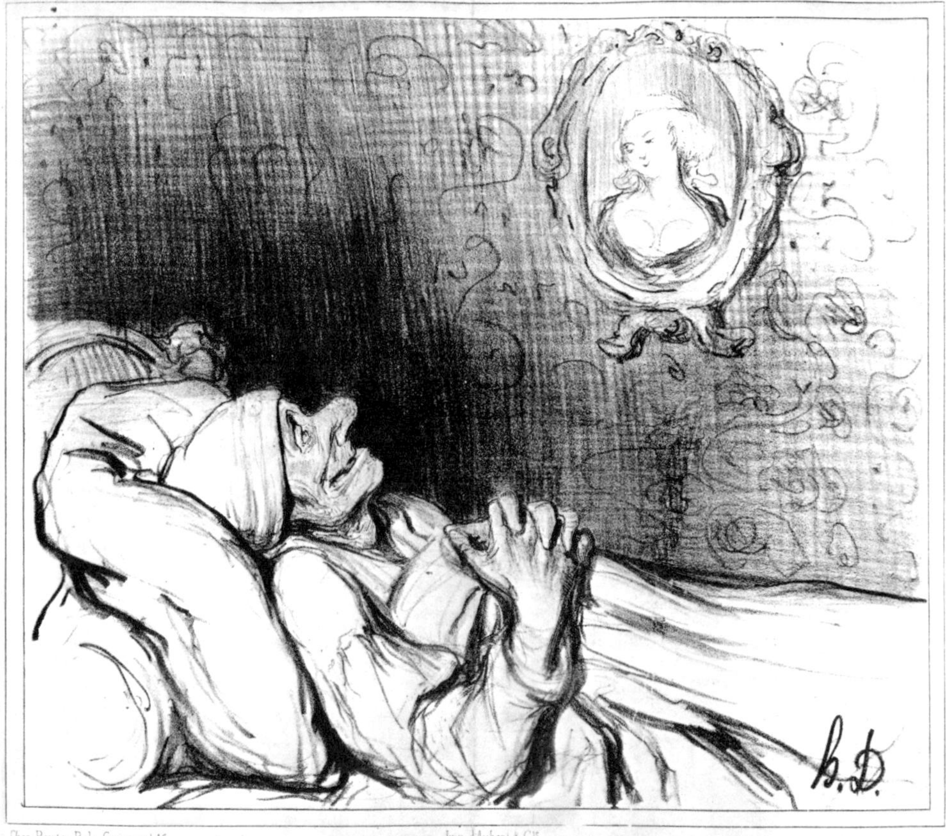

aside his strategies of challenging the authority of the past in favor of scenes that emphasize the values of love and fidelity, shared by both his heroes and heroines of antiquity and his upright bourgeois citizens of the present. Furthermore, Daumier's placement of women in the "Histoire ancienne" series in roles more in keeping with nineteenth-century middle-class values is not without its own humor. In his version of the scene from Plutarch in which a mother declares to another woman that her children are her jewels, *La Mère des Gracques* (cat. 40), Daumier depicts a robust Roman matron who gestures grandly to her squalling, nose-picking progeny. And when the nymph Thetis dips Achilles in the river Styx to assure his immortality in *Le Baptême d'Achille* (cat. 41), the mother's protective action is translated into the mundane activity of bathing a child, since, as the legend informs us, "a bath is good for everything."

Throughout the "Histoire ancienne" series Daumier reduces the stature of the heroes and heroines of antiquity by refusing to idealize his subjects. Much of the humor lies in the unexpected realism of the physiognomies and physiques of his characters. In *Présentation d'Ulysse à Nausica* (cat. 42), Daumier creates a parody of an episode in the *Odyssey* in which the naked Ulysses, covering himself with a branch, appears to Nausicaa (daughter of King Alcinous who will eventually help Odysseus return to Ithaca) and her handmaidens as they are washing her clothes. Ulysses is not the male figure made beautiful by Athena whom Nausicaa later indicates she would like to marry; he is flabby and hairy. Nausicaa spreads her fingers in amazement, and her companion hides her face behind a laundry beater. Whereas in paintings and drawings Daumier conveyed the dignified bearing of the laundresses he observed along the quais of mid-nineteenth-century Paris (fig. 6.3), in this print he emphasizes the laundresses' shock and horror when confronted by the all-too-human creature before them. In *Enée aux enfers* (cat. 43) a scrawny Aeneas with an oversized nose opens his hands in amazement when Dido's grimacing shade scorns him with her gesture (after being Aeneas's mistress, Dido killed herself when he deserted her). As in his depiction of Ulysses and Nausicaa, here, too, Daumier carefully avoids any idealization of Aeneas and Dido, thus stripping them of the physical and conceptual perfection that would be conveyed by ideal form.

The issues of authority, idealism, and gender reversal seen in the prints discussed above converge in Daumier's version of the Pygmalion myth (cat. 44). As the

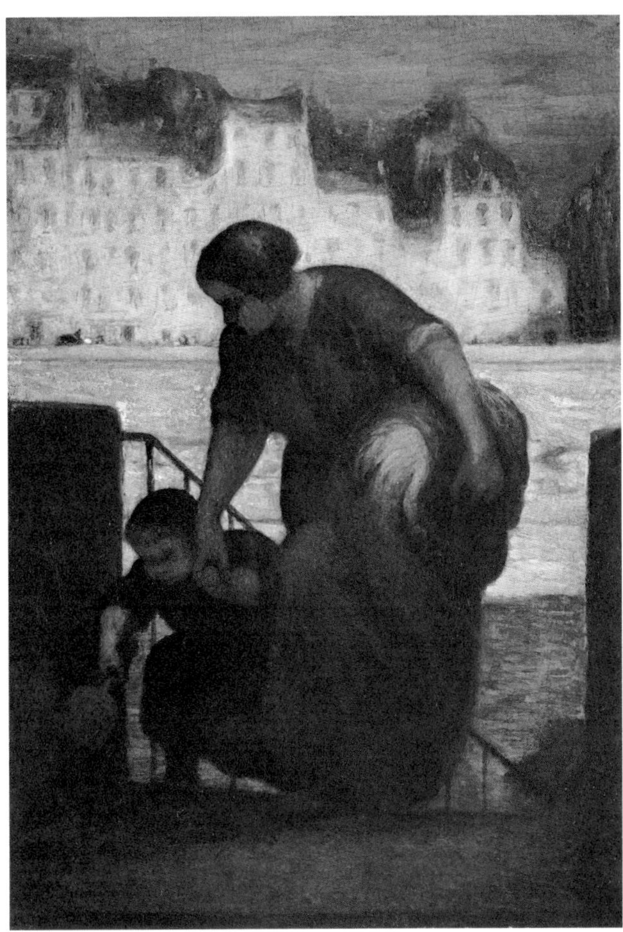

Fig. 6.3 Honoré Daumier.
The Laundress, 1863.
Oil on panel, 19½ x 13 in. (49.8 x 33 cm).
The Metropolitan Museum of Art, Bequest of Lizzie P. Bliss, 1931 (47.122).

beautiful statue comes to life before the open-mouthed, disheveled sculptor, the woman leans down, the legend tells us, to ask for a pinch of snuff. Thus Daumier's classical figure literally descends from her pedestal to seek the pleasures of the street—an apt metaphor for the devaluation of classical idealism that occurs throughout the "Histoire ancienne" series. Moreover, despite her graceful pose and ample female proportions, Galatea enters the masculine sphere by asking to share a male vice. Like the bluestockings who drink and smoke (see cat. 34), her personal liberation leads to social impropriety when she oversteps the boundaries of a gender-related activity.

Oddly enough, this exchange between Pygmalion and Galatea is paralleled in attitudes about modern copies of classical sculptures of women. In 1841 an article in *L'Artiste* discussed a reproduction of the Venus de Milo, made in reduced size with Achille Collas's newly invented pointing machine.[32] The author praised antique sculpture in general, noting its superiority to modern creations, and compared the Venus de Milo to other classical works. But the article concluded on a surprising note: "This is not just the woman of antiquity, still consecrated to the pleasure of man; this is woman after her emancipation, with freedom from her love and her body, as the modern world has presented her."[33] Thus the classical Venus is an idealized version of the emancipated woman, one who is beyond physical desires. While Daumier and his contemporaries made modern progressive women into unpleasant, promiscuous creatures (cat. 26), the Venus de Milo represented a freedom for women that was at once personal, universal, and pure. Daumier drew on these associations late in his career when he published *La République de Milo ou l'idéal de la droite* (D. 3873) in *Le Charivari*. Here the classical merges with the allegorical, as the armless Venus becomes a type for the Republic in 1871.[34]

Daumier's representations of the women of antiquity demonstrate the complexity and ambiguity of his views about women of the past and present. His female characters mock and are mocked. They often help defuse the authority of the past by reversing gender expectations. Unlike the limp piles of wilting neoclassical women in David's *Oath of the Horatii* (1784–1785, Paris, Musée du Louvre) and his *Lictors Returning to Brutus the Bodies of His Sons* (1789, Paris, Musée du Louvre), Daumier's classical women are predominantly active, engaged, and willing to take matters into their own hands. At times they anticipate the powerful allegorical women seen in Daumier's work after 1848, who take to task politicians, generals, and even emperors. In other instances they show unexpected affinities to the bourgeois wives and mothers of Daumier's prints of contemporary life. And in still other prints, women help to point up the ironically unidealized forms of the men of Daumier's ancient world. Above all they contradict the negative views Daumier reflected in his *bas-bleu* prints done only a year or two later. The role of women in the "Histoire ancienne" series highlights the artist's willingness to reverse neoclassical stereotypes of the passive women of antiquity, while upholding the stereotypes that define the proper place and activities of his contemporaries. Throughout the series mockery implies a loss of authority, and together with other progressive artists, writers, and reformers of the mid-

nineteenth century who worked to extinguish the twilight of the gods, Daumier offered his audience an irreverent, humorous, and ultimately modern revision of the place of women in the classical world.

NOTES

1   "Qui nous délivrera des Grecs et des Romains?" Charles Baudelaire, "Quelques Caricaturistes français," in *Oeuvres complètes,* 2 vols. (Paris: Gallimard, 1976), 2:556. The same sentiment appears in "Elégie sur les Grecs et les Romains" by Joseph Berchoux (1765–1839): "Qui me délivra des Grecs et des Romains? / Du sein de leurs tombeaux, ces peuples inhumains / Feront assurément le malheur de ma vie." See Louis Provost, *Honoré Daumier: A Thematic Guide to the Oeuvre,* ed. Elizabeth C. Childs (New York and London: Garland Publishing, 1989), p. 136.

2   "Un blasphème très amusant, et qui eut son utilité"; Baudelaire, "Quelques Caricaturistes français," p. 556. For a general discussion of Baudelaire's theories of caricature, see Ainslie Armstrong McLees, "*Argot plastique*: Baudelaire and Caricature," Ph.D. diss., University of Virginia, 1980.

3   Baudelaire explores the idea of the superiority of laughter in part three of "De l'essence du rire," in *Oeuvres complètes,* 2:530–31. This idea is elaborated at greater length in Freud's analysis of laughter and humor in *Jokes and Their Relation to the Unconscious,* trans. James Strachey (New York: Norton, 1960). James Cuno makes an interesting application of Freud's theories to French caricature between 1820 and 1840 in "Charles Philipon and La Maison Aubert: The Business, Politics, and Public of Caricature in Paris, 1820–1840," Ph.D. diss., Harvard University, 1985.

4   King Louis-Philippe was first caricatured as a pear by Charles Philipon in 1832, when the artist drew a series of portraits of the heavy-jowled monarch showing the gradual transformation of his face into a pear.

5   For a recent discussion of mechanisms of political caricature in revolutionary France, see James Cuno's introduction to *French Caricature and the French Revolution, 1789–1799* (Los Angeles: University of California Grunwald Center for the Graphic Arts, 1988), pp. 13–22.

6   Klaus Herding, "Daumier, critique des temps modernes. Recherches sur l' 'histoire ancienne,'" *Gazette des Beaux-Arts* 113 (January 1989): 29–44. See also Klaus Herding, "'Inversionen.' Antikenkritik in der Karikatur des 19. Jahrhunderts," in Klaus Herding and Gunter Otto, eds., *Nervöse Auffangsorgane des inneren und äusseren Lebens—Karikaturen* (Giessen, 1980), pp. 131–71. Other general studies of the "Histoire ancienne" series include Philippe Roberts-Jones, "L'Antiquité selon Grandville et Daumier," *Gazette des Beaux-Arts* 109 (January–February 1988): 71–75, *Honoré Daumier: "Histoire ancienne,"* exh. cat. (Malibu: J. Paul Getty Museum, 1975), and R. K. Chambers, "Daumier's 'Histoire Ancienne': Art and Politics," *Arts* 55 (September 1980): 156–57.

7   See cat. 36 and D. 954.

8 Among the authors cited are the poet Casimir Delavigne (D. 928), Abel-François Villemain, until 1844 minister of instruction under Guizot (D. 930), and Auguste Trognon, historian and tutor to the prince de Joinville, son of Louis-Philippe (D. 941).

9 The pedagogical ideals behind the study of the classics had their origins in the ancien régime. It was believed that the works of classical authors expressed the highest truths and moral statements and were therefore models of thought, conduct, and style. Study of the classics could result in an enthusiasm for truth and virtue, brought about by the beauty of expression of ancient writers. As R. D. Anderson has observed, it was hoped that the memory of noble and elevated ideals would survive even after the Latin and Greek language skills had faded. Thus, the educator's aim was to isolate the student from the real world and make him live in an idealized, heroic, classical one. According to Anderson, educators "were not worried by charges that their teaching was out of touch with the spirit of the age, because that was, in a sense, its whole point." See R. D. Anderson, *Education in France, 1848–1870* (Oxford: Clarendon Press, 1975), p. 27.

10 Claire Moses, *French Feminism in the Nineteenth Century* (Albany, N.Y.: S.U.N.Y. Press, 1984), pp. 32–33, and passim.

11 "La Grèce et Rome sont la bonne compagnie de l'esprit humain, et au milieu de la chute de toutes les aristocraties, il faut tâcher que celle-là demeure debout"; quoted in Pierre Chevallier and B. Grosperrin, eds., *L'Enseignement français de la Révolution à nos jours*, 2 vols. (Paris: Mouton, 1971), 2:150.

12 "J'ai le sentiment d'avoir été élevé dans un milieu noble, étranger et lointain. J'ai vécu à Athènes au temps de Périclès, à Rome, au temps d'Auguste, à Versailles, au temps de Louis XIV"; Ernest Lavisse, "Souvenirs d'une éducation manquée," in Antoine Prost, ed., *Histoire de l'enseignement en France, 1800–1967* (Paris: Librairie Armand Colin, 1968), p. 62.

13 Foremost among the voices that promoted the importance of classicism was Quatremère de Quincy, elected secrétaire perpétuel of the Académie des beaux-arts in 1816, a position he held until his retirement in 1839. According to Albert Boime, "Conservative Quatremère believed that Academies existed in order to preserve traditions, not to create new ones. He consistently denounced the romantic movement, and considered the Revolution of 1830 a victory for innovating trends and a defeat for the academic tradition." See Albert Boime, *The Academy and French Painting in the Nineteenth Century* (London: Phaidon Press, 1971), p. 7.

14 "Toujours la Grèce et toujours Rome antique: — jamais la France! jamais le dix-neuvième siècle! Quel étrange aveuglement! Dans nos lycées, les rhétoriciens en lisière reçoivent, pour programmes de leurs compositions, des scènes de mélodrames ajustées à l'antique. Là encore toujours la Grèce et Rome: — de la France, où ces enfans doivent vivre un jour, pas un mot"; "Beaux-Arts. Grands Prix. Concours d'architecture," *L'Artiste* 2 (1831): 73.

15 "Soyons français, soyons de notre époque"; "Concours d'architecture," p. 73.

16 "Il faut être de son temps." For a discussion of this motto and its ramifications, see George Boas, *Wingless Pegasus: A Handbook for Critics* (Baltimore: The Johns Hopkins Press, 1950), pp. 194–210.

17 *Le Charivari* (December 22, 1841). The article is paraphrased in Oliver Larkin, *Daumier: Man of His Time* (New York: McGraw-Hill, 1966), p. 60.

18 This range of responses to the classical world had already been widened by J. J. Grandville's satirical versions of themes from ancient mythology in his "Galerie mythologique" of 1830. For a discussion of these prints, see Roberts-Jones, "L'Antiquité selon Grandville et Daumier," pp. 72–73.

19 Other prints from the "Histoire ancienne" series are also based on neoclassical paintings. See works cited in Provost, *A Thematic Guide to the Oeuvre*, pp. 136–37. For a discussion of sources for Daumier's *La Mort de Sapho* (D. 973) see Jacquelynn Baas Slee, "Daumier's 'Sapho' and Academic Painting," *Print Collector's Newsletter* 8 (November–December 1977): 138–39.

20 This gesture is repeated in *Mariage chinois,* plate 7 from the "Voyage en Chine" series (fig. 2.1; D. 1195). The gesture in *Ménélas vainqueur* has also been interpreted as an allusion to the sentiments of modern Hellenes who had just been forced to accept a Bavarian monarch. See *Honoré Daumier: "Histoire ancienne,"* p. 8.

21 The caption text is credited to the Bareste translation, no doubt the translation of the *Iliad* by Eugène Bareste, with illustrations by Célestin Nanteuil, published in 1841.

22 This poet was probably Théodore de Banville. See Slee, "Daumier's 'Sapho' and Academic Painting," p. 139 n. 1., and Jonathan Mayne, trans. and ed., *The Painter of Modern Life and Other Essays by Charles Baudelaire* (London and New York: Phaidon, 1965), p. 179 n. 1.

23 "Je me rappelle qu'un poète lyrique et païen de mes amis en était fort indigné. Il appelait cela une impiété et parlait de la belle Hélène comme d'autres parlent de la Vierge Marie. Mais ceux-là qui n'ont pas un grand respect pour l'Olympe et pour la tragédie furent naturellement portés à s'en réjouir"; Baudelaire, "Quelques Caricaturistes français," p. 556.

24 See, for example, the articles on censorship: "Ils en veulent beaucoup à la presse," *Le Charivari* (January 7, 1842); an untitled article about suppression in *Le Charivari* (January 16, 1842); "Les Condamnations d'hier," *Le Charivari* (January 17, 1842); and "La Parisienne de la presse," *Le Charivari* (February 7, 1842).

25 For a discussion of Daumier's uses of distanced subjects (either through time or geography) to veil criticism of contemporary France, see Elizabeth C. Childs, "Honoré Daumier and the Exotic Vision: Studies in French Caricature and Culture, 1830–1870," Ph.D. diss., Columbia University, 1989.

26 L. Lecuyer, "Du beau et de son rôle dans l'éducation (1856)," quoted in Anderson, *Education in France,* p. 22.

27 Amable Tastu, *Le Livre des femmes, choix de morceaux extraits des meilleurs écrivains français sur le caractère, les moeurs, et l'esprit des femmes,* 2 vols. (Ghent: chez G. de Busscher et fils, 1823).

28 Tastu, *Le Livre des femmes,* 1:11–12.

29 In 1840 Patin published *Mélanges de littérature ancienne et moderne* and between 1841 and 1843 his *Etudes sur les tragiques grecs ou examen critique d'Eschyle, de Sophocle et d'Euripide, précédé d'une histoire générale de la tragédie grecque. Grand Dictionnaire du XIXᵉ siècle,* s.v. "Patin, Henri-Joseph-Guillaume."

30 Although this print appeared in *Le Charivari* on April 24,
    1842, the lithograph stone bears the date April 14, 1842, indi-
    cating that Daumier actually drew the caricature on this earlier
    date. See Provost, *A Thematic Guide to the Oeuvre,* p. 170.

31 For a discussion of antique sources for Daumier's representation
    of Penelope, see Jody Maxmin, "A Hellenistic Echo in Dau-
    mier's Penelope?" *Art International* 27 (August 1984): 38–47.

32 "La Vénus de Milo et les réductions de M. Achille Collas,"
    L'Artiste 22 (1841): 159–61. Daumier himself may have owned
    one of the Collas reductions of the Venus de Milo. Such a sculp-
    ture appears in two works, a sketch entitled *Un Amateur* (Rot-
    terdam, Museum Boymans-van Beuningen; see K. E. Maison,
    *Honoré Daumier: Catalogue Raisonné of the Paintings, Watercolours,
    and Drawings,* 2 vols. [Greenwich and London: New York
    Graphic Society, (1967–1968)], 2:no. 369) and a watercolor,
    Un Amateur (New York, The Metropolitan Museum of Art;
    Maison, 2:no. 370). Herding (see note 4) suggests that these
    works present a different relationship between Daumier and the
    classics, in which private, quiet contemplation and admiration
    of the work of an ancient sculpture is appropriate and aesthet-
    ically satisfying.

33 "Ce n'est point la femme de l'antiquité, consacrée encore aux
    jouissances de l'homme; c'est la femme après son émancipation,
    avec sa liberté de son amour et de sa personne, comme le
    monde moderne l'a pressentie"; "La Vénus de Milo," p. 161.

34 This type is repeated in *Tirez, ça fait équilibre* (cat. 48).

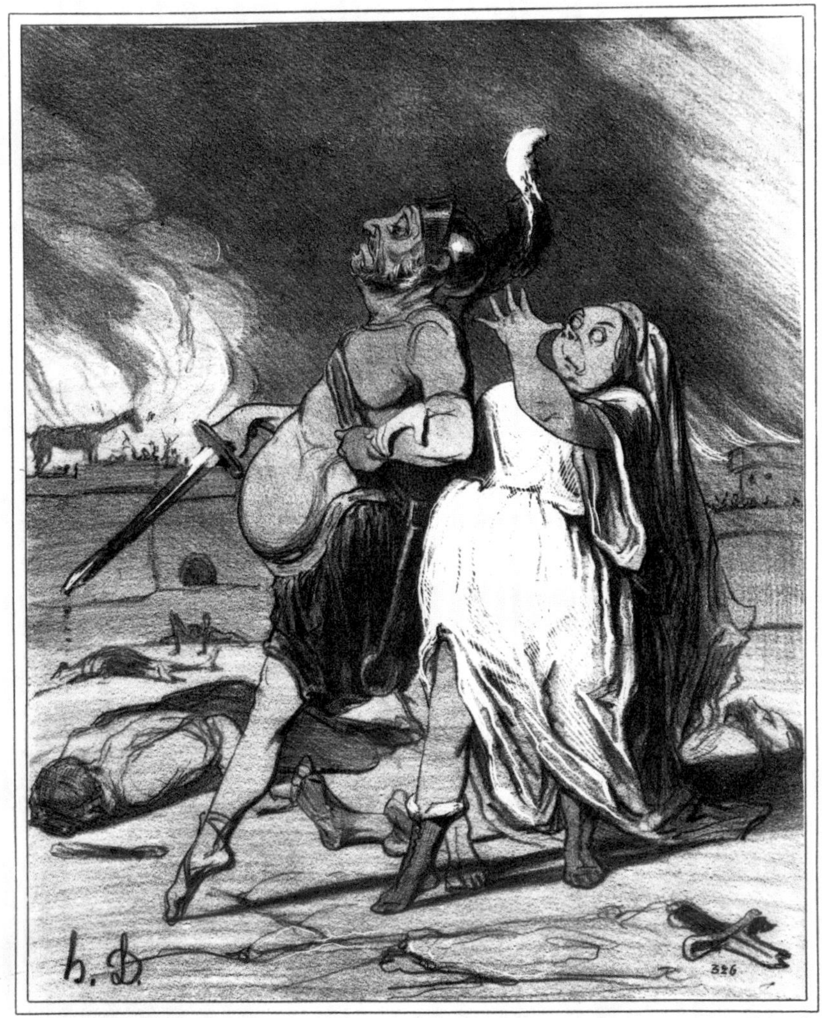

Cat. 35

MÉNÉLAS VAINQUEUR

Sur les remparts fumants de la superbe Troie,
Ménélas, fils des Dieux, comme une riche proie,
Ravit sa blonde Hélène et l'emmène à sa cour
Plus belle que jamais de pudeur et d'amour.

Illiade (Traduction Bareste)

MENELAUS VANQUISHER

On the smoking ramparts of superb Troy,
Menelaus, son of the gods, like a rich prize,
Carried off his blond Helen and took her to his court
More beautiful than ever with modesty and love.

The Iliad (Bareste translation)

"Histoire ancienne" (Ancient history), no. 1; published in
Le Charivari, December 22, 1841 (D. 925).

LENDER: Print Collection, Miriam and Ira D. Wallach
Division of Art, Prints and Photographs. The New York
Public Library, Astor, Lenox, and Tilden Foundations.

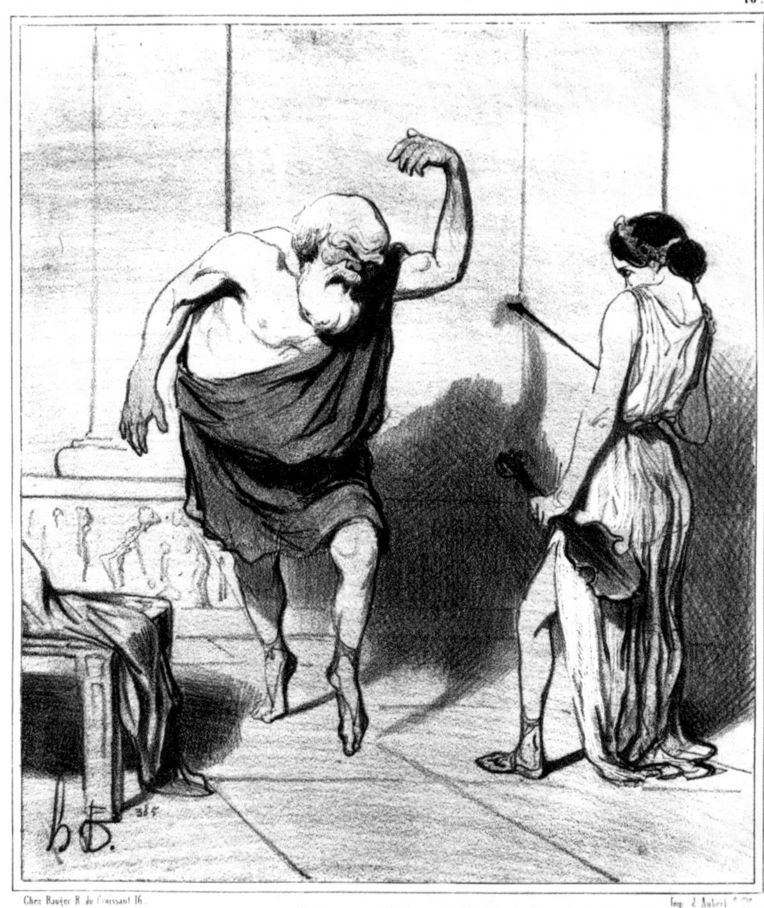

Cat. 36

SOCRATE CHEZ ASPASIE

Aimant le vin et les fillettes,
Socrate après dîner laissait sagesse en plan,
Et comme un Débardeur chez d'aimables Lorettes,
Il pinçait son léger cancan.
(Poésies badines de Mr Vatout)

SOCRATES AT ASPASIA'S HOUSE

Liking wine and young girls
Socrates after dinner leaving wisdom behind
And like a docker at a friendly tart's
He danced a lively cancan.

(Gay verses by Mr. Vatout)

"Histoire ancienne" (Ancient history), no. 10; published in *Le Charivari,* June 5, 1842 (D. 934).

LENDER: Print Collection, Miriam and Ira D. Wallach Division of Art, Prints and Photographs. The New York Public Library, Astor, Lenox, and Tilden Foundations.

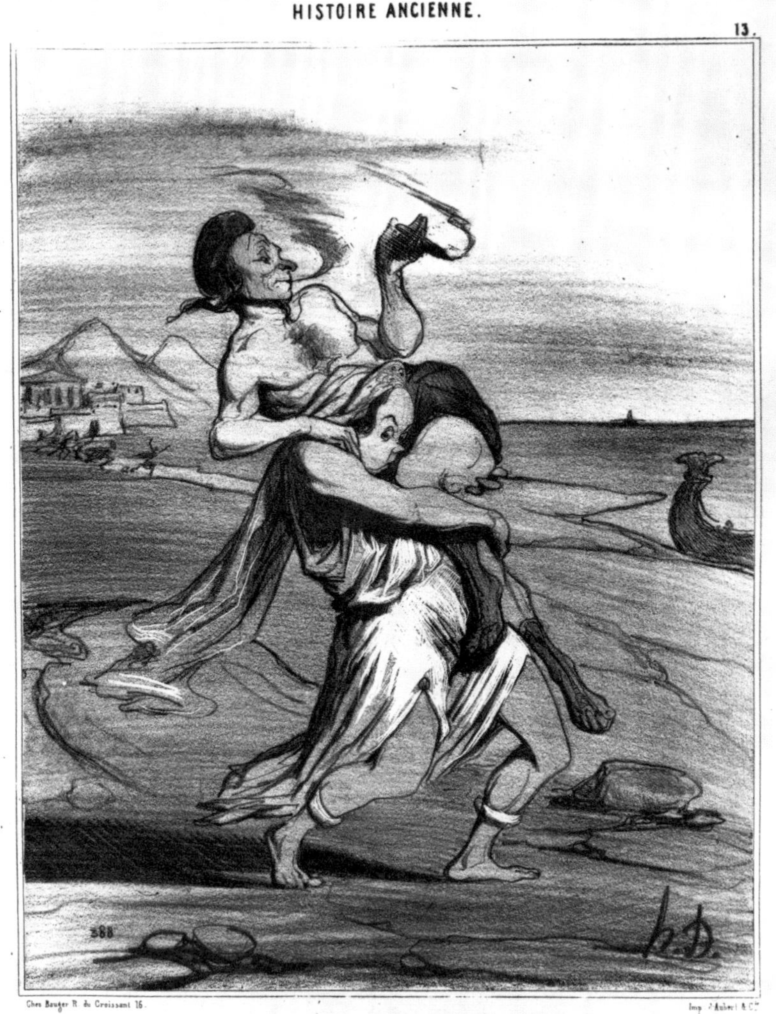

Cat. 37

L'ENLÈVEMENT D'HÉLÈNE

Pâris qui par amour sur les dents s'était mis,
N'était plus guère bon qu'à fumer un cigarre.
Hélène le savait aussi sans crier gare,
Sur ses robustes bras elle enleva Pâris.

(Eneide, travestie par M' Patin)

THE RAPE OF HELEN

Paris, who had worn himself out with love
Was good for nothing but smoking a cigar.
Helen knew it too; without warning,
In those robust arms she bore off Paris.

(The Aeneid, parodied by Mr. Patin)

"Histoire ancienne" (Ancient history), no. 13; published in
Le Charivari, June 22, 1842 (D. 937).

LENDER: Print Collection, Miriam and Ira D. Wallach
Division of Art, Prints and Photographs. The New York
Public Library, Astor, Lenox, and Tilden Foundations.

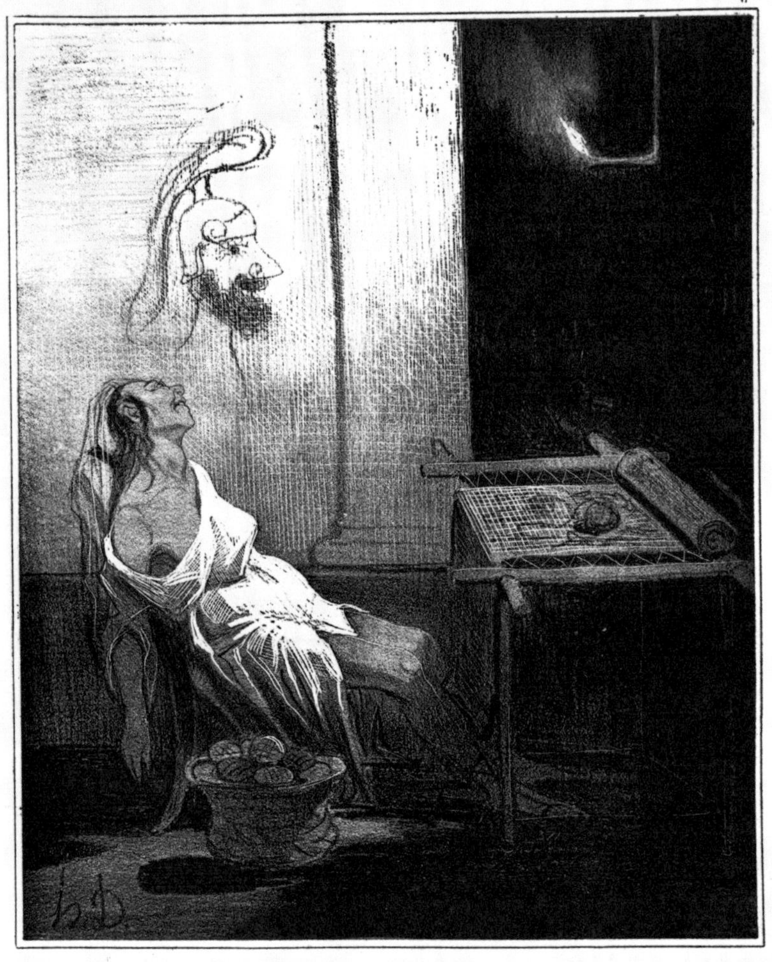

Cat. 38

LES NUITS DE PÉNÉLOPE

De son époux absent l'adorable profil,
Toujours à ses doux yeux brillait comme une étoile.
Mais pour tramer trois ans et sa ruse et sa toile
Il fallait qu'elle eut un fier fil.
(Odyssée, Ch. II. Trad. indiscrète de Mr Villemain)

THE NIGHTS OF PENELOPE

The adorable profile of her absent spouse,
In her sweet eyes shone always like a star.
But to weave for three years both plot and tapestry
She must have had quite a thread.
(The Odyssey, Ch. II. Indiscreet trans. by Mr. Villemain)

"Histoire ancienne" (Ancient history), no. 6; published in *Le Charivari,* April 24, 1842 (D. 930).

LENDER: Print Collection, Miriam and Ira D. Wallach Division of Art, Prints and Photographs. The New York Public Library, Astor, Lenox, and Tilden Foundations.

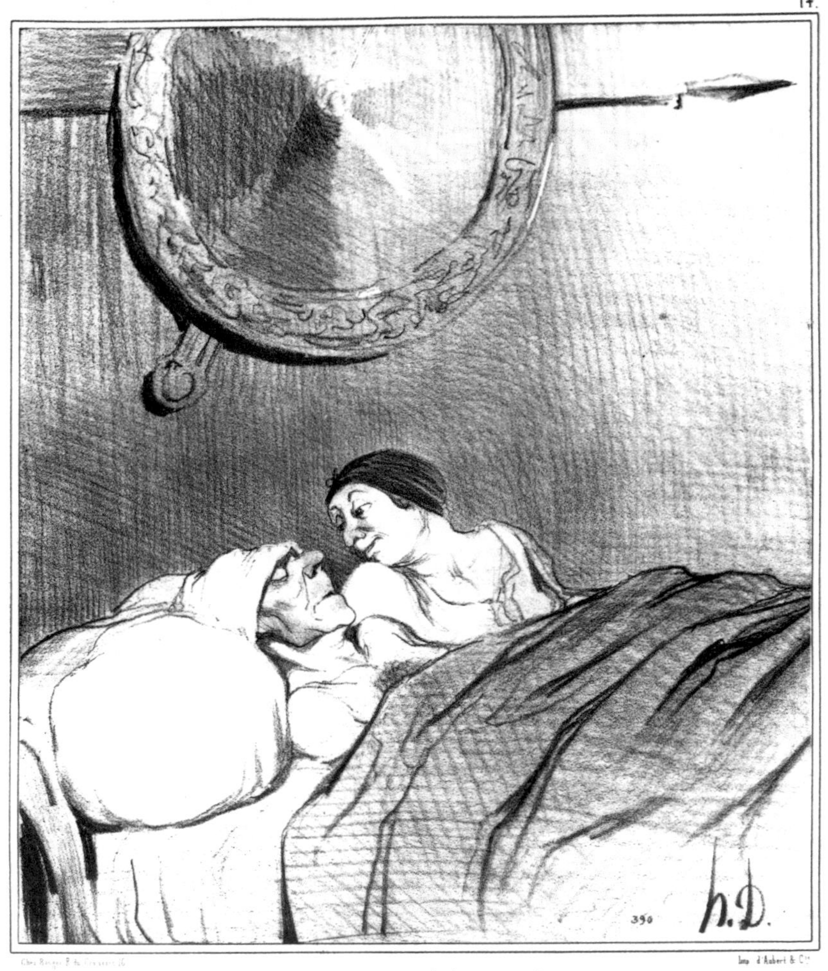

Cat. 39

ULYSSE ET PÉNÉLOPE

Chastement étendus sur leur pudique couche
Ces deux nobles époux se retrouvaient enfin,
Et quand Ulysse ronfla, sur sa charmante bouche
Pénélope commit un amoureux larcin.

(Oeuvres badines de Mr Vatout)

ULYSSES AND PENELOPE

Chastely lying upon their unsullied couch
The noble couple found each other again
And when Ulysses snored, on his charming mouth
Penelope committed an amorous theft.

(The Gay Works of Mr. Vatout)

"Histoire ancienne" (Ancient history), no. 14; published in *Le Charivari,* June 26, 1842 (D. 938).

LENDER: Print Collection, Miriam and Ira D. Wallach Division of Art, Prints and Photographs. The New York Public Library, Astor, Lenox, and Tilden Foundations.

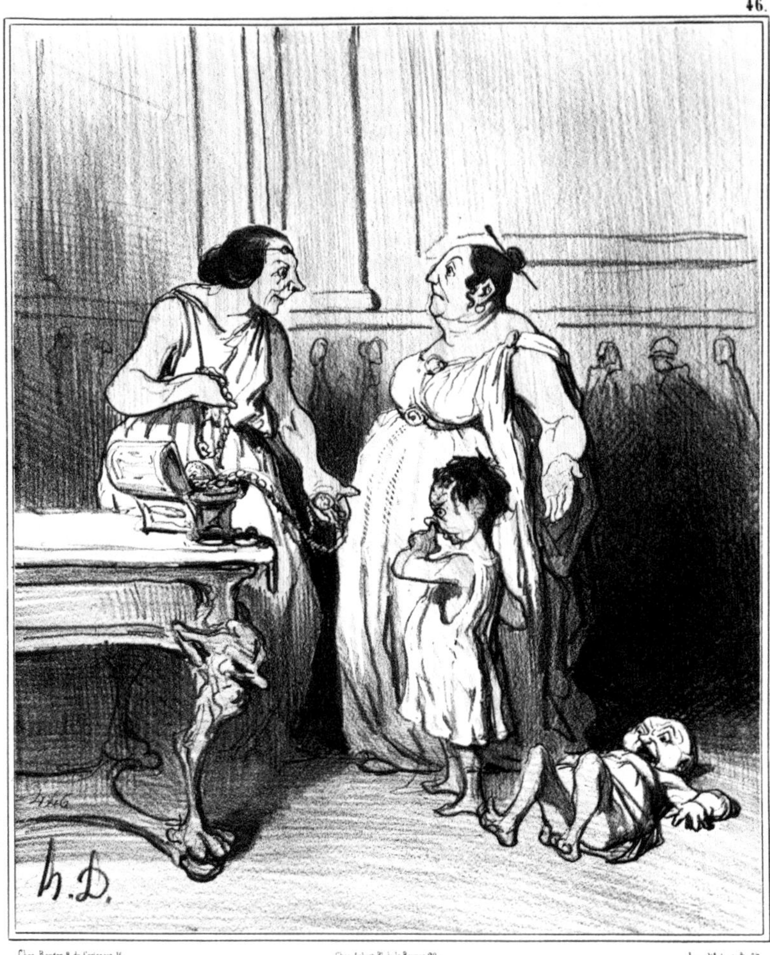

Cat. 40

LA MÈRE DES GRACQUES

Un jour qu'une lorette avec effronterie
Lui vantait des joyaux qui valaient quelques sous;
En montrant ses deux fils, l'espoir de la patrie
Cette Romaine dit: Voilà mes seuls bijoux!!
(Plutarch)

THE MOTHER OF THE GRACCHI

One day when a prostitute shamelessly
Bragged to her of jewelry worth pennies;
Pointing to her two sons, the hope of the country,
The Roman woman said: here are my only jewels!!

(Plutarch)

"Histoire ancienne" (Ancient history), no. 46; published in
Le Charivari, December 23, 1842 (D. 970).

LENDER: Print Collection, Miriam and Ira D. Wallach
Division of Art, Prints and Photographs. The New York
Public Library, Astor, Lenox, and Tilden Foundations.

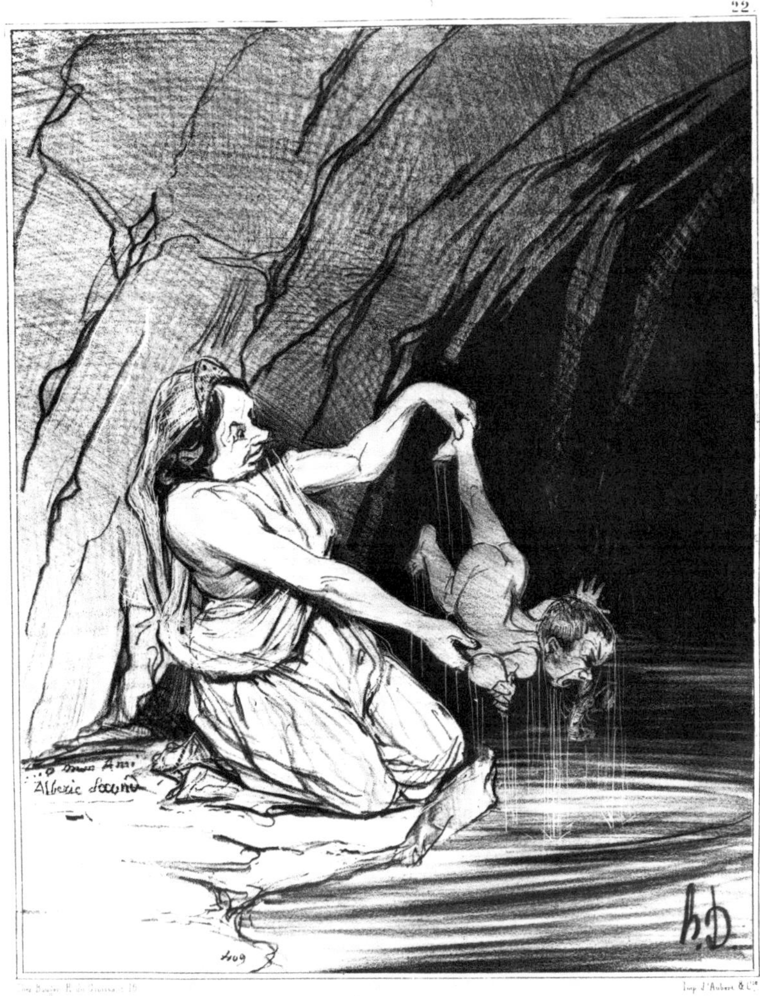

Cat. 41

LE BAPTÊME D'ACHILLE

Comme on trempe une arme de guerre,
Thétis de son moutard voulant faire un héros,
Le trempa dans le Styx dès qu'il vit la lumière;
Ce qui prouve qu'un bain est bon à tout propos.
(De l'influence des bains, Poème par Mr Vigier)

THE BAPTISM OF ACHILLES

As a weapon of war is quenched,
Thetis, of her brat wishing to make a hero,
Dipped him in the Styx as soon as he was born;
Which proves that a bath is good for everything.

(On the influence of baths, a poem by Mr. Vigier)

"Histoire ancienne" (Ancient history), no. 22; published in
Le Charivari, August 28, 1842 (D. 946).

LENDER: Print Collection, Miriam and Ira D. Wallach
Division of Art, Prints and Photographs. The New York
Public Library, Astor, Lenox, and Tilden Foundations.

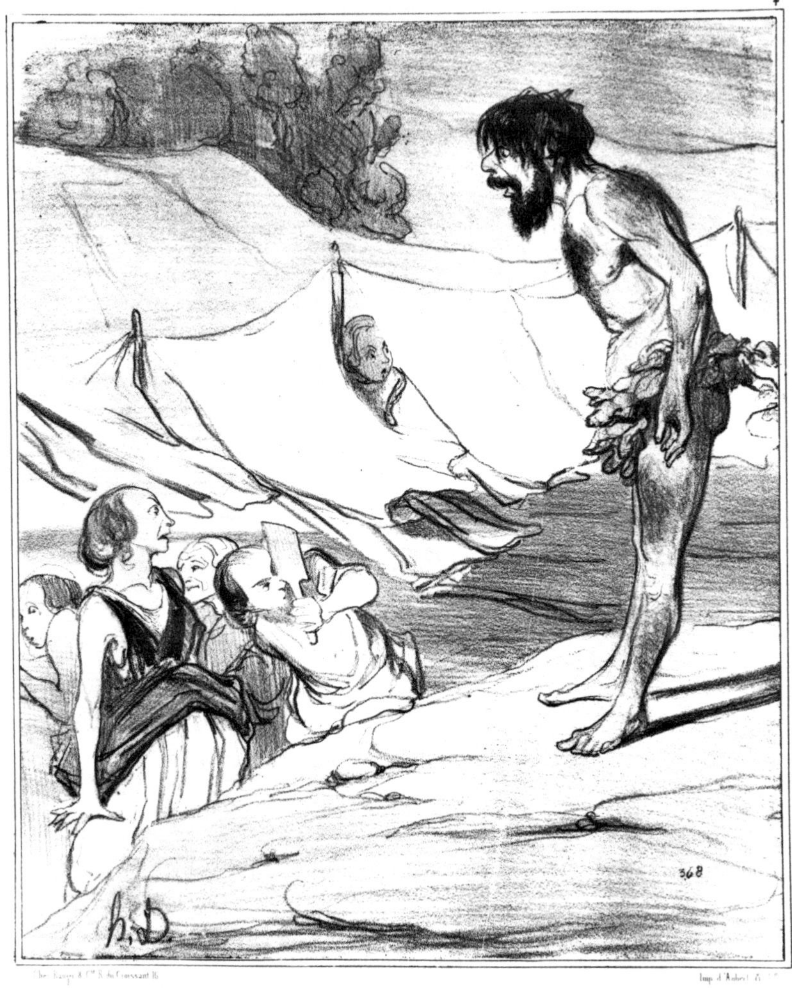

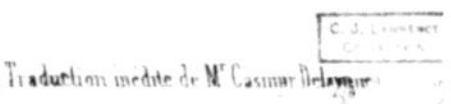

Cat. 42

PRÉSENTATION D'ULYSSE À NAUSICA

A l'aspect du héros souillé de limon noir,
Tout fuit, mais Nausica dans sa pudeur naive;
Lui dit en rougissant sans quitter sa lessive:
Quel Dieu noble étranger t'amène en mon lavoir?
(Traduction médite de Mr Casimir Delavigne)

INTRODUCTION OF ULYSSES TO NAUSICAA

At the sight of the hero, dirty with black silt,
Everyone flees, but Nausicaa in her naive modesty
Asks him, blushing, without leaving her laundry:
What strange noble God brings you to my washing place?

(Translation mistakenly attributed to Mr. Casimir Delavigne)

"Histoire ancienne" (Ancient history), no. 4; published in
Le Charivari, March 30, 1842 (D. 928).

LENDER: Print Collection, Miriam and Ira D. Wallach
Division of Art, Prints and Photographs. The New York
Public Library, Astor, Lenox, and Tilden Foundations.

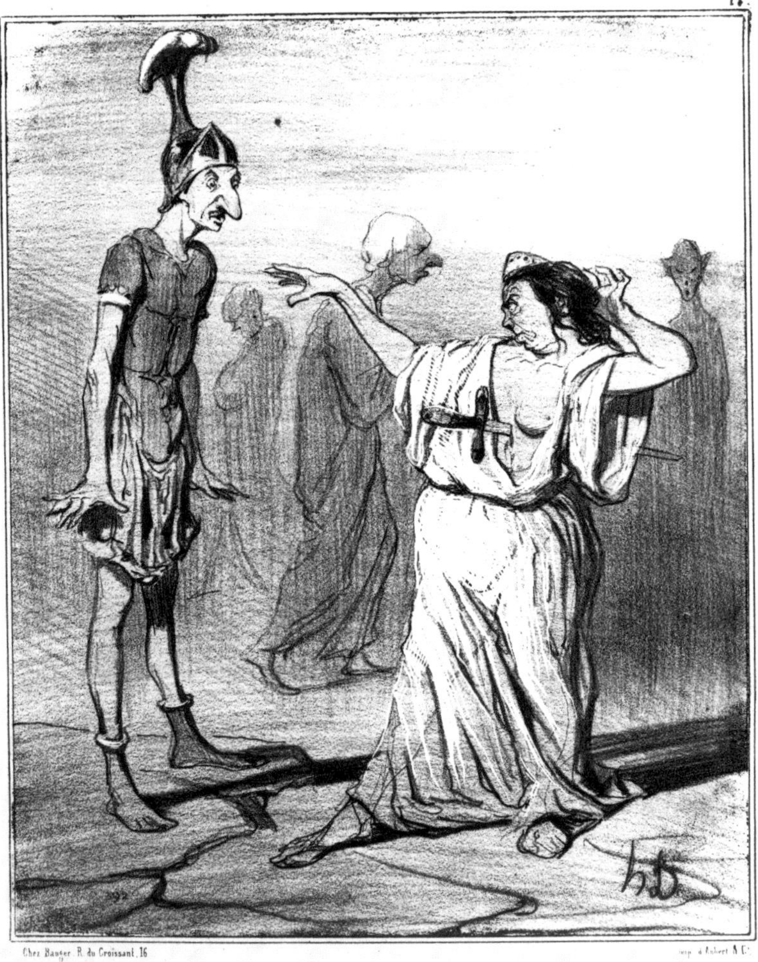

Cat. 43

ENÉE AUX ENFERS

Horreur! il aperçoit la femme qui l'adore!
Un poignard dans le coeur et les yeux pleins d'émoi;
Qui d'un geste charmant que la pudeur décore,
Lui dit: cher bien aimé, je me fiche de toi!

(Eneide, trad. de M. Trognon)

AENEAS IN HELL

Oh horror! He spies the woman who adores him!
A dagger in her heart and her eyes filled with emotion;
Who, with a charming gesture, adorned with modesty,
Says: dear beloved, I don't give a damn about you!

(The Aeneid, trans. by Mr. Trognon)

"Histoire ancienne" (Ancient history), no. 17; published in
Le Charivari, July 15, 1842 (D. 941).

LENDER: Print Collection, Miriam and Ira D. Wallach
Division of Art, Prints and Photographs. The New York
Public Library, Astor, Lenox, and Tilden Foundations.

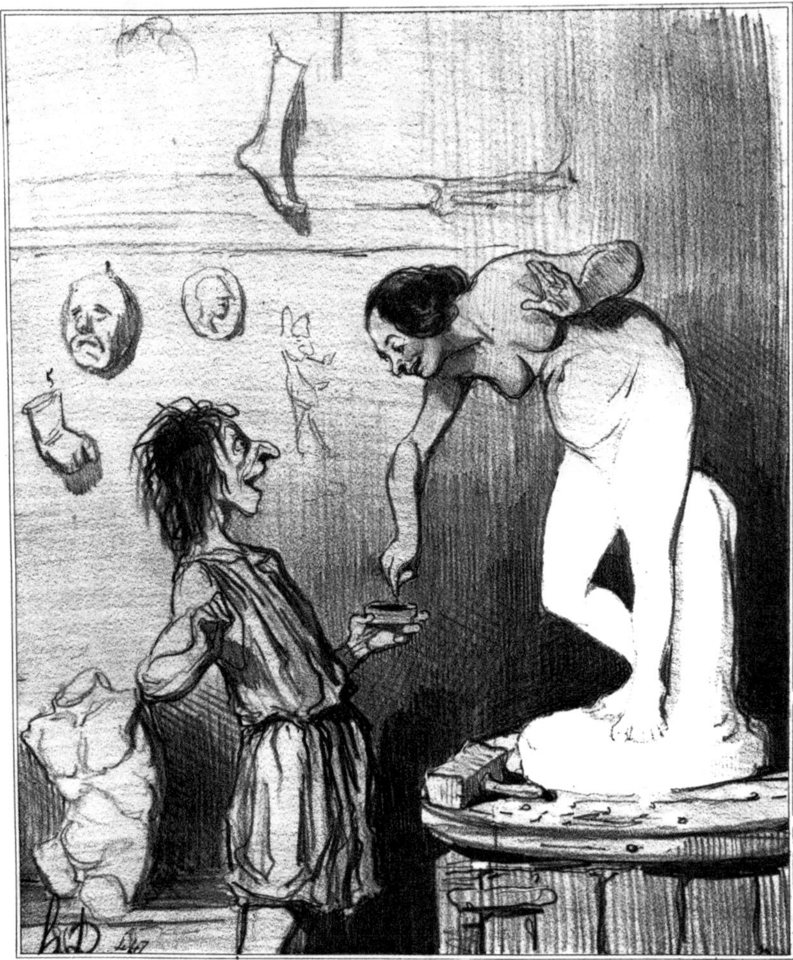

Cat. 44

PYGMALION

O triomphe des arts! quelle fût ta surprise,
Grand sculpteur, quand tu vis ton marbre s'animer,
Et, d'un air chaste et doux, lentement se baisser
Pour te demander une prise.

(Comte Siméon)

PYGMALION

Oh, triumph of the arts, what a surprise,
Great sculptor, when you saw your marble come to life,
And with a chaste, sweet air, slowly bend down
To ask you for a pinch of snuff.

(Count Siméon)

"Histoire ancienne" (Ancient history), no. 47; published in
Le Charivari, December 28, 1842 (D. 971).

LENDER: Print Collection, Miriam and Ira D. Wallach
Division of Art, Prints and Photographs. The New York
Public Library, Astor, Lenox, and Tilden Foundations.

Women in the Modern Allegory

ELIZABETH C. CHILDS

DAUMIER'S FEMALE ALLEGORICAL FIGURES are among the most profound and moving images in his lithographic oeuvre.[1] They assume particular importance during the periods when Daumier was able to produce political satire without the threat of rigid censorship laws—that is, during the early years of the July Monarchy (1830–1835), the Second Republic (1848–1852), the late Second Empire (1867–1870), and the Franco-Prussian War (1870–1871).[2] When he sought forms to clothe the political concepts he advocated, such as Peace, Liberty, or the Republic, Daumier used predominantly female imagery to reinforce the symbolic power of his compositions. Women were excellent candidates for these ideated roles, in part because Daumier's audience could not easily confuse them with the real players in world politics, who were primarily men. With a few exceptions, such as Queen Victoria of England, women in Daumier's world did not wield political clout. Moreover, as we stress in our introductory essay in this catalogue, Daumier did not support the demands of women for increased legal rights. Because of their forced exclusion from the political arena, women's appearance in political satire was unexpected. Their mere presence signaled that the caricature had abandoned the sphere of literal human action and had moved into a symbolic realm.

Drawn primarily in the later years of Daumier's career, these monumental satirical personages are characterized by an increasing boldness of caricatural line and a suppression of anecdotal detail. These imposing allegories dominate strikingly simple compositions. Proud, sober, often tragic characters, they star in satires that are often more grotesque or poignant than amusing. Their meanings are varied: Daumier's statuesque women embody such abstract concepts as Peace, Liberty, and Diplomacy; they sometimes represent his ideal form of government, the Republic; they also symbolize temporal units, such as years, or geopolitical areas, such as Paris, France, or even all of Europe.[3] These abstractions inhabit female bodies in the human worlds of the home, the circus, and the battlefield. His mixture of universalizing symbolism with the circumstances of contemporary life results in a provocatively modern allegory.

In his symbolic use of women Daumier draws on a long-standing tradition of allegory in the visual arts. Allegorical figures represent abstract ideas through the substitution of a personage for a concept; the artist transposes meaning onto the figure, which then becomes a formal means to the artist's symbolic end.

These figures do not necessarily illustrate or translate into action the concepts they have been assigned; rather, they are transformed into new entities through the processes of correspondence and personification.[4] Widely accepted codes of meaning allow viewers to identify many classical, Renaissance, and baroque allegories—such as Virtue and Vice—by standard dress, attributes, or settings.[5]

Just as traditional allegorical figures are often based on classical prototypes, Daumier's allegorical females are predominantly classical in appearance; they are usually dressed in the timeless costumes of formless shifts or billowing drapery.[6] In this way Daumier distances them from the contemporary world he so masterfully portrays elsewhere in his social satire. Moreover, these imaginary women are physically distinct from the contemporary women in Daumier's caricature of *moeurs*—their well-developed musculature, imposing stature, and massive hands reflect his study of classical sculpture, Michelangelo, and Delacroix more than his depictions of *parisiennes* do. These symbolic figures inhabit a Parnassus of Daumier's imagination. Their actions often force our attention away from the particularity of current events to broader reflections on the struggle for and survival of ideals in the modern world.

Daumier's use of allegorical symbolism is part of a larger artistic enterprise at mid-century. As realist artists challenged academic tradition, they rejected the historical and mythological themes still favored by the academy in favor of contemporary ones. Yet the desire to address universal issues through the authority and grandeur of symbolic representation remained. Gustave Courbet's canvas *The Painter's Studio* of 1855 (Paris, Musée d'Orsay) demonstrates that symbolism could also be fashioned into a new form of personal expression using realist subjects and styles. In a complex and highly individualized system of allegory, Courbet freely constructed and assigned meaning, using a wide range of modern and seemingly ordinary persons.[7]

Like Courbet, Daumier devises his own symbolic forms out of the tradition of allegory. His women are not strictly defined by any fixed iconographical system; thus they cannot be consistently distinguished by one set of attributes. For example, the same crenellated crown appears on women labeled alternately as Paris (cat. 45), France (D. 3813), Europe (cat. 46), and Peace (D. 3644). The generically symbolic forms of these women are vessels for shifting meanings that are then usually clarified either by the legend or by a word written across their bodies, such as *Paix* or *L'Europe*. Dau-

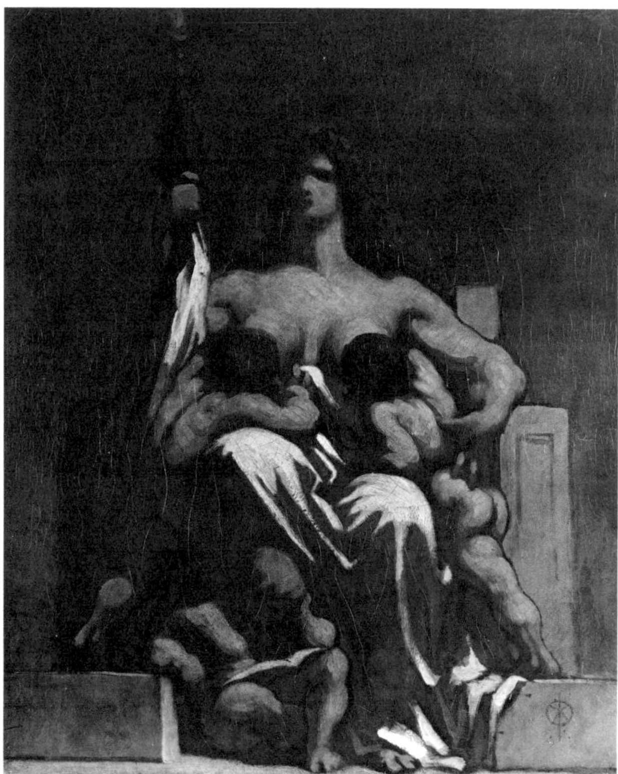

Fig. 7.1 Honoré Daumier.
La République (The Republic), 1848.
Oil on canvas, 28¾ x 23⅝ in. (73 x 60 cm).
Musée d'Orsay, Paris, Donation Etienne Moreau-Nélaton
(Courtesy Photo Bulloz).

mier bends their identities to suit his will and provides the viewer with a label to clarify his intentions. Daumier granted these fictional women powerful voices and essential roles as commentators on their society.[8] They inhabit the man's world: in caricatures that feature actual male politicians and world leaders, Daumier often used a female allegorical figure—a nonhistorical entity—as a vivid foil to the image and actions of specific men. One example is Daumier's dramatic contrast of the generic figure of the Republic with the well-known features of Louis-Philippe's ministers (cat. 47).

While the figures of Daumier's allegorical women are largely interchangeable, those of his male personae are not. He adopts established satirical types, such as Robert Macaire, Monsieur Prud'homme, or Ratapoil, all of whom have easily recognizable physiognomies and costumes. Similarly, the caricatures of actual men tend to be more particularized than those of allegorical women in Daumier's satire, in part because such detail was needed to distinguish the large cast of male characters in the theaters of national and international politics. Even in the few instances when Daumier created male allegorical figures, he codified them more rigorously than his female allegories through a greater adherence to standard iconographical convention.[9]

The French Republic is one of the most important allegorical women in Daumier's work. In French culture, the representation of the Republic as a female dates to the Revolution of 1789.[10] In Daumier's time a classically inspired, goddess-like figure was often merged with the image of Marianne, the popular representation of the French Republic. Marianne is typically depicted in French art as wearing a red Phrygian bonnet, the revolutionary symbol derived from the caps worn by freed slaves in ancient Rome. In some of the popular cults devoted to Marianne, she assumed a quasi-religious status as a mother figure who combined the virtues of the Virgin Mary with the democratic principles of republicanism.[11]

This popular image of a nurturing Marianne informs Daumier's most famous representation of the Republic (fig. 7.1), the oil sketch he entered in the competition of 1848 for a symbolic figure of the new Republic. Daumier's work won eleventh place out of several hundred entries.[12] The new government then commissioned Daumier to enlarge the sketch to a full-scale painting, a task he never completed. The artist's fervent idealism expressed in this canvas had mellowed into resigned cynicism about the Republic by 1849, when Louis-Napoléon Bonaparte had consolidated his power as president.

But in 1848 Daumier's republican idealism found its full expression in the figure of a partially clothed woman sitting squarely on a monumental throne, holding the tricolor flag of France. Two children suckle at her ample breasts; at her feet a third child reads. She is *La Patrie* incarnate, nurturing her offspring, the people of France. Daumier does not articulate her facial features; part of her power derives from the indeterminacy of her countenance. While most of the paintings entered in the competition were painted with a tighter, more Ingresque precision, Daumier's Republic resists detailed definition. Moreover, unlike his fellow artists, Daumier needed no iconographical apparatus beyond the simple French flag to identify his subject. Other depictions of the Republic feature not only flags but sheaves of wheat, lions, scales of justice, stone tablets, and jeweled scepters; Daumier's Republic asserts her authority through more austere means, such as her monumental proportions and her resemblance to the traditional symbol for Charity, a nursing mother.

The Republic, who had appeared in a few of Daumier's lithographs in the July Monarchy, became more prominent in his caricature of the Second Republic.[13] In contrast to the noble and static seated figure of Daumier's painted oil sketch, the Republic of his caricature is an active and dynamic personage. This dualistic view of the Republic—as both passive icon and dynamic heroine—is common in the popular imagery of the French Revolution in the female figure of Liberty, who served as the prototype for the allegorical figures of the First Republic of 1792.[14]

The model of the more dynamic heroine inspires several of Daumier's caricatures of the Republic during the revolutionary year 1848, including *Dernier Conseil des ex-ministres* (cat. 47).[15] This print, published five days after universal suffrage was granted to French men, celebrated the fall of the monarchy and its replacement by the Republic.[16] The resilient Marianne, identifiable by her Phrygian cap, interrupts the last meeting of the counselors of the deposed Louis-Philippe. As she abruptly opens the doors into the darkened house of the French government, brilliant light illuminates the exterior, announcing both the arrival of the new order and the departure of the old through an open window. The generalized physiognomy of the fictional woman, the Republic, contrasts with the specified features of actual men, most notably Adolphe Thiers, whose spectacles, pointed chin, and long nose immediately identified him to the readers of *Le Charivari*. Dramatically opposing the Republic's confident stride with the frenzied panic of fleeing men, Daumier asserts the rightful occupant of the symbolic space.

Not surprisingly, the image of the Republic was proscribed during the Second Empire. She reappears in Daumier's art in the caricatures published in 1870–1871 (cat. 48). Yet her generalized features, imposing form, and classical dress begin to reappear, in only slightly altered form, in many of Daumier's allegorical images of the late, Liberal Empire. Although they are labeled alternately as Peace, France, and Liberty, and although they lack the revolutionary Phrygian cap, these veritable *femmes d'esprit* carry on the spirit of Daumier's Republic. Many of his emblematic women of the late 1860s (D. 3733 and 3747) lack only a shield or an identifying label to symbolize the Republic. The highly flexible nature of Daumier's modern allegory allows him to exploit the multiplicity of associations conveyed by this figure to his republican readers. His allegories still carry the authority and impact of traditional symbology—they represent those entities with whose names they are inscribed. Yet their repetitive and generalized appearance also permit an important inflection of additional meaning by invoking the viewer's memory of earlier, similar, republican symbols.

Daumier's allegorical women (including both the Republic and her manifestations as France, Peace, Paris, and Liberty) often appear in conventional female roles as wives, mothers, homemakers, and lovers. This domestication of the Republic is consistent with Daumier's idealization of her as a maternal figure in his canvas of 1848 (see fig. 7.1). Some of his allegorical women appear as modern *parisiennes,* in many of the same situations found in Daumier's satires of the bourgeoise discussed in my essay earlier in this catalogue. Her presence in a domestic setting invited interpretation of her as symbolic mistress and homemaker. For example, the historian Jules Michelet characterized the power of Daumier's Republic in *Dernier Conseil des ex-ministres* through such a metaphor of domestic authority. In a letter to Daumier that reveals Michelet's convictions that women belonged *only* in the home, he wrote:

You have demonstrated, even to the simple-minded, the rights of the Republic. She is returning home; she finds thieves at the table, who fall back in disarray. She has the strength and assurance of the mistress of the house. Here at last she is shown as she is, and her right to be here is clear to all. She alone is at home in France.[17]

The metaphor of France as a tidy housekeeper also appears in several of Daumier's caricatures of the late Second Empire, in which France sweeps out the trash of imperialism (D. 3813 and 3903). Daumier's France is not just a housecleaner; she can be as refined a mistress of her home as any well-raised bourgeoise: she sings and plays the piano (D. 3717); she entertains her guests with a magic-lantern show (D. 3745), and, as Peace she coyly plays shuttlecock with War (D. 3701). Again as Peace, she exchanges polite "kisses of circumstance" with Europe, in the manner of acquaintances fulfilling the obligations of etiquette (D. 3565). And in a gesture worthy of any fashion-conscious bourgeoise, Liberty instructs her seamstress, the Constitution, not to shorten her dress too much (cat. 49).

Daumier also feminizes his allegories by casting the figures as young girls being courted or, ultimately, as mothers. The personages receive the attentions of suitors with varying degrees of tolerance and interest. Liberty may discourage a flock of men seeking her hand (D. 3712). In one stirring image of 1851 the Republic disdainfully rejects the arm of the sleazy Ratapoil, Louis-Napoléon's fictional agent, whose passion is too sudden for her to believe (cat. 18).[18] Later, in 1870, France appears as a pregnant woman beginning labor, delivering a new Republic (D. 3784). Although the imposing statures of these allegorical figures assert their symbolic missions, these beings gesture as ordinary women do. Moreover, their bodies are "feminine" according to nineteenth-century conventions: supple arms and prettified faces appear on many of these figures. A comparison of the graceful bearing of Liberty in cat. 49 with the robust figure of the weight-lifting Europe in cat. 46 suggests that Daumier saved the heavily muscled bodies for symbolic women engaged in conventionally masculine activity.

Not all of Daumier's allegorical women occupy the traditional feminine domains of domesticity and love. Many of them frequent the more glamorous and artificial realms of carnival, circus, and sideshow. Filling the foreground of the compositions, their figures often occupy a clearing ringed by distant observers (cat. 50). Thus the viewer becomes an extension of this audience. In these prints, Daumier establishes a fictional circus in the journal aptly called *Le Charivari,* a name that implies both an uproarious din and the satiric rituals of folk celebration. Under the big top of Daumier's satire, parody, comedy, and burlesque combine harmoniously. His noble allegories step into their roles as clowns, acrobats, and magicians. As in a real circus, they titillate their audience through a combination of comic behavior and physical risk—the viewer's excitement is heightened by the realization that behind all the glamor of the performance the possibility of injury is very real.

During the late Second Empire, as threats of war shook Europe, the circus was an excellent metaphor for the arena of international politics. In 1867, the year in which Paris hosted an elaborate International Exhibition, Europe's powers put their differences aside long enough to participate in the fair. In Daumier's print *Aussi forte que le chinois de l'hippodrome,* Peace performs a sword-swallowing act to entertain the crowd, identified by their diverse hats as various European nations (cat. 50). The brave feat of Peace's daring spectacle temporarily disarms Europe, as indeed the International Exhibition did that summer. Yet as many of Daumier's caricatures from that same year stress, this peaceful

hiatus is only temporary (D. 3583); just as a sword swallower never actually ingests a knife blade, Daumier's performer must soon remove the blade from her throat.

The precariousness of European peace is a central theme in Daumier's work of 1867. In one bold and simplified composition (fig. 7.2), he transforms Europe into an acrobat who struggles to keep her balance. She risks losing control of a ball which is actually a smoking bomb. In a print of the following year, a female Europe assumes the guise of a strongman lifting an enormous weight (cat. 46). This heavily muscled Europe supports the obese, seated figure of the Turkish sultan, leader of the Ottoman Empire, which had been draining the resources and patience of Europe over the previous several decades.[19] Although these circus acts were traditionally performed by men, Daumier's caricatures often reject and reverse typical gender roles. This transgression of convention underscores the fictional

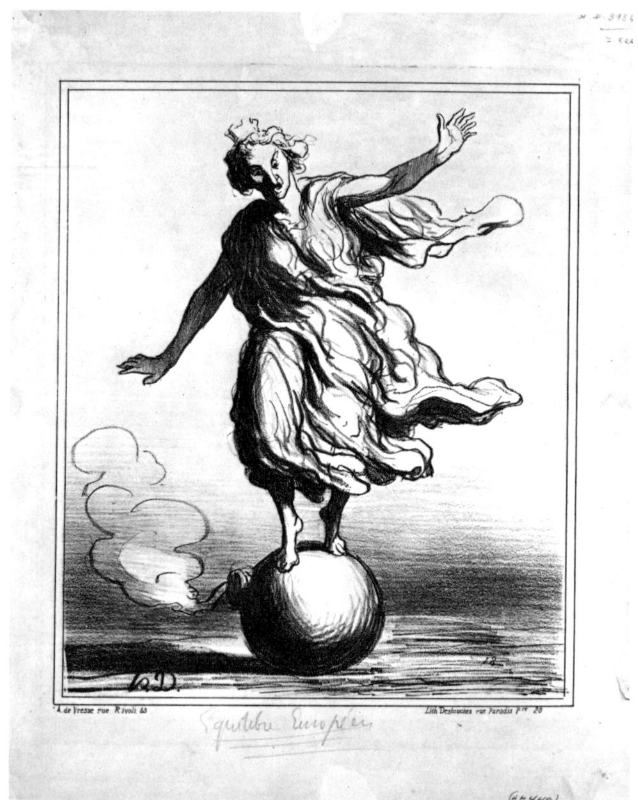

Fig. 7.2 Honoré Daumier.
Equilibre européen (European equilibrium), 1867.
Proof before letters of lithograph published in *Le Charivari,*
April 3, 1867 (D. 3566).
National Gallery of Art, Washington, D. C., Rosenwald Collection.

and symbolic nature of his allegories. Daumier's show also includes, however, the more usual female circus performers, such as the Fat Lady, who personifies the aggressive Prussia (D. 3607), and the hypnotized figure of Europe, who sleeps in a trance, magically suspended over the bayonets of war (D. 3552).

The world of the circus and traveling saltimbanques, one of Daumier's favorite motifs, appears throughout his prints, paintings, and drawings. The circus performer in Daumier's art may be interpreted as a surrogate figure for the artist himself—the clown, like the caricaturist, amuses his audience with wit and skill. Yet Daumier's focus on the saltimbanque has a more poignant dimension, for these popular entertainers were repressed by Second Empire law. In Daumier's images of clowns, comic facades often mask the personal tragedies of these victims of Napoléon III's modernization, which did not accommodate this raffish form of folk entertainment.[20]

This paradox of a comedy tinged with tragedy also applies to the sober humor of Daumier's clowning allegories. As the more tolerant Liberal Empire of Napoléon III unshackled political commentary once again, Daumier's clowns and entertainers came on stage to mount a critique of the circus of world politics. With his allegorical troupe, Daumier gives new form to his own double identity as entertainer and serious critic:

these fictional beings embody the artist's ideals, while the danger of their performances suggests his fears. These women who juggle and balance international crises at their own peril not only amuse and impress us, but they also elicit our sympathy for Daumier's views— those of a committed pacifist who dreads the loss of international peace.

Daumier's prophecies about the outbreak of war came true in 1870–1871 with the Franco-Prussian War. The German defeat of Napoléon III at Sedan in September 1870 was followed by two brutal sieges of Paris—first, by the Germans throughout the fall and early winter of 1870–1871; and then by the French government troops against the Communards of Paris in the late spring of 1871.[21] The cost in human life and suffering was immense. Yet throughout these desperate months, *Le Charivari* continued publication, though in a smaller format that required less paper, a precious commodity during the siege.[22]

During the siege of Paris, the image of Marianne reappears in the pages of *Le Charivari* to inspire and comfort her people.[23] Yet as the death and illness caused by the blockade increased, the caricatures in the journal reflected an increasingly sober and despairing mood. Daumier again invoked his repertoire of symbolic females to comment on the crisis. In blatant mockery of Napoléon III's famous campaign slogan,

Fig. 7.3 Honoré Daumier.
Rue Transnonian, le 15 avril, 1834.
Lithograph; published in *L'Association mensuelle,* plate 24, July 1834.
The Armand Hammer Collection, Los Angeles, California.

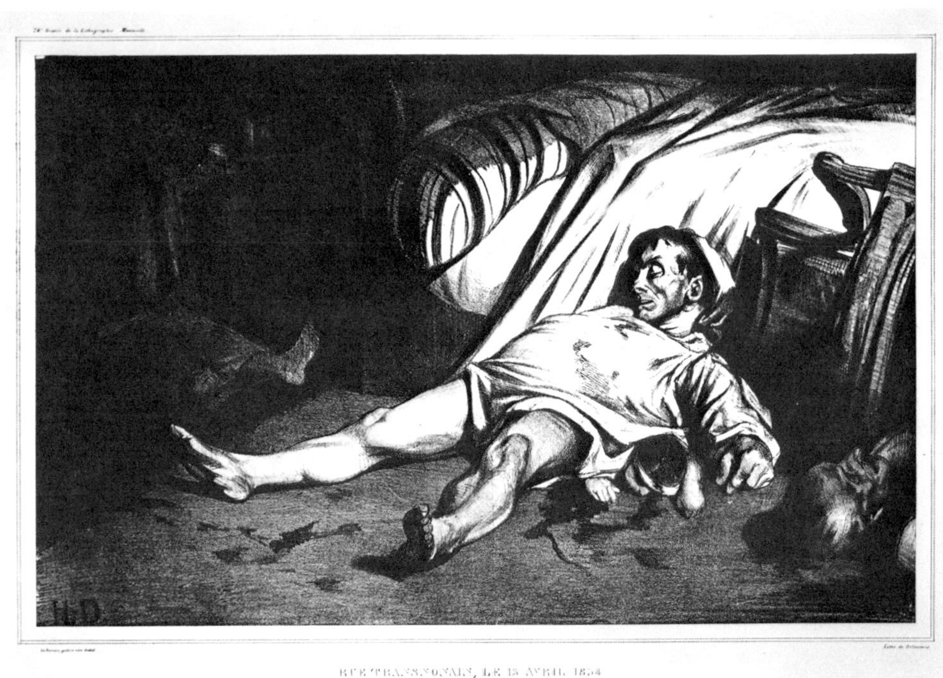

"The Empire Means Peace," Daumier creates a vivid landscape of the destruction of Paris (cat. 51). The intensely black rubble in the foreground and the blackened clouds of the sky create a startling frame for our oblique view of a ravaged street. In the right foreground lies a dead woman, whose loosely draped clothing is hauntingly reminiscent of Daumier's figures of Peace and Paris, as if they too have been vanquished along with this victim.

Elsewhere, in an image of poignant and compelling simplicity, a grief-stricken figure representing the year 1871 steps onto a battlefield strewn with corpses, her inheritance from the bloody previous year (cat. 52). Her cloak and hands completely hide her face; Daumier achieves the emotional intensity of this figure through the brilliant device of the shuddering contour of her garment and weeping body. Her dark, shrouded figure, silhouetted against a chillingly empty horizon, recalls the austerity of Parisian neoclassical mortuary reliefs, in which weeping women are similarly isolated against a symbolically blank background.[24]

In several grim scenes Daumier's heroic figures of Paris and France become emblematic victims of the war. In the devastated landscape of *Autres Candidats,* a flock of crows sweeps toward the body of France, lying dead on her shield (cat. 53).[25] The diagonal placement of the brutalized corpse in the foreground echoes in reverse the composition of Daumier's famous commemoration of an earlier massacre, the *Rue Transnonain* of 1834 (fig. 7.3), which represents the innocent victims of a violent government reprisal.[26] Although both scenes reverberate with the pathos of martyrdom, the earlier lithograph requires the depiction of an entire family: a dead father collapses across the body of his son, while the head of his own murdered father appears in the right foreground. Through a network of crossing diagonal lines and a sweeping shaft of light, Daumier emphasizes the body of the fallen father, who symbolizes the tragedy of both this particular family and the French people in general. The only woman in this scene lies strewn over the threshold at the upper left, in the same dramatically foreshortened position as that of France in *Autres Candidats.* Although also a victim of the same catastrophe, she is peripheral to Daumier's patriarchal metaphor for the disruption of the social fabric by this bloody massacre.

Although inspired by the Franco-Prussian War and the Commune, Daumier's later work is generally less literal in its references to particular events. In the forty years that separate the *Rue Transnonain* and *Autres Can-*

didats, as Daumier's work grew increasingly symbolic, he developed the expressive potential of female allegory. It is as if the dead woman in the periphery of the *Rue Transnonain* has slid from her position of shadowed obscurity into the foreground of symbolic presence. In the earlier image, woman was a marginalized detail in a predominantly male tragedy; in Daumier's later work women take center stage in the popular theater of his political satire. In allegorical form they play out the farces of the collapsing Second Empire and the tragic encores of the Commune.

NOTES

1   An exhaustive list of Daumier's allegorical figures is found in Louis Provost, *Honoré Daumier: A Thematic Guide to the Oeuvre,* ed. Elizabeth C. Childs (New York and London: Garland Publishing, 1989), pp. 61–62.

2   The most comprehensive survey of the impact of censorship on French caricature is Robert Goldstein, *Censorship of Political Caricature in Nineteenth-Century France* (Kent, Oh.: The Kent State University Press, 1989). For a discussion of the impact of censorship on the history of *Le Charivari,* see Elizabeth C. Childs, "Daumier and the Exotic Vision: Studies in French Caricature and Culture, 1830–1870," Ph.D. diss., Columbia University, 1989, chap. 1.

3   A brief discussion of Daumier's allegorical women is Ann Morrissey, *Daumier on Women: The Lithographs,* exh. cat. (Los Angeles: University Art Galleries, University of Southern California, 1982), pp. 18–20. An excellent study of Daumier's representations of Europe is André Stoll, *Die Rückkehr der Barbaren: Europäer und "Wilde" in der Karikatur Honoré Daumiers,* exh. cat. (Hamburg: Hans Christians for the Kunsthalle der Stadt Bielefeld, 1985), pp. 425–63. He discusses the following lithographs included in the present exhibition: cat. 46, 50, and 53.

4   A useful general discussion of the theory of allegory is Angus Fletcher, *Allegory: The Theory of a Symbolic Mode* (Ithaca, N.Y.: Cornell University Press, 1964).

5   A classic study of allegory in Renaissance and baroque art is Rudolf Wittkower, *Allegory and the Migration of Symbols* (London: Thames and Hudson, 1977). An important study of the representation of women in allegorical art is Marina Warner, *Monuments and Maidens: The Allegory of the Female Form* (New York: Atheneum, 1985).

6   Exceptions to this generalization include a few European countries symbolized as women who appear in contemporary nineteenth-century dress, such as Spain (D. 3677) and Austria (D. 3511).

7   Courbet described his painting *The Painter's Studio* as a "real allegory" of seven years of his life as an artist. In a curious fusion of the symbolic and the literal, Courbet uses contemporary figures not only to describe his personal world of family,

friends, and patrons but also to allude to broader issues such as famine and political corruption. See Hélène Toussaint, "The Dossier on *The Studio* by Courbet," in *Gustave Courbet,* exh. cat. (London: Arts Council of Great Britain, 1978), pp. 249–79. The painting is clearly intended to be symbolic, but its meaning is tantalizingly hermetic, as demonstrated by the wide range of interpretations offered in subsequent art-historical analysis. The allegorical role of the central nude female model who gazes over the artist's shoulder as he paints is an especially enigmatic combination of realism and symbolism. She is both an ordinary and unidealized woman, who has disrobed to model, and a muse-like presence, symbolic of Truth, Nature, and perhaps even of Representation itself. See Michael Fried, "Representing Representation: On the Central Group in Courbet's *Studio,*" in *Allegory and Representation,* ed. Stephen J. Greenblatt, Selected Papers from the English Institute, 1979–1980, new series, no. 5 (Baltimore: The Johns Hopkins University Press, 1981), pp. 94–127.

8   An interesting parallel emerges between Daumier's manipulation of the image of women with his racist appropriation of exotic personages for political satire. For example, during the Second Empire, Daumier transformed the image of the black Haitian emperor, Faustin Soulouque, into a surrogate figure for Emperor Napoléon III. See Elizabeth C. Childs, "The Secret Agents of Satire: Daumier, Censorship, and the Image of the Exotic in Political Caricature, 1850–1860," in the forthcoming *Proceedings of the Western Society for French History, 1989.*

9   A minority of Daumier's symbolic personages are male, such as Father Time, or Mars, the embodiment of war. Unlike the allegorical women, however, the allegorical men generally require no labels for the viewer to understand the image; one can identify them by their standard attributes based on iconographical convention—Father Time carries his scythe (D. 3754), and Mars wears his armor and helmet (D. 3716). A few symbolic male figures are based on classical mythology, such as a depiction of the year 1869 as the mythological character Sisyphus, who pushes the budget up the hills of hell (D. 3694). Men appear most commonly in Daumier's caricature not as allegorical figures but as general types, characteristic of their age, class, or métier; as famous men, such as politicians or monarchs of the day; or as the embodiments of specific nations or political parties, such as Austria or Bonapartism. Although one can isolate various exceptions to this broad generalization, it is nonetheless true that Daumier particularizes his symbolic male personages more than his symbolic females.

A few of Daumier's allegorical figures are hermaphroditic. Despite long hair and flowing drapery, their bodies are so heavily muscled and so distinctly flat-chested that a clear identification of the figures as female is impossible. In one instance, Daumier fuses the female personification of France with a male mythological character, Prometheus, to create a tragic figure whose sex is ambiguous (D. 3847). Such generalization distances these allegorical figures even further from daily reality.

10 See Maurice Agulhon, *Marianne into Battle: Republican Imagery and Symbolism in France, 1789–1880,* trans. Janet Lloyd (Cambridge: Cambridge University Press, 1981).

11 Agulhon, *Marianne into Battle,* pp. 128–29. Agulhon demonstrates how flexible the character and roles of Marianne could be in the hands of republican writers. For example, the ardent republican Félix Pyat praises Marianne alternately as the Republic, a Virgin, a Goddess, and a Mother. Similarly, Daumier's allegorical Republic fills many roles.

12 The most comprehensive study of the painting competition for the figure of the Republic in 1848 is Marie-Claude Chaudonneret, *La Figure de la République: Le Concours de 1848,* Notes et Documents des Musées de France, no. 13 (Paris: Editions de la Réunion des musées nationaux, 1987). There was also a sculptural competition for the figure of the Republic. The close connection between the figures of the Republic and those of Liberty or Justice is confirmed by the directive of Nieuwerkerke, head of the fine arts under Napoléon III, to the artist Soitoux to transform his figure of the Republic, which had won the competition of 1848, into a figure of Justice or Liberty. See Albert Boime, *Hollow Icons: The Politics of Sculpture in Nineteenth-Century France* (Kent, Oh.: Kent State University Press, 1987), p. 58.

13 The figure of the Republic—usually Marianne wearing a Phrygian bonnet—appears earlier in Daumier's caricatures of 1834 and 1835 in D. 84, 93, 111, and 210. The related allegorical figure of France wearing a crenellated crown appears in Daumier's early work of the July Monarchy in D. 114, 206, and 237. A thorough examination of Daumier's representation of the Republic throughout his entire career is Helmut Hartwig, "Die Republik und andere allegorische Frauengestalten: Zum Verhältnis von Bild und Begriff bei Daumier," in *Honoré Daumier und die ungelösten Probleme der bürgerlichen Gesellschaft,* exh. cat. (Berlin: Neue Gesellschaft für bildende Kunst for the Schloss Charlottenburg, 1974), pp. 80–100.

14 In his study of the popular imagery of Marianne, Maurice Agulhon distinguishes two traditions of the allegorical figure of Liberty at the time of the French Revolution. One is a solemn, calm, and grand woman, often seated, who is fully clothed in the classical style. The other is a young, active, semi-clothed woman, whose dress is often short, and whose breasts are often partially exposed; Agulhon, *Marianne into Battle,* p. 16. This latter personification informs romantic representations of a militant Marianne as an Amazon-like warrior, as in Delacroix's *Liberty Leading the People* of 1830 (Paris, Musée du Louvre). In a recent study of the convention of the "slipped chiton" of female allegorical figures, Marina Warner argues that the frequent exposure of the breast of the autonomous and powerful figures of Liberty and the Republic reinforces their allegorical identity; the semi-nudity of these fictional women is more an emphatic sign of their inviolacy than an erotic signal of a sexualized body; Warner, "The Slipped Chiton," in *Monuments and Maidens.* Similarly, there is nothing erotic about Daumier's semi-nude depiction of the Republic in his oil sketch of 1848. Her bare chest facilitates her symbolic action of nourishing her children. Enthroned in an abstract world, her body is liberated from the sexualized conventions of more earthly domains. Yet significantly, when Daumier transports her from her noble Olympian throne to the domestic and social circumstances of ordinary life, he slips the chiton back up on her shoulder. The Republic of his caricatures is a modest, chaste, and fully

clothed lady, whose classical dress conforms to nineteenth-century notions of propriety.

15 For a discussion of Daumier's other figures of the Republic in his caricature of the Second Republic, see Judith Wechsler's essay in this catalogue.

16 On the history of the early Second Republic, see Maurice Agulhon, *The Republican Experiment, 1848–1852,* trans. Janet Lloyd, The Cambridge History of Modern France series (Cambridge: Cambridge University Press, 1983), chap. 2.

17 As quoted in Roger Passeron, *Daumier* (New York: Rizzoli, 1981), pp. 157–58. Michelet's views that the natural and necessary domain of all women should be home and family were widely circulated during the Second Empire in his books *L'Amour* (1858) and *La Femme* (1860). See Claire Moses, *French Feminism in the Nineteenth Century* (Albany, N.Y.: S.U.N.Y. Press, 1984), pp. 158–61.

18 On the development of Ratapoil, see T. J. Clark, *The Absolute Bourgeois* (Greenwich, Conn.: The New York Graphic Society, 1973), pp. 116–17; and Joachim Heusinger von Weldeg, *Kunst + Documentation: Honoré Daumier, Ratapoil um 1850/1851,* exh. cat. (Mannheim: Städtische Kunsthalle, 1980).

19 On Daumier's caricatures of the Ottoman Empire and the Eastern Question, see Childs, "Daumier and the Exotic Vision," chap. 6.

20 Paula Hays Harper, "Daumier's Clowns: *Les Saltimbanques et Les Parades,* New Biographical and Political Functions for a Nineteenth-Century Myth," Ph.D. diss., Stanford University, 1976.

21 Following Napoléon III's defeat by the Germans at the Battle of Sedan in September 1870 the emperor was deposed. The Germans surrounded Paris and conducted a relentless siege against the famine- and disease-ridden city until January 28, 1871. Adolphe Thiers, the new chief executive of the provisional national government, negotiated a peace with the Germans, but resistant factions in Paris refused to submit to the new government of Thiers. These Parisians established a governing council known as the Commune, and Thiers mounted a second siege against the city which lasted from April to May of 1871. Thiers's troops finally succeeded in penetrating Paris, but only after the Communards had burned the Tuileries Palace and other major governmental buildings. In the bloody reprisals that followed, some 17,000 Parisians were executed, and many more were exiled or imprisoned. In August 1871 Thiers became president of the Third Republic. See Robert Baldick, *The Siege of Paris* (London: The History Book Club, 1964). On caricatures of the Commune, see Susan Lambert, The *Franco-Prussian War and the Commune in Caricature, 1870–1871,* exh. cat. (London: Victoria and Albert Museum, 1971).

22 *Le Charivari* (September 25, 1870).

23 See, for example, the caricature of Marianne by Alfred Grevin in *Le Charivari* (September 25, 1870).

24 An example is the bronze relief *Femme voilée devant un tombeau,* made by Paul Cabet in 1866 for his wife's tomb in the Montparnasse Cemetery of Paris. See *La Sculpture française au XIXe siècle,* exh. cat. (Paris: Editions de la Réunion des musées nationaux, 1986), p. 270.

25 Daumier's portrayal of a flock of scavenging birds sweeping toward the corpse of France recalls a gruesome caricature by Grandville, *La France livrée aux corbeaux de toute espérance,* published in *La Caricature* (October 15, 1831). The body of Grandville's France, chained to a barren plain, is pecked by monstrous crows who wear the decorations of Louis-Philippe's ministers.

26 For a discussion of the Rue Transnonain, see Edwin de T. Bechtel, *Freedom of the Press and L'Association Mensuelle—Philipon Versus Louis-Philippe* (New York: The Grolier Club, 1952), pl. XXIV.

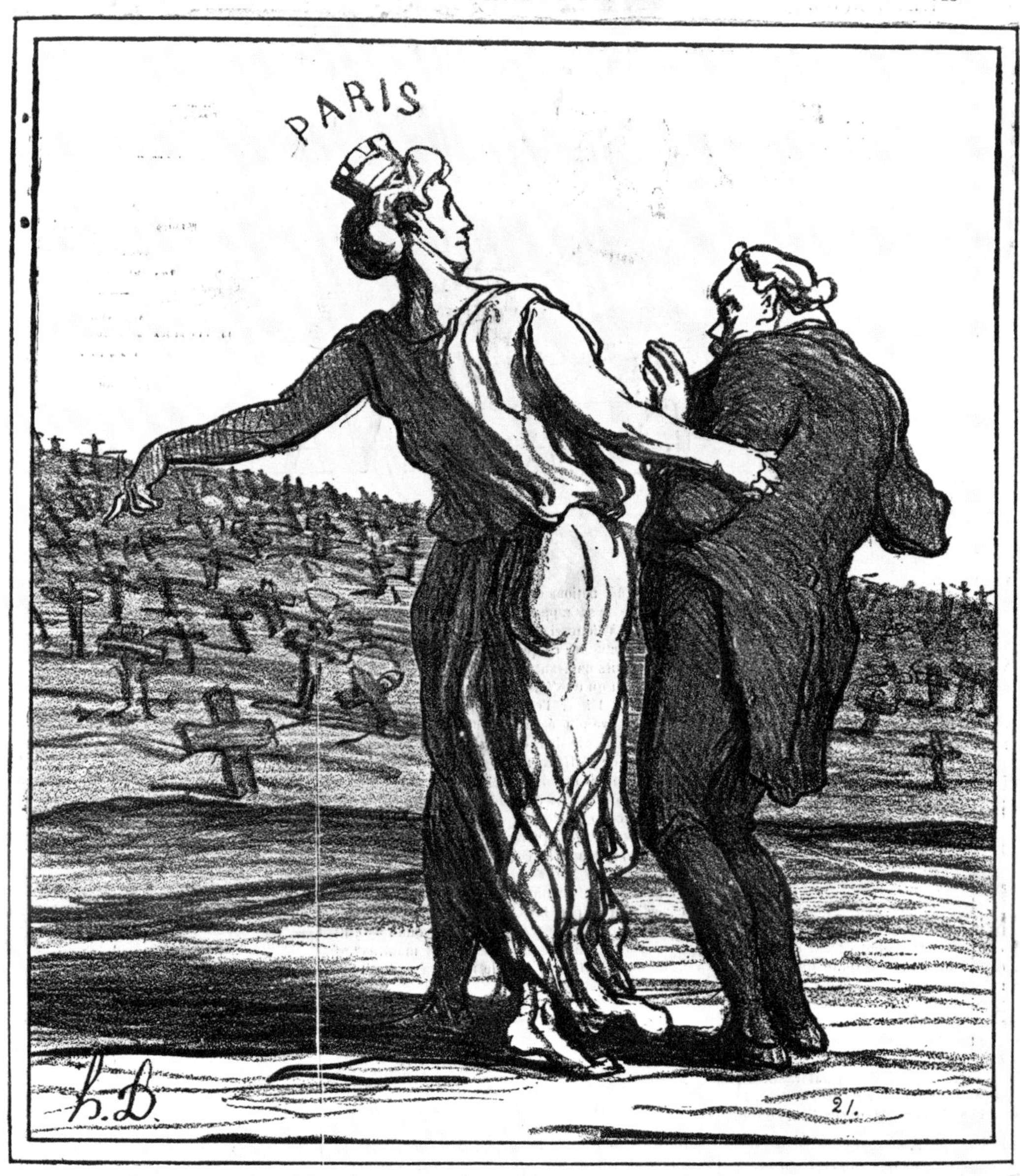

— Voyons, monsieur Réac, il y en a pourtant bien assez !

Cat. 45

—*Voyons, Monsieur Réac, il y en a pourtant bien assez!*

—Come on, Monsieur Reactionary, there are enough already!

"Actualités" (Current events), no. 343; published in
Le Charivari, March 30, 1871 (D. 3858).

LENDER: The Rose Art Museum, Brandeis University,
Waltham, Massachusetts, The Benjamin A. and
Julia M. Trustman Collection.

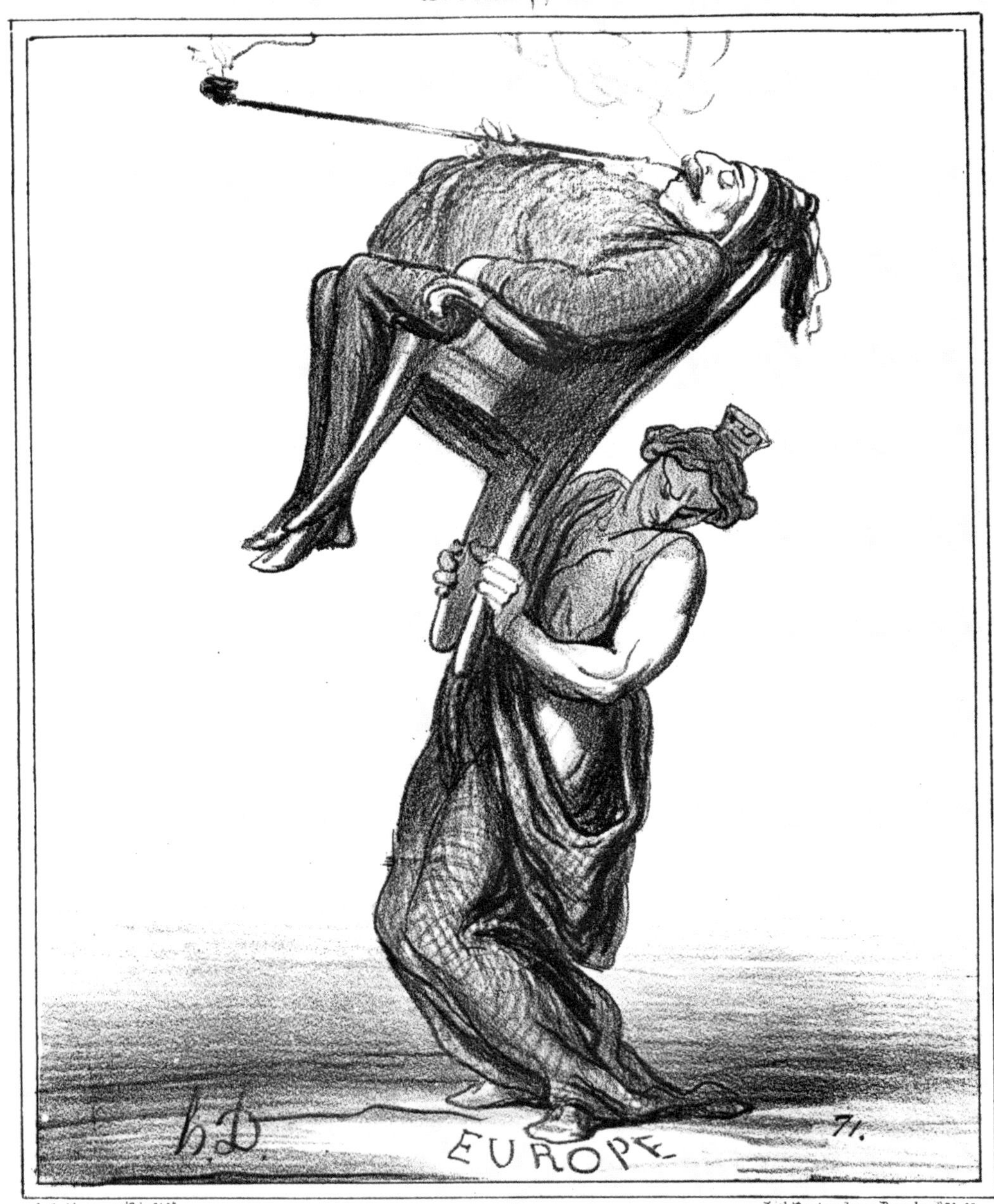

Une situation qui commence à devenir fatigante

Cat. 46

Une Situation qui commence à devenir fatiguante.

A situation that is beginning to get tiring.

Published in *Le Charivari,* January 10, 1868 (D. 3617).

LENDER: Museum of Fine Arts, Boston, Bequest
of William P. Babcock.

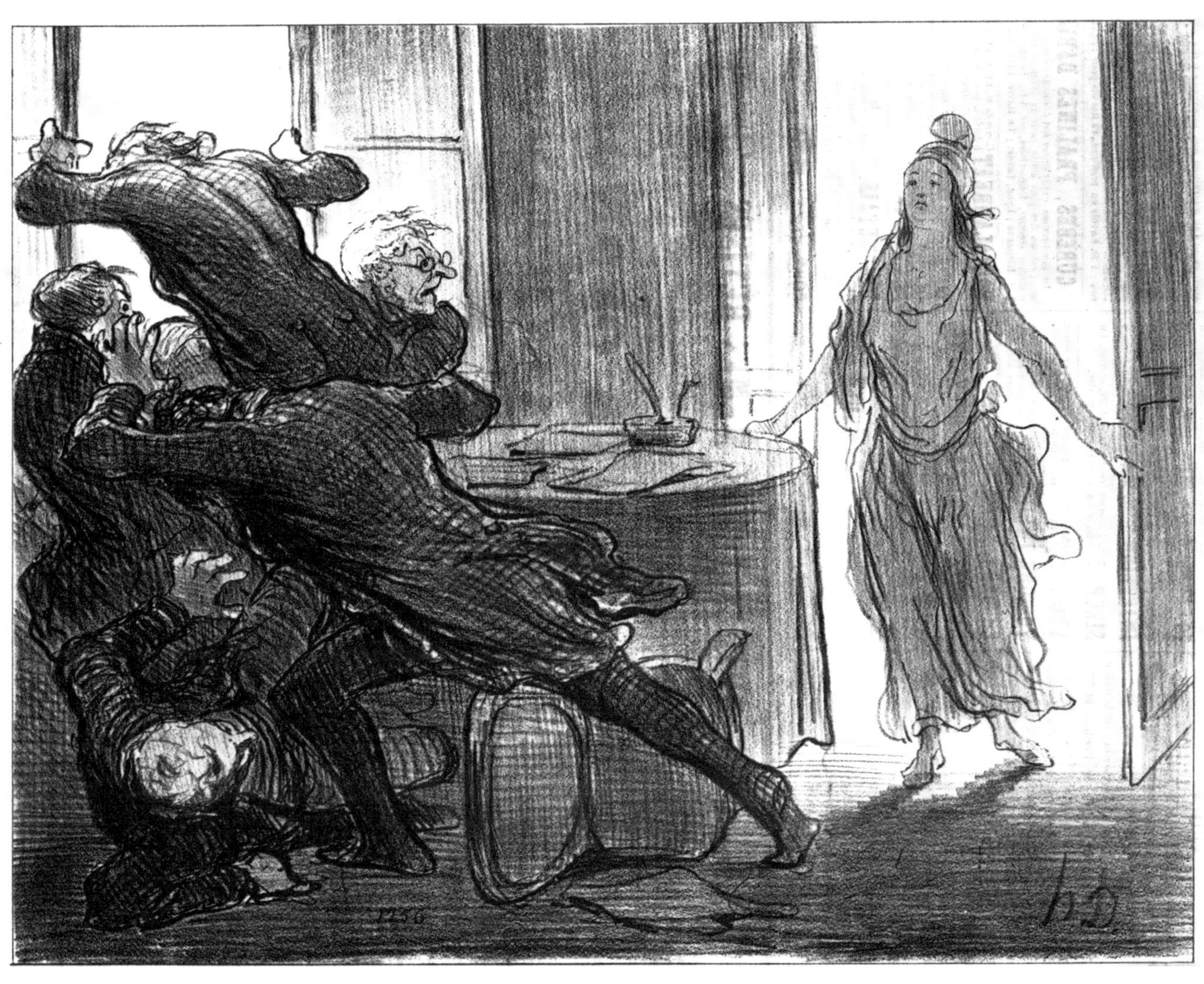

Cat. 47

Dernier Conseil des ex-ministres.

The last meeting of the ex-ministers.

Published in *Le Charivari,* March 9, 1848 (D. 1746).

LENDER: Museum of Fine Arts, Boston.

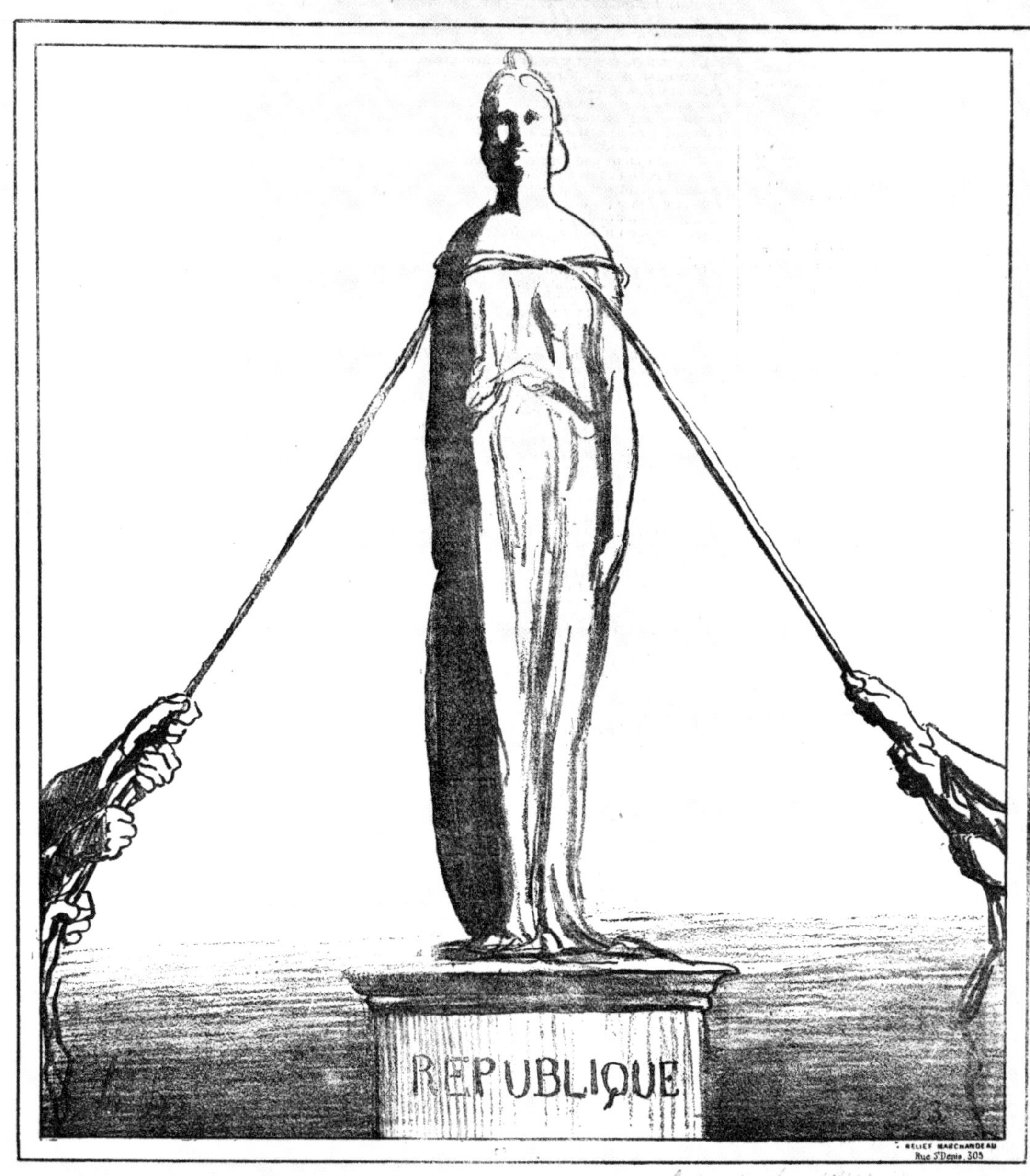

— Tirez, ça fait équilibre.

Cat. 48

—*Tirez, ça fait équilibre.*

—Pull, that will bring it into balance.

"Actualités" (Current events), no. 668; published in
Le Charivari, November 25, 1871 (D. 3891).

LENDER: Museum of Fine Arts, Boston, Bequest
of W. G. Russell Allen.

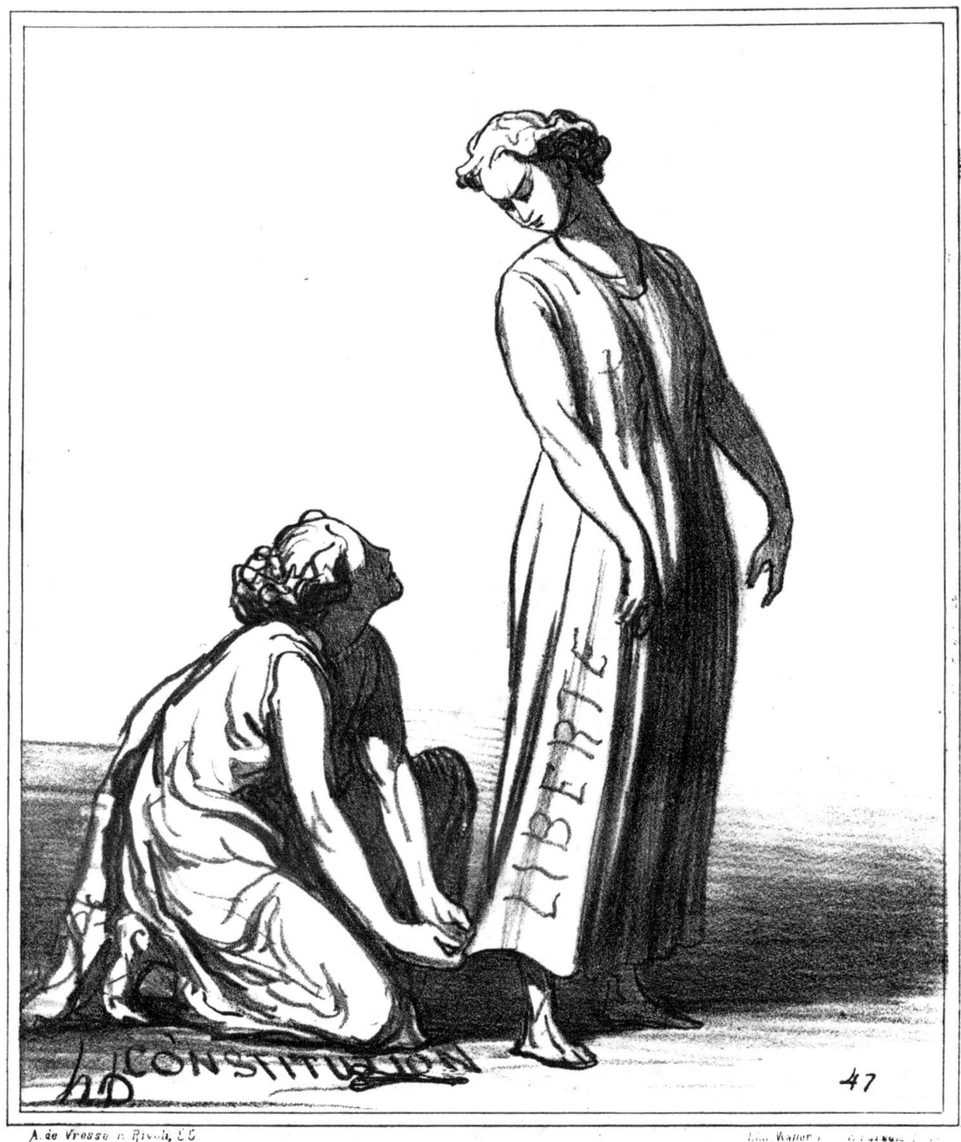

Cat. 49

Pas trop écourté, s'il vous plait.

Not too short, please.

"Actualités" (Current events), no. 192; published in
Le Charivari, August 23, 1869 (D. 3731).

LENDER: Museum of Fine Arts, Boston, Bequest
of William P. Babcock.

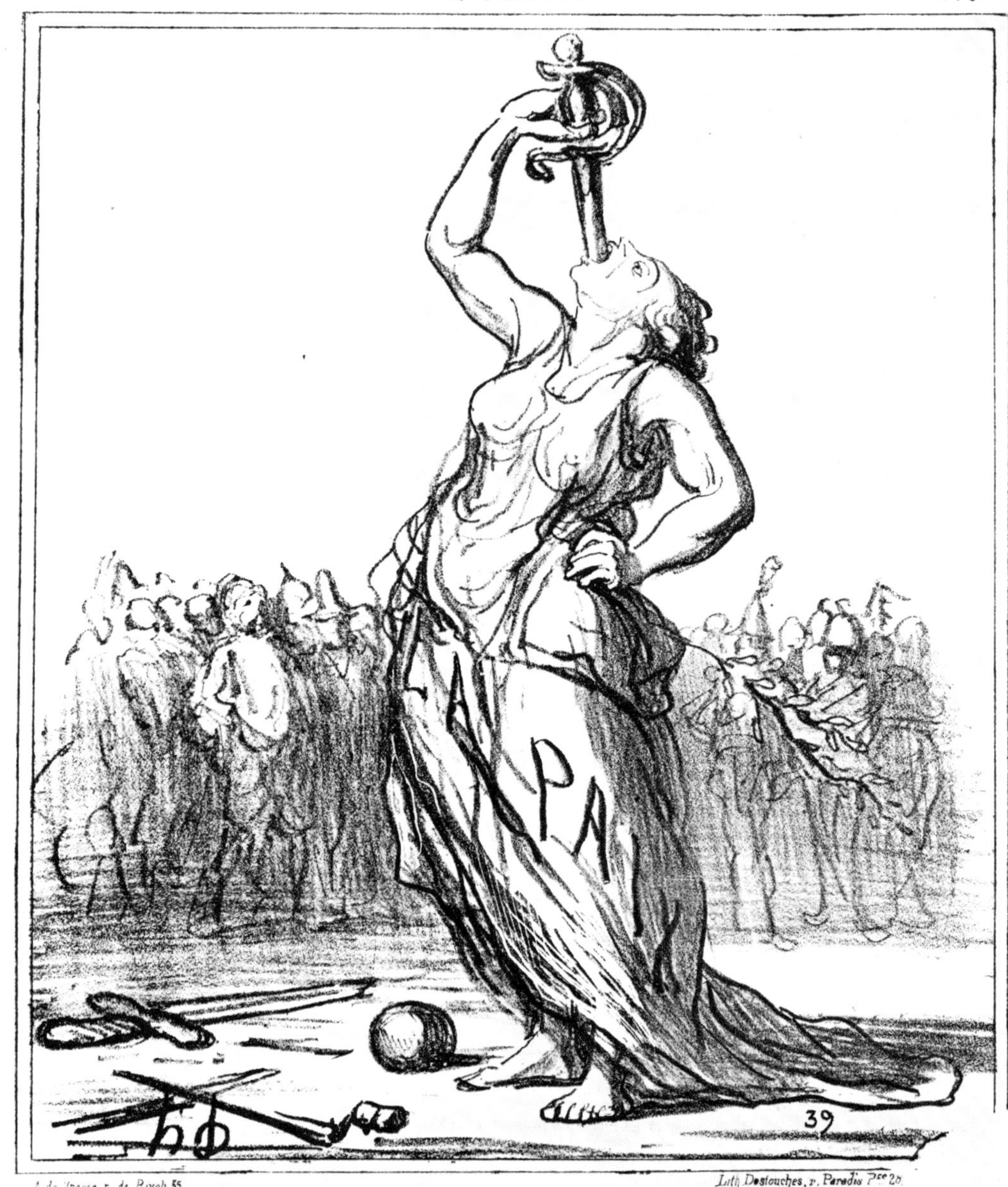

Aussi forte que le Chinois de l'Hippodrome la paix! en avale t'elle de ces lames de sabre !

Cat. 50

Aussi forte que le Chinois de l'Hippodrome, la paix! en avale t'elle de ces lames de sabre!

As strong as the Chinese man at the Hippodrome, peace! She swallows these sabre blades for you!

Published in *Le Charivari,* August 1, 1867 (D. 3585).

LENDER: The Metropolitan Museum of Art, Bequest of Edwin De T. Bechtel, 1957 (57.650.249).

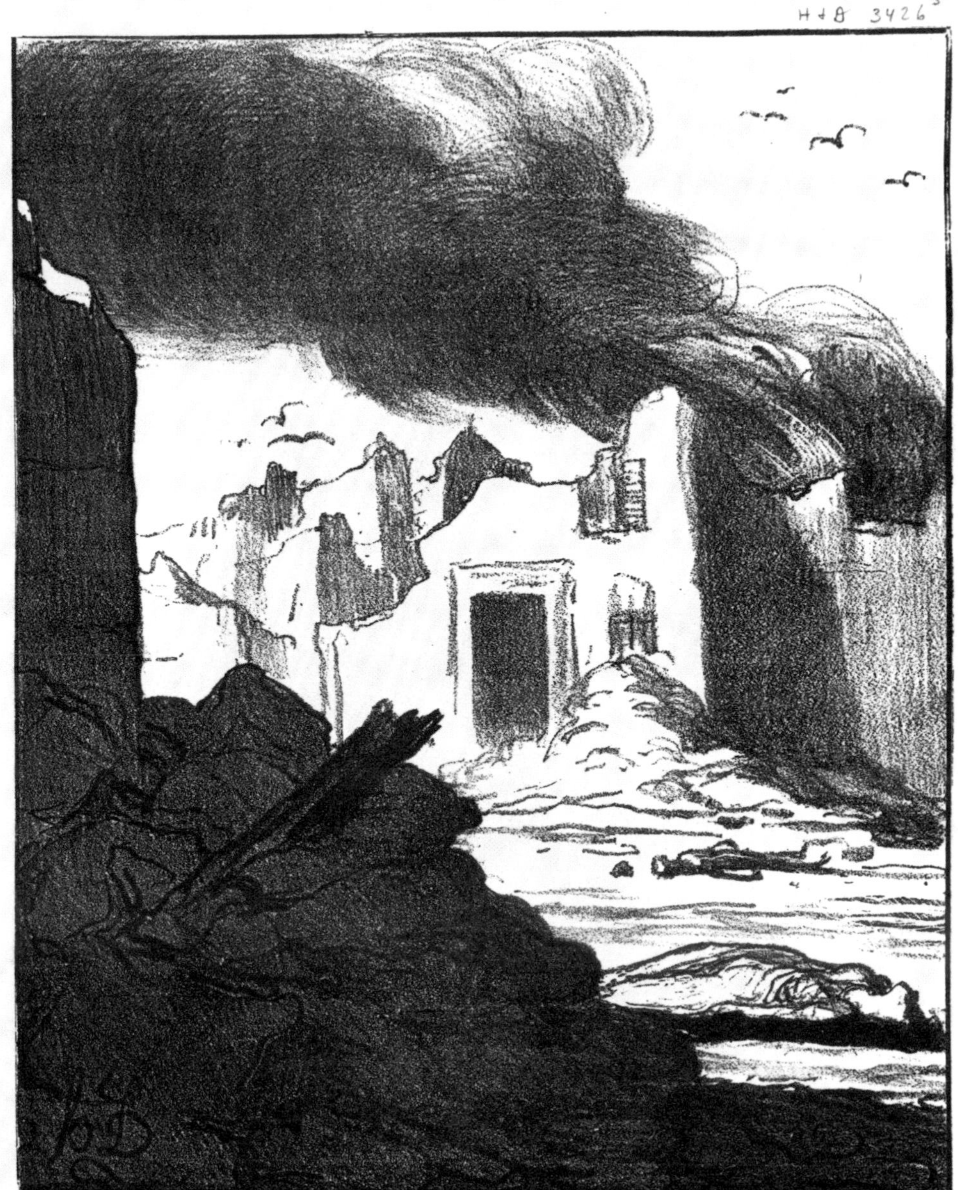

Cat. 51

L'Empire, c'est la paix.

The empire: peace.

"Actualités" (Current events), no. 232; published in
Le Charivari, October 19, 1870 (D. 3814).

LENDER: Print Collection, Miriam and Ira D. Wallach
Division of Art, Prints and Photographs. The New York
Public Library, Astor, Lenox, and Tilden Foundations.

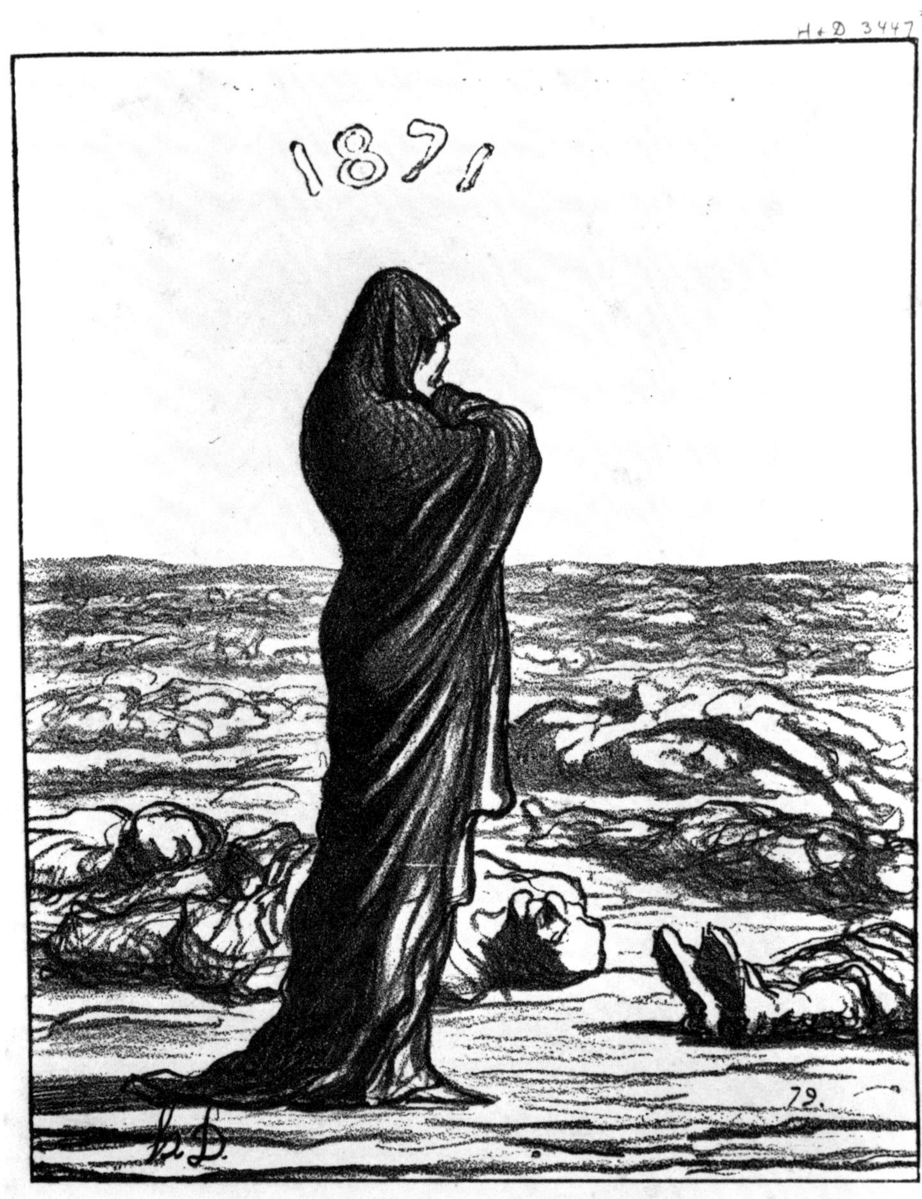

ÉPOUVANTÉE DE L'HÉRITAGE.

Cat. 52

Epouvantée de l'héritage.

Horrified at the legacy.

"Actualités" (Current events), no. 280; published in
Le Charivari, January 11, 1871 (D. 3838).

LENDER: Print Collection, Miriam and Ira D. Wallach
Division of Art, Prints and Photographs. The New York
Public Library, Astor, Lenox, and Tilden Foundations.

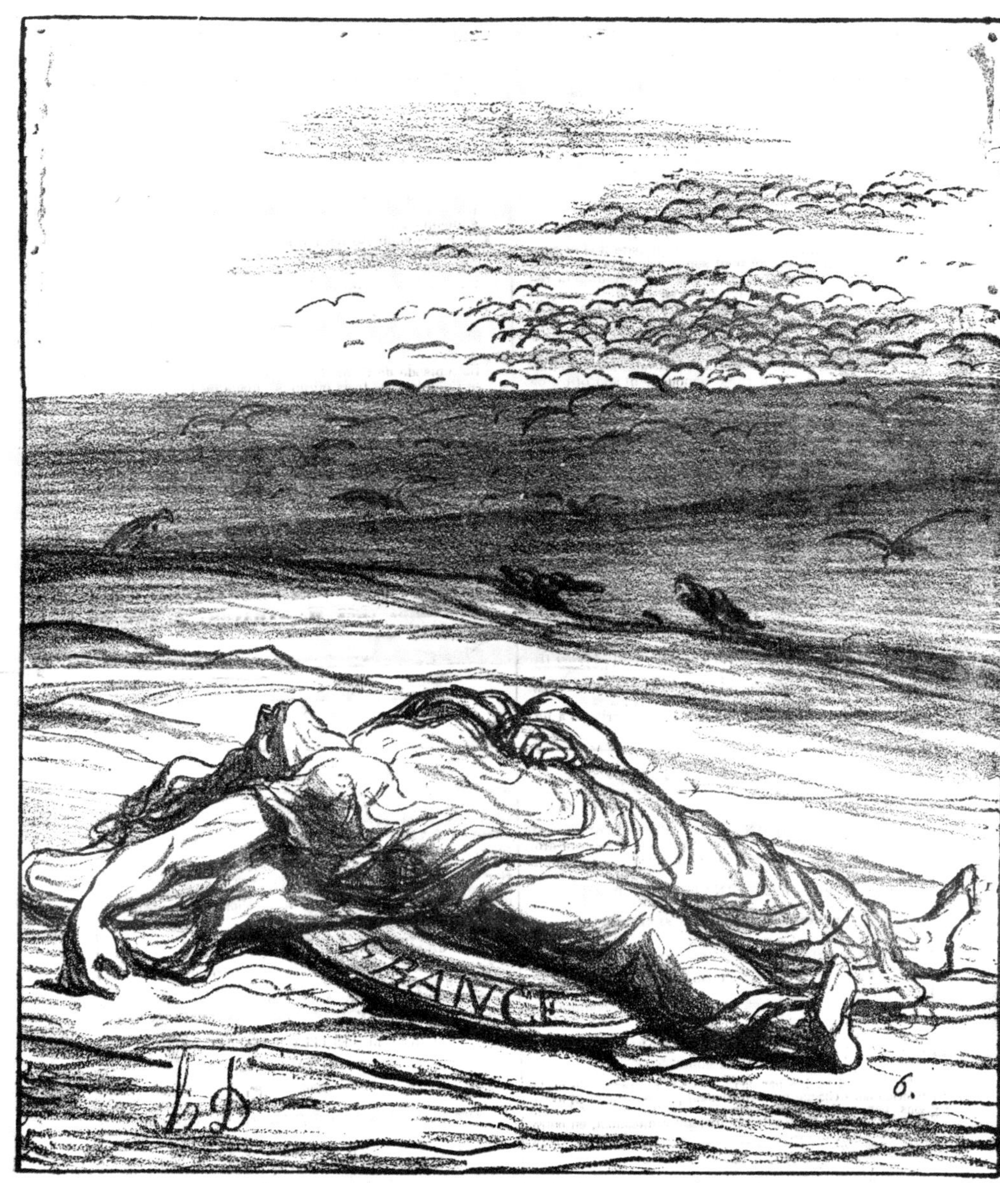

Cat. 53

Autres Candidats.

Other candidates.

"Actualités" (Current events), no. 301; published in
Le Charivari, February 3, 1871 (D. 3844).

LENDER: The Rose Art Museum, Brandeis University,
Waltham, Massachusetts, The Benjamin A. and Julia M.
Trustman Collection.

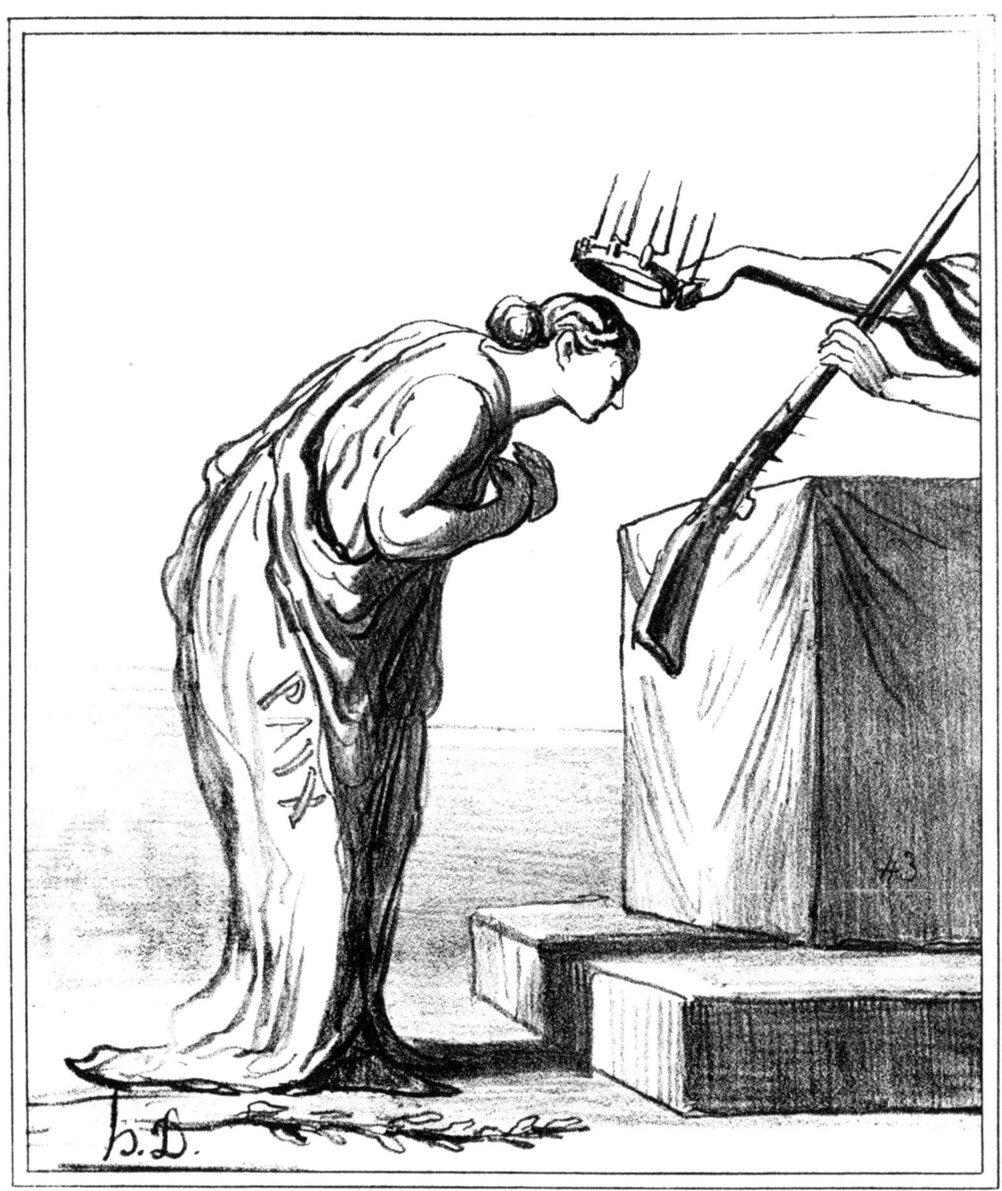

Une lauréate en 1868.

Cat. 54

Une Lauréate en 1868.

A prizewinner in 1868.

"Actualités" (Current events), no. 187; published in
Le Charivari, September 1, 1868 (D. 3659).

LENDER: The Christian A. Johnson Memorial Gallery,
Middlebury College, Gift of Dr. Jay Leyda.

Checklist of the Exhibition

D. = Loys Delteil, *Le Peintre-Graveur illustré: Daumier,* 11 vols. (Paris: Chez l'auteur, 1925–1930).

D. 566. Intérieur d'un omnibus (cat. 15)

D. 629. Je me fiche bien de votre Mme SAND . . . (cat. 12)

D. 630. Six Mois de mariage (cat. 4)

D. 654. Malheureux! Tu veux donc tuer le père de tes enfants? (cat. 6)

D. 669. Le Mari du bas-bleu (cat. 13)

D. 678. Un Intérieur parisien (cat. 14)

D. 711. C'est unique! J'ai pris quatre tailles . . . (cat. 5)

D. 924. Si vous saviez combien vous êtes jolie . . . (cat. 1)

D. 925. Ménélas vainqueur (cat. 35)

D. 928. Présentation d'Ulysse à Nausica (cat. 42)

D. 930. Les Nuits de Pénélope (cat. 38)

D. 934. Socrate chez Aspasie (cat. 36)

D. 937. L'Enlèvement d'Hélène (cat. 37)

D. 938. Ulysse et Pénélope (cat. 39)

D. 941. Enée aux enfers (cat. 43)

D. 946. Le Baptême d'Achille (cat. 41)

D. 970. La Mère des Gras (cat. 40)

D. 971. Pygmalion (cat. 44)

D. 1196. Mariez-vous donc . . . en Chine (cat. 2)

D. 1222. Dis donc . . . mon mari . . . j'ai bien envie d'appeler mon drame . . . (cat. 25)

D. 1227. La mère est dans le feu de la composition . . . (cat. 23)

D. 1231. Emportez donc ça plus loin . . . il est impossible de travailler . . . (cat. 24)

D. 1233. Monsieur, pardon si je vous gêne un peu . . . (cat. 20)

D. 1235. Femme de lettre humanitaire se livrant sur l'homme . . . (cat. 27)

D. 1244. Depuis que Virginie a obtenu le septième accessit . . . (cat. 21)

D. 1248. Une femme comme moi . . . remettre un bouton? . . . (cat. 22)

D. 1249. Ma bonne amie, puis-je entrer! . . . (cat. 26)

D. 1674. La Cinquième Acte à la Gaité (cat. 19)

D. 1746. Dernier Conseil des ex-ministres (cat. 47)

D. 1371. Vous avez perdu votre procès c'est vrai . . . (cat. 17)

D. 1769. Citoyennes . . . on fait courir le bruit . . . (cat. 31)

D. 1770. Voilà une femme qui, à l'heure solennelle . . . (cat. 32)

D. 1771. Les maris ne sont pas ce qu'un vain peuple pense! (cat. 33)

D. 1773. Toast porté à l'émancipation des femmes . . . (cat. 34)

D. 1918. L'Insurrection contre les maris . . . (cat. 28)

D. 1920. Il parait que les clubs vont être . . . fermés . . . (cat. 30)

D. 1924. Ah! vous êtes mon mari, Ah! vous êtes . . . (cat. 29)

D. 2153. Belle dame, voulez-vous bien accepter mon bras? (cat. 18)

D. 2429. Voilà pourtant notre chambre nuptiale . . . (cat. 8)

D. 2566. A la mairie . . . (cat. 3)

D. 2594. Laissez-moi, Madame Prudhomme . . . (cat. 9)

D. 2626. Plus que ça d'ballon . . . excusez! . . . (cat. 11)

D. 2973. Saprelotte! si les femmes continuent . . . (cat. 10)

D. 3193. La Dame. — Oh! mon ami . . . quel beau turco! . . . (cat. 7)

D. 3252. En chemin de fer . . . un voisin agréable (cat. 16)

D. 3585. Aussi forte que le chinois de l'hippodrome, la paix! (cat. 50)

D. 3617. Une Situation . . . fatiguante (cat. 46)

D. 3659. Une Lauréate en 1868 (cat. 54)

D. 3731. Pas trop écourté, s'il vous plait (cat. 49)

D. 3814. L'Empire, c'est la paix (cat. 51)

Design and Typography by Catherine Waters
Typeset by Highwood Typographic Services
Printer's negatives by Robert Hennessey
Printed and bound by Meriden-Stinehour Press